PARTNER___ N __NITIAL TEAC_____

Also available in the Cassell Education series:

P. Ainley and M. Corney: *Training for the Future: The Rise and Fall of the Manpower Services Commission*

G. Antonouris and J. Wilson: *Equal Opportunities in Schools*

N. Bennett and A. Cass: *From Special to Ordinary Schools*

D. E. Bland: *Managing Higher Education*

M. Bottery: *The Morality of the School: The Theory and Practice of Values in Education*

L. Burton (ed.): *Gender and Mathematics*

C. Christofi: *Assessment and Profiling in Science*

G. Claxton: *Being a Teacher: A Positive Approach to Change and Stress*

G. Claxton: *Teaching to Learn: A Direction for Education*

D. Coulby and S. Ward: *The Primary Core National Curriculum*

C. Cullingford (ed): *The Primary Teacher*

L. B. Curzon: *Teaching in Further Education* (4th edition)

B. Goacher *et al.*: *Policy and Provision for Special Educational Needs*

H. Gray (ed): *Management Consultancy in Schools*

L. Hall: *Poetry for Life*

J. Nias, G. Southworth and R. Yeomans: *Staff Relationships in the Primary School*

J. Sayer and V. Williams (eds): *Schools and External Relations: Managing the New Partnerships*

R. Straughan: *Beliefs, Behaviour and Education*

H. Thomas: *Education Costs and Performance*

H. Thomas, G. Kirkpatrick and E. Nicholson: *Financial Delegation and the Local Management of Schools*

M. Watts: *The Science of Problem-Solving*

J. Wilson: *A New Introduction to Moral Education*

S. Wolfendale (ed): *Parental Involvement*

Partnership in Initial Teacher Training

Edited by

M. B. Booth, V. J. Furlong and M. Wilkin

CASSELL

Cassell Educational Limited
Villiers House
41/47 Strand
London WC2N 5JE

First published 1990

British Library Cataloguing in Publication Data
Partnership in initial teacher training. – (Cassell
  Education series).
  1. Teachers. Professional education
  I. Booth, M. B. (Martin Butler) *1936–*   II. Furlong, V. J.
  (V. John)   III. Wilkin, M. (Margaret)
  370.71

  ISBN 0–304–31984–8

Typeset by Fakenham Photosetting Limited, Fakenham, Norfolk
Printed and bound in Great Britain by Page Bros, Norwich

Contents

The Contributors   vii

Introduction   ix

Section I – The Context of Partnership

1 The Development of Partnership in the United Kingdom   3
Margaret Wilkin

2 The Two Routes into Teaching   24
Ted Wragg

3 Partnership: A CNAA Perspective   33
Len Wharfe and Alison Burrows

4 Changing Partnership   44
Gill Crozier, Ian Menter and Andrew Pollard

Section II – The Principles of Partnership

5 Partnership in Initial Teacher Education: Confronting the Issues   59
Robin Alexander

6 The Theory–Practice Relationship in Teacher Training   74
Paul H. Hirst

7 School-Based Training: The Students' Views   87
John Furlong

8 Partnership and the Training of Student History Teachers   99
Martin Booth, Gwenifer Shawyer and Richard Brown

9 The Oxford Internship Scheme and the Cambridge Analytical
Framework: Models of Partnership in Initial Teacher Education   110
Donald McIntyre

Section III – The Practice of Partnership

10 Partnership and Reflective Practice in the Subject Training Group:
Some Opportunities and Obstacles   131
Peter Lucas

11 A Training Course for School Supervisors: Two Perspectives   143
Martin Booth and Nicolas Kinloch

12 Practical School Experiences: Who Teaches the Student Teacher?   153
Colin Terrell

13 A Double Vision: The Experiences of a Head and Principal   166
Ray Stirling

Name Index   173

Subject Index   175

The Contributors

Robin Alexander is Reader in Primary Education at the University of Leeds.

Martin Booth is Lecturer in History Methods in the University of Cambridge Department of Education.

Richard Brown is School College Integrated Link Co-ordinator at Manshead School, Bedfordshire and previously Seconded Teacher in the ESRC Training of History Teachers research project.

Alison Burrows is Assistant Registrar at the Council for National Academic Awards.

Gill Crozier is Senior Lecturer in Education at Bristol Polytechnic.

John Furlong is Lecturer in the Sociology of Education in the University of Cambridge Department of Education.

Paul Hirst is Emeritus Professor of Education in the University of Cambridge Department of Education.

Nicolas Kinloch is Head of History at The Netherhall School, Cambridge.

Peter Lucas is Director of the Postgraduate Certificate in Education course in the University of Sheffield Division of Education.

Donald McIntyre is Reader in Education in the University of Oxford Department of Educational Studies.

Ian Menter is Senior Lecturer in Education at Bristol Polytechnic.

Andrew Pollard is Reader in Education at Bristol Polytechnic.

Gwenifer Shawyer is Tutor in History at the John Leggatt Sixth Form College,

Scunthorpe and previously Senior Research Associate in the ESRC Training of History Teachers research project.

Ray Stirling is Principal of Bushfield Community School, Peterborough.

Colin Terrell is Dean of the Faculty of Education and Health at Cheltenham and Gloucester College of Higher Education.

Len Wharfe is Registrar for Education and the Built Environment at the Council for National Academic Awards.

Margaret Wilkin is Co-Director of an Inservice Course for Teacher Supervisors in the University of Cambridge Department of Education.

Ted Wragg is Professor of Education and Director of the School of Education at the University of Exeter.

Introduction

The training of teachers has been an issue of major debate and controversy over the past decade. Much of the discussion has centred round the roles of the training institution and the school in providing a coherent, relevant and effective course. Some now argue that training should focus mainly on the school with the experienced classroom teacher playing the major role; others believe that the emphasis should be on an equal partnership between training institution and school and that the theory/practice divide should give way to a situation in which theory is derived from the practical experience of the school and classroom. The Department of Education and Science is promoting both these approaches through its articled student and licensed teacher schemes – where the majority of the training will be 'on site' – and through its encouragement of school-based training courses such as are run at the Universities of Sussex and Oxford. Yet in all these schemes some form of partnership between school, training institution and local education authority is envisaged. Just what that partnership will entail is at present far from clear; the rhetoric of the politicians has done little to tease out the complexities and variations in practice which the word encompasses. It is the intention of the essays in this book to address these issues in the hope of illuminating and clarifying the debate.

The book is divided into three sections. The first section explores the historical and political context of partnership. Margaret Wilkin sets the scene by tracing the evolution of partnership, its roots in the theory/practice debate and the way it is being influenced by the political context. She stresses the tension that exists between the profession with its concerns for quality of training and the creation of teachers capable of critically reflecting on and developing their skills and knowledge and a government which seems to be promoting alternative models, one of which parallels developments in training institutions, the other of which reflects much more directly the New Conservatism.

Ted Wragg argues that the late 1980s led to a situation where two parallel models of teacher training were under consideration. Model A was a response to the increasing demands of the profession; it looked to a training which was well-structured, wideranging and continued throughout the teacher's professional career. Model B was based on the nineteenth-century idea of apprenticeship – that all that was needed was for a trainee to spend time with an experienced teacher in school to pick up 'tips on teaching'.

Wragg argues that a significant move to Model B could easily deprofessionalize both teaching and teacher training.

The chapter which follows explores the significant contribution that the Council for National Academic Awards (CNAA) has made to the theory and practice of partnership. The Council first engaged in debate about the validation of teacher education courses in 1966. Len Wharfe and Alison Burrows show how CNAA took a leading role in the 1970s and 1980s in making public the debate on partnership, partly in response to outside pressures, partly as a result of its own research and evaluation of the teacher training courses it validates.

Gill Crozier, Ian Menter and Andrew Pollard argue that partnership has often been developed unquestioningly by local authorities, schools and training institutions, responding to the promptings of central government. In their chapter they raise questions about the notion of partnership and, by examining its origins and practice, develop a critique which emphasizes that partnership is a complex, problematic and profoundly ideological phenomenon. It must, they argue, be transformed into a dynamic alliance if teacher education is to survive.

The second section of the book explores some of the principles underlying the practice of partnership. Robin Alexander advances a framework or matrix for analysing partnership. His framework explores two main levels of partnership – enabling procedures and structures and day-to-day interactions – and the four main dimensions which cut across the two levels. These he terms structural, attitudinal, personal and conceptual. Such a matrix serves to highlight both the challenges of bringing institutions and people together for a common enterprise and the ways in which effective partnership can be achieved.

Paul Hirst then goes on to make a detailed examination of the relationship between theory and practice in teacher training. He argues that all teacher practices must be rationally defensible in terms of the concepts, beliefs and principles which inform them if the teacher is to be deemed to be acting professionally. Mastery of practices by students requires not the application of general theories but the acquisition through observation, practice and discussion of a range of approaches which must then be submitted to critical reflection in different ways. In the first instance this may be an appraisal of personal performance against given criteria; later it may be more wideranging; finally, the practices are considered in the light of the basic disciplines.

John Furlong's chapter focuses on the students' views of partnership, looking particularly at the issues of practice, theory and reflection. Drawing on data from a research project examining school-based training, he shows that the students in his sample had an equally strong concern with all three dimensions and clear ideas as to how they should be interrelated. The evidence also shows that the students considered that both lecturers and teachers each have a vital, though different, contribution to make to the students' professional development.

The chapter which follows also draws on a research project into the one-year Postgraduate Certificate in Education. Martin Booth, Gwenifer Shawyer and Richard Brown show how ill-defined, limited and erratic the supervision was which the students in their sample received when in school on block teaching experience or practice. Supervisors both from the schools and training institutions rarely addressed subject-specific issues of pupils' learning and progress, concentrating for the most part on the immediate issues of classroom management and control. Understanding by teacher supervisors of the institutions' role in training was often limited or distorted. The authors conclude that there is an urgent need for a national programme of inservice training for teachers who supervise students in school.

Oxford University's Department of Educational Studies scheme of school-based training, where students become 'interns' and the teacher supervisors 'mentors', has excited much interest and debate. Donald McIntyre examines the course in the light of an analytical framework developed by a research team in Cambridge. The framework postulates training on four levels, ranging from training through direct, practical experience in the classroom – Level (a) – through to introducing students to an essential content of theoretical knowledge – Level (d). Though McIntyre acknowledges the insights gained through the use of the framework, he questions its hierarchical nature and the emphasis on academic knowledge as the 'superior arbitrating kind of know-ledge'. The Oxford course, he argues, stresses the importance and diversity of know-ledge and of learning opportunities in the context of practice.

In the final section of the book, we move to examples of the practice of partnership. Peter Lucas describes and evaluates a particular model of partnership developed with postgraduate students at Sheffield University's Division of Education. Students engage in a collaborative inquiry project in schools; the teachers are then invited to attend the sessions where the projects are presented to the rest of the group. Lucas shows how the teachers are regarded by the students as both a resource whose experience and knowledge can be drawn on and as participants learning alongside the students.

In contrast, Cambridge University's Department of Education runs an inservice training course of about seven days spread over the year for teachers involved in the supervision of students. Martin Booth describes the rationale behind the course and presents its main features; Nicolas Kinloch, a recent participant, gives his reactions to the training and the ways in which it affected his approach to supervising students.

At Cheltenham and Gloucester College of Higher Education an action research project which attempted to improve the quality of supervision offered to students on teaching practice also led to the development of a training course for co-operating classroom teachers. The emphasis of the course is on the teachers' role and skills as supervisors and their own personal development as classroom practitioners. Colin Terrell's chapter highlights some of the myths which often seem to underpin the way in which teaching practices are now conducted and describes the way in which an inservice course was developed which satisfies both the college's need for effective supervisors and the local authority's inservice training concerns.

In the concluding chapter, Ray Stirling, a secondary comprehensive school head and former principal of a training college, looks back over three decades at the fortunes of partnership. He highlights the pressure for increased professional interdependence between schools and training institutions which emerged with the new education initiatives in the 1960s and the early 1970s – the move towards comprehensive schools, the increasing use of mixed-ability teaching in secondary schools, the establishment of a new national examination for the less able, the raising of the school leaving age; and he recalls how the James Report on the training of teachers (1972) seemed to herald the realization of a new partnership. Stirling recalls that the James proposals had little effect because of professional conservatism, public expenditure cuts and, later, a fall in the birth rate. During his time in the late 1970s as a training college principal he became convinced that a genuine partnership could not be achieved within the confines of an establishment devoted solely to initial teacher education; the enterprise of training must be conceived much more widely. Today there is a new emphasis on partnership; but Stirling believes that a 'covenant of partnership' can be achieved only if a rational and co-ordinated programme is drawn up in which planned release, professional development and proper funding are the key features.

Section I

The Context of Partnership

Chapter 1

The Development of Partnership in the United Kingdom

Margaret Wilkin

By the later 1980s, it would have been difficult to find an institution which was responsible for initial teacher training that did not claim that it was engaged in some form of partnership with its associated schools. This is not just because 'partnership' was made a mandatory requirement of training courses by the government in Circular 3/84 (DES, 1984) – a requirement subsequently endorsed and strengthened in Circular 24/89 (DES, 1989a) – and that therefore all institutions were by then obliged to make provision for it. It is also because teachers in schools and tutors within colleges and departments of education have for many years regarded a close association between the two types of institution as a necessary characteristic of the good training course. When Circular 3/84 advocated partnership, it was not therefore suggesting any innovative break with current practice. Rather it was, first of all, confirming a professional trend which had been gaining in strength and robustness for many years.

But it was not only in terms of general sentiment that the Circular reflected the status quo. In suggesting that the experienced practising teacher should share responsibility for the various aspects of the student's teaching practice, should contribute to the training of the student within the training institution and should participate in the selection of students for the course, it also affirmed what were by then well-established goals in many institutions. Courses were already planned 'to allow for a substantial element of school experience and teaching practice'. The time that the trainee spent in school had been increasing steadily for at least a decade, and it had long been an aim that education and professional studies should be clearly linked with each other and with a student's practical experience in schools (DES, 1984, Annex). In a second respect, therefore, this Circular was very much of its time. By selecting for enforcement the unobjectionable minimum of existing collaborative activities and structures it captured the drift to partnership as it already existed.

Thirdly, it is clear from the presentation of partnership in the Circular that the training institution will be expected to cede responsibility to the school, that partnership entails the transfer of power from the lecturer or tutor to the teacher. Its recommendations therefore subsumed the existing power differential between the two types of institution, and in this respect the Circular also reflected the current teacher training scene. There is no suggestion for example that the school grants further or alternative rights to the tutor (except in providing a context in which to gain recent and relevant experience). Circular 3/84 was thus very much a watershed. It acknowledged the current aspirations and practices of the profession and – in endowing these with mandatory status – legitimated them. But in assuming the constitutionally innovative right to determine the training curriculum, it transferred into the political domain what previously had been a matter of professional debate and decision.

Although in professional terms the Circular did little more than echo existing good practice, it forced the active confrontation of partnership by all those engaged in teacher education. Over the years the movement towards partnership within the colleges and the university departments had been fired by a desire to improve the quality of training and had evolved through a process of pragmatic incrementalism. But it had now become an issue for conscious consideration. Since its implementation was obligatory it had become necessary to explore the meaning and the implications of the term more fully than hitherto, and since the Circular was issued it has become apparent that the deceptively simple notion of partnership subsumes a great many tensions and contradictions. The range, complexity and controversial nature of these issues has become increasingly evident as theoretical base and practical example are analysed and articulated. There is, first of all, the tension between structure and practice which is overlaid but not synonymous with that between rhetoric and reality. To construct a partnership-conducive curriculum is no guarantee that partnership practices – which are themselves problematic – will follow. Then there is the longstanding tension between training institution and school, a tension that is as much a cultural gap as a direct reflection of structural opportunities for teachers and tutors to meet and co-operate. This tension itself subsumes a further tension – that of the ownership of knowledge and expertise. Who is best qualified to convey to the trainee which professional skills and how their respective responsibilities can be co-ordinated? There is the further tension between the professionals' perception of partnership and that of the politicians which seems to reflect their opposing viewpoints about the whole nature of the teaching enterprise. As has already been implied, there are further disagreements amongst the professionals themselves about the form partnership should take. There is, finally, potential for controversy in the functional definition of partnership itself. Is partnership to be construed as a relation of interdependence or complementarity, or as a relation of logical equivalence? It is the purpose of this chapter to make a limited attempt at clarifying some of the issues mentioned above. The emergence of 'partnership' and the functional advantage of the concept will be discussed; a brief consideration of the nature of partnership follows. Finally partnership is located in the current political context.

THE EVOLUTION OF PARTNERSHIP

As at least two of the chapters in this volume imply, the relationship between training institutions and schools has evolved over the last two or three decades from one of distant wariness and expediency to one of mutual co-operation and respect; from one where 'all the training institutions seemed to want was a ticket of access to the classroom' and where 'It was a bonus if we, the teachers, were invited to contribute to the assessment of the student' to one where 'there is a shared recognition of the different contributions which practising teachers and university lecturers are each well placed to make'. Recently this development has been conceptualized as the growth of partnership, but during the 1960s and 1970s, when the term 'partnership' was rarely used, it can more readily be represented as shifts in the balance between the theory and practice elements of the training curriculum, 'practice' being represented by professional or methods courses and time spent in schools, 'theory' by the disciplines of education. Partnership is the theory–practice relationship reformulated, and the altered terminology is itself indicative of the changes that have taken place. The phrase 'theory–practice relationship' suggests an academic concern, a matter for analysis or theoretical debate. 'Partnership' on the other hand suggests action or active involvement. The hastening redistribution of responsibility for student training in favour of the schools is signified in the current preference for the latter formulation over the former.

Retrospectively, the shift away from theory and into practice or the drive towards partnership can be seen as a steady cumulative pressure over a quarter of a century to reassert the importance of competency in the classroom as the essential outcome of initial training. The influences which have shaped this trend have in the main been internal, within the profession itself, those of central government being limited until recently to the unintended consequences of implementing other education policy measures. It had been the professionals in the colleges and departments of education who had supported the revision of the curriculum content in favour of education theory during the post-Robbins era and who had accepted the accompanying relative marginalization of practical work. It had been in their interests to do so since the disciplines of education were the means of remedying the lack of rigour in the existing curriculum and hence of ensuring the academic status of the new BEd degree when it was introduced. But during the following two decades the challenge to a curriculum dominated by the disciplines also came from within the teacher training movement. As the gradual erosion of theory and the strengthening of 'practice' gathered momentum, and as teachers as a consequence were drawn into more active involvement in training, the term partnership was used more and more frequently.

The weakening of the status and power of the disciplines of education over this period, the dilution of their impact, may be considered from two interrelated perspectives. The first of these concerns the rhetorical attack on theory, or, more generously, the challenge to it. The other concerns the patterns of curriculum practice within the institutions.

The dominance of theory over practice was undermined rhetorically from two quarters. It suffered an epistemological or logical challenge from the philosophers of education and others engaged in academic debate. It also suffered what might be called a 'moral' challenge. This challenge could alternatively be regarded as 'professional' for it concerns the views of those engaged in teacher training about the best way to undertake this task. But in as much as the premises on which courses are constructed and according to which they are justified reflect certain values, and more particularly will demonstrate at their heart a positive or negative valuation of teachers' contribution to training, discussion on the distribution between teacher and tutor responsibilities in the training of teachers can also be considered a moral matter. It is convenient to separate these two domains, the epistemological and the moral, though throughout the development outlined above they have been mutually interrelated. The former, the epistemological, has been and still is evoked to justify the latter, and the latter dimension, the professional or moral, has in turn influenced the course of the former. These challenges, although at the level of rhetoric, undoubtedly influenced the practical activity of teacher training itself.

In the epistemological debate, the movement away from the claim – in any case tenuously held and occasionally rather than consistently stated – that the theory of education determined practice, was rapid. Amongst the philosophers of education this was a form of the theory–practice relationship which was short-lived, though as a straw man it remained common currency for much longer. It had served its purpose in helping to establish standards of 'degree worthiness' in teacher education in the post-Robbins phase. That theory which is general cannot dictate practice which is specific was quickly acknowledged. This of course does not imply that education theory must be jettisoned, although there were those in the colleges of education with their tradition of practical rather than academic training who felt that this should be so. The challenge was that its relationship to practice needed to be reformulated. Thus as early as the mid-1960s, the form of the relationship which was later neatly epitomized as 'raiding the disciplines' became the accepted orthodoxy. The theory–practice relationship was now reversed. Primacy was given to practice, the logical limitation of theory being acknowledged. Its function was now the illumination, clarification or refinement of professional activity.

Within the moral dimension, there had remained some limited opposition to the dominance of the disciplines even as they were in the ascendant. In the colleges particularly, with their history of training for the less able pupil, of recruitment of the (allegedly) less able student and of allegiance to metaphysical rather than scientific 'theory', the new theory was alien. Students declared that they had little interest in it. It was regarded as irrelevant and distant from the classroom. Their preference was to draw guidance and understanding from the teachers with whom they had contact in schools. The same critical view of the current curriculum was found in some of the university departments of education (UDEs), it being argued that the disciplines of education 'appear to offer relatively little guidance to the individual teacher on how to go about his work *in the classroom*' and that, although contextual understanding is important, 'students may reasonably ask also for something that contributes more directly to the most pressing of their problems' (Sutton, 1975, 343). Again the primacy of practice is emphasized. Theory was deemed 'irrelevant' quite simply because too much was being expected of it, technically. This was now accepted as self-evident. Rather, the new task of theory was to extend the student's understanding of the problems which were being met in practice. The once proud disciplines of education which had spawned their own organizational structures in the institutions and had dominated the curriculum were now reduced to the task of servicing practice although in this role theory had both epistemological and moral legitimacy.

By the mid-1970s, it was being acknowledged that educational theory in the form of the disciplines was 'a disaster area': 'In practice [trainees] know that they learn the theory to pass the theory exams, not to help them in their practice. In practice they rely not on theory, but on their native wit and energy, plus the support of "real" teachers in their practice schools' (Wilson and Pring, 1975, 3). The failure of theory to provide the answers to the problems of the classroom had forced a reconsideration of its value within the curriculum. Training to be a teacher should after all be about learning to teach, and this should mean less time spent studying the disciplines of education in the training institution and more time spent on practice in the school. But training had long since moved away from any form of apprenticeship and into the arena of higher education, and so closer association with schools could not imply the mere learning of tips from teachers. Unquestioning acceptance is not the stuff of higher education. Rather it is critical awareness and analysis. The professional activity of the teacher should not therefore be viewed as a collection of random acts. It was patterned and justifiable. Wilson and Pring continue: 'There exists another possibility, namely that theory already exists in practices – any practices – and that it can be found there if one looks for it. The improvement of one's practice in that case would consist in the first instance of becoming aware of the theory which ones practice already embodied'. Enter the theorizing teacher!

This shift of both focus and kind in the relationship between theory and practice represented a convenient marrying of the two perspectives. It was a solution to the dilemmas posed by the need for theory and the simultaneous rejection of the disciplines of education, and by the need to make training more school-focused. It was a view that rapidly attracted adherents. The truism that any activity is 'theory laden' was repeated as frequently as a mantra. Given teachers' practical and evaluative justifications of their practices, inferences could be made about their implicit theory. Theory was no longer only a body of research-based knowledge to which reference could be made in times of trouble as it were. It was, alternatively and additionally, articulated 'craft knowledge', the very rationale of practice.

There thus emerged from the epistemological and moral challenges to the disciplines of education two models of the relationship between theory and practice which became the bases of alternative models of training and hence of the relationship or partnership between school and training institution. They can be represented as the poles of a *continuum*, which ironically are not so dissimilar in one respect. They both have at their heart the theorizing teacher. In the first 'traditional' representation of theory and its use, the teacher logically *must* theorize about his or her practice since only if he or she does so does it make any sense to talk about reference to the disciplines for clarification of that practice. But this theorizing is implicit; it is theory-as-product which is fore-grounded. The alternative 'radical' (because subsequent) perspective is that which emphasizes theory-as-process. The poles differ however in other respects. The former clings on to the disciplines while the latter lets them go, emphasizing rather the articulation and systematization of the teacher's own theory. These alternative perspectives on the form and use of theory must have implications for the respective roles of tutors and trainees. In the traditional model, the tutor remains the expert on theory and by extrapolating from the current practical situation guides the trainee to a deeper understanding of his or her practice. In the radical model, however, it is the practitioner who is the expert, since he or she is the owner of a personal theory, and the task of the tutor is to work with the trainee in articulating, structuring and refining this theory. There are therefore also consequences here for the degree and type of collaboration between the two forms of institution, and for the distribution and location of power. In the era of the disciplines, theory and practice remained different areas of expertise; in the era of the 'theorizing teacher' there is only one domain for investigation, that of practice itself. This continuum therefore subsumes a number of alternatives. These concern the type of theory emphasized and also the role of the tutor *vis-à-vis* that of the teacher or student within that theoretical domain; also the relative status and power of the two types of institution and their respective representatives, and the form of collaboration between them.

The second perspective on the development of partnership can now be considered. It concerns the way in which the curricula of the institutions evolved – and since this development was uneven across institutions, the distribution of the institutions themselves within the framework outlined above. The focus is now the reality of the teacher training programme rather than the rhetoric, and inevitably there will be a lack of coincidence between these dimensions. It is a relatively simple matter to devise and justify theoretical schemes. Putting them into operation is altogether different. For example, a powerful *ideal* of collaboration had emerged as the discussion on theory *vis-à-vis* practice progressed during the 1970s. In keeping with the model of the theorizing teacher, it was suggested that the tutor and the teacher 'should share the same practical theory – a somewhat ambitious model of partnership in which the respective members would be equals who peered at the world through identical pairs of spectacles' (Webster, 1975). A less challenging and perhaps more realistic alternative was also proposed which did not depend on either side relinquishing their areas of expertise but on complementarity. This was to be a form of collaboration or partnership in which school and training institution had 'full knowledge and maximum understanding' of each other's roles and in which tutor and teachers jointly planned the course and accepted joint responsibility for it (Hirst, 1975). Aside from the exuberant exaggeration in the latter proposal (*full* knowledge, *maximum* understanding) there is no evidence that any training institution then in existence (except perhaps Sussex University) ran a course which remotely met the standards of collaboration indicated here by either writer. At the level of action, these sorts of proposals could only remain goals. Nevertheless, some institutions came much nearer to achieving these ideals than others.

Diversity across institutions seems always to have been an intrinsic characteristic of teacher training in the UK. Comments to this effect have been a regular feature of surveys and reports on initial training since the Robbins Report, and the various reports themselves may even have encouraged it as did the dissension on the administration of teacher education between the members of the McNair Committee (1944). There were first of all the very different traditions of training within the colleges and the universities. The two systems of training recruited different types of students, prepared them for different types of teaching posts, were predicated on different notions about the nature of training. And within each of these groups there was further variety. Prior to the Area Training Organisation (ATO) system, many of the colleges were not only small but geographically and professionally isolated. Yet although association with the universities encouraged in general the development of the academic curriculum in the colleges, the ATO system itself did little to reduce diversity since the university schools of education operated autonomously, being accountable only to their respective governing bodies. Nor did a university school of education necessarily function consistently within its twin training capacities. Its own students did not receive the same form of training as the students in the colleges under its auspices.

The James Report (DES, 1972) was highly critical of these arrangements, raising pertinent questions about the lack of co-ordination within the system. It also suggested that the reality of the association between university and public sector institution differed considerably from the rhetoric supporting it. The 'argument from prestige by association' was found to be wanting since 'placing undue emphasis on the present link with universities has its own attendant dangers. The most obvious of these is that some colleges have been encouraged to strive for the wrong kind of excellence. Their courses have in many cases become too academic' (para. 5, 17). The 'argument from academic freedom' for retaining links with the universities was also dismissed. 'There has been no indication that the colleges need the kind of bulwark against outside pressures that the present structure is said to provide' (para. 5, 19). In the view of the committee, the close association of the public sector institutions with the universities had perpetuated an undesirably theoretical curriculum and moreover was no longer necessary since the colleges were now powerful enough and of sufficient reputation to be able to fend for themselves. In so forcibly making these two points, the Report not only encouraged but also legitimated the transfer of public sector institutions to the Council for National Academic Awards (CNAA) for the purposes of course validation. The early 1970s saw the first tentative applications to CNAA. By the middle of the decade, this trickle had become a flood.

In its operation, the CNAA perpetuated the two characteristics of initial training discussed above: the trend away from theory and towards a more school-focused curriculum, and the diversity across institutions. Its early commitment to involving practising teachers in the operation of courses in a variety of ways promoted the closer association between colleges and polytechnics and schools. There was, secondly, the nature of its own involvement with the training institutions. As the responsive partner in this relationship, its aim has always been to validate courses in terms of their intrinsic worth, and this means accepting a well argued and supported case on that basis rather than on whether it fits a particular model of training. Thus institutions which were dissatisfied with their position under the ATO system because, amongst other reasons, they met with reluctance when wishing to reduce or redefine the theoretical element of the course, could now approach CNAA in anticipation of a receptive hearing for an alternative, more school-focused approach to training which the institution had itself devised with its own students' needs and staff expertise in mind. In an interesting paper written in 1975, Gorbutt justifies the transfer of the PGCE course at his institution, a polytechnic, to CNAA for validation on the grounds that: 'The first question which can be asked of any course is does it equip a student to do a job? Thus courses for intending professionals must clearly be seen to develop a professional competence' (p. 47). A model of teacher as 'self-critical problem solver' was therefore devised. This did not entail the complete rejection of the disciplines of education, but the investigation of personal practice was to take precedence over theory, reference to which would then provide the means of sharpening up the analysis.

Subsequent submissions of courses in initial training from the polytechnics and colleges to CNAA for validation appeared only to strengthen the direction in which teacher training was moving. In these institutions particularly, the desire to see training take a more practical 'relevant' form was very real, and this was exemplified in the changes that occurred in course proposals. 'Teaching practice' became 'school experience' – a significant change in terminology signifying that time should be spent in school for purposes other than and additional to the traditional form of block teaching practice. Teachers were to be appointed to internal committees, where although outnumbered heavily they could nevertheless make their views known, and they were to assume more responsibility for student assessment. Moreover the whole operation of CNAA course application and approval itself tends to stabilize these trends further. For example, the initial requirement that courses remained in operation for a prescribed period of years only served to further sediment – to render almost 'common sense' – the developments already in train.

Government-sponsored events which fuelled a reassessment of the training curriculum in favour of practitioner competence and which could not be ignored by the training institutions although they were not necessarily directed at them included the expansion of the comprehensive school movement during the 1960s and 1970s. The new schooling arrangements introduced new challenges and new practical problems for the training institutions to consider: mixed-ability teaching, classroom management and control. Moreover the James Report, by relegating theory to the proposed second cycle of training, also found for the 'pragmatists' as it were. Neither of these events could be said to have redirected current training practices. Rather they appeared to license a trend already in progress. Whether this was also the case with respect to the effect of the demographic and economic pressures to rationalize the whole public sector training system during the 1970s is more difficult to tell. Since the direction of the relationship was by now from the particular to the general – for both logical and technical reasons, referring practice to theory for the enhancement of understanding rather than claiming that theory determined practice – it became possible to justify reorganizing the curriculum according to the thematic approach in which a single (usually) school-focused problem could act as the focus for several theoretical or even subject perspectives. This alternative form of curriculum was more flexible across the new diversified courses. Was this fortuitous coincidence, or was this curriculum change an unintended consequence of government policy? It seems likely that the reorganization of the public sector institutions nudged the curriculum in the direction in which it was already moving.

An overview of the status quo with respect to the development of school–institution links as the 1980s approached indicates that, in terms of their curricula, institutions were scattered along the hypothetical continuum outlined above (which it will be recalled subsumed two different types of theory and the respective roles of tutor and teacher or student within each particular theoretical domain; these two types of theory also had implications for forms of collaboration and the distribution of power between the two types of institution). Given the tradition of diversity within teacher training this distribution comes as no surprise. From what has already been said about the consequences of the public sector institutions seeking validation under CNAA, it might also be expected that the courses in the colleges and polytechnics would tend to be variable but overall be more centrally placed than those in the UDEs which would tend to bunch towards the 'traditional' end of the spectrum. With respect to the UDEs the SPITE (Structure and Process in Teacher Education) survey of PGCE courses in university departments of education (Patrick, Bernbaum and Reid, 1982) seems to suggest that this was indeed the case. There is no mention of 'partnership' in the text: the single long block practice was still a common form of school placement, and 'it is worth noting that there are large numbers of students who appeared to do no [school] visiting at all' (ibid., 49). The disciplines of education were still well entrenched and 'tutors were clearly unwilling to give up their teaching practice responsibilities . . . they disagreed strongly that school staff should take the main responsibility for supervision' (ibid., 197). Nevertheless, 'there was a deliberate attempt to collaborate with schools on the subject of teaching practice' and 'inducting the student into the disciplines of education' received minimal support as an aim of training. An exception to this overall pattern was of course the PGCE programme at Sussex which had been operating as a 'partnership with schools' since 1965. Students spent three days a week in school for a large part of the year and responsibility for their supervision was entrusted to the practising teacher. They kept personal 'reflective' accounts of their teaching experience, there was considerable collaboration and exchange of function between the staffs of the two types of institution, and there were no specialist education tutors.

It was clear, then, that at the end of the decade the practice of partnership in the UDEs at least fell far short of the rhetoric, and this was itself acknowledged in the report of the PGCE working party of the Universities Council for the Education of Teachers (1979). This working party was 'transbinary', drawing its members from both university and public sector institutions, and the report represented 'the general direction of the Working Party's thinking'. It was unequivocal in its promotion of partnership ('there needs to be far greater co-operation than at present between schools and training institutions'), and in its commitment to discharging responsibility on to the school where this is appropriate ('it is clearly the case that it is in schools that the vast majority of [training in practical skills] must be done, and that primarily under the day to day supervision of school staff'). It stressed particularly the importance of utilizing the respective expertise of the teacher and the tutor for the benefit of the student ('We need to find ways in which the different forms of knowledge and expertise brought to the course by teachers and tutors are effectively integrated') (pp. 9–10). There then follows a series of recommendations 'for experiment' which include, for example, collaboration on course construction and the suggestion that tutors and teachers should work together with students in school.

If the courses in the UDEs did not attain these dizzy heights, indeed were still struggling on the nursery slopes, what was the position with respect to the public sector institutions? Since there were no extensive surveys of colleges and polytechnics which yielded this sort of information, the position here is rather less clear and conclusions must rest as much on argument as on data. The limited studies of public sector initial training courses which were undertaken at about this time (e.g. DES, 1979; McCulloch, 1979) seem to confirm that partnership was indeed on the way, but that the development of collaborative links with schools was cautious and slow – a conclusion that seems to be at odds with the general level of interest in partnership and the degree of claimed commitment to it. For example, the recorded instances of poor communication or of failure to reach a common understanding and agreement on the aims of school experience contrast sharply with institutions' optimistic statements concerning their own practices (e.g. Alexander and Whittaker, 1980).

Does this therefore suggest that after all CNAA-validated courses scarcely differed *in practice* from those in the UDEs with respect to school–college liaison? This is unlikely for a number of reasons. There were, first of all, certain 'partnership requirements' that CNAA made of its submitting institutions. They have already been mentioned and include for example the requirement that serving teachers should contribute to student assessment. Secondly, the way in which CNAA operates needs to be taken into account. While there will inevitably be a distinction between statements of intent about practice and the enactment of those intentions, on CNAA-validated programmes of training the gap between the two is likely to be relatively narrow. This is because the degree of detail in which institutions present their programmes for validation and the rigour of the monitoring procedures encourage coincidence – though obviously cannot ensure it – between planned programme and practical action. Thirdly, the studies of the public sector institutions sometimes included both CNAA- and university-validated courses. General statements in these surveys about the degree or quality of partnership may therefore be misleading since the (perhaps high) incidence of teacher–tutor collaboration on CNAA courses may be negated by the (perhaps low) incidence of collaboration on university-validated courses. There is on the other hand some indication that the 'CNAA emphasis on the need for academic rigour and honours standards was felt by colleges to inhibit the use of school based work as the central focus for B.Ed. programmes. This view contrasted with CNAA policy on the professional focus of the B.Ed.' (McCulloch, 1979, 55; also Alexander, 1979).

The situation with respect to CNAA-validated courses is therefore complex, and in the absence of evidence it is difficult to draw conclusions. Course submissions indicate that although by the mid-1970s some institutions were well advanced in their 'partnership thinking' others were clearly far from even considering entering into a collaborative relationship with schools. Those institutions which had moved towards partnership had done so principally by making incremental adjustments of a structural nature to their courses, for example by increasing the time spent by the student in school. This is not surprising since this sort of relatively minor change required much less disruption to the curriculum, to current patterns of thinking and to power relations than anything so innovative as a model of training built on the articulation, analysis and refinement of personal practical principles. This latter, the more radical form of partnership at the opposing end of the continuum, has in general been limited to action research projects or to inservice training with experienced teachers (e.g. Elliott, 1976). But that it may be the model of initial training that is preferred by the professionals in the future is suggested by the fact that it has recently been the basis of an element within a programme of initial training (Tickle, 1987), and that a whole programme of initial training has been constructed along these lines at Oxford.

The points above can be summarized: until the beginning of the 1980s, the incidence of *active* committed partnership in the teacher training system as a whole appears to have been limited, despite the long-term and widely articulated commitment to it, though in the public sector institutions collaborative links were more advanced than in the UDEs.

THE NATURE OF PARTNERSHIP

It is now necessary to investigate more thoroughly and systematically what 'partnership' had come to mean. The discussion above suggests that during the 1960s and 1970s 'partnership' had emerged as a concept which conveniently summarized the diverse ways in which the training institutions were incorporating the shifting balance between theory and practice into their respective curricula. It was a shorthand which both justified and explained the expanding range of liaison practices between the schools and the colleges, and because partnership is perceived as something intrinsically admirable, implying as it does a degree of autonomy within a framework of co-operation for the benefit of both sides, it attracted claimants whose respective interpretations of what it entailed varied considerably. 'Partnership' had come to subsume a variety of practices, but its popularity gave a misleading unity to the teacher training scene. This lack of clarity was also functionally convenient for those engaged in teacher training for it permitted any institution to announce quite credibly that it was subscribing to that desirable state although the ways in which it did so may have differed quite significantly from the partnership practices of its neighbours.

Yet despite the advantages to the various parties concerned of retaining a flexible interpretation of the partnership relationship, the cloudiness of the concept became an irritant and, as the partnership bandwagon gathered momentum, the need to clarify what it might or should entail became evident. A reasoned and explicit consideration of the components of partnership would introduce some order in a very disordered world and would also help those engaged in course construction. It is not surprising therefore that one of the first attempts to explore the issue of partnership and articulate its problems and principles was made by CNAA. In 1984 the Council issued what was in effect a policy statement on partnership. This document stresses particularly the interactive nature of the school–college link. For CNAA, not only should teachers share responsibility for all aspects of students' work when they are in school, but the maximum benefit will be derived only when teachers are 'actively involved in helping to devise the work which is done in schools . . . [which] implies that they must understand the purpose of the college based work *and be able to influence it*' (p. 27, emphasis added). In terms of the redistribution of power in favour of the school, the form of partnership proposed by the Council would therefore go beyond that recommended in Circular 3/84, which suggests only the *sharing* of responsibility. (To share responsibility for something must of course entail the opportunity to influence it, but the explicit stating of this truth indicates the underlying sentiment of the Council.) It also stresses the importance of the briefing of the school by the training institution prior to the student's school experience. It was considered inadequate to transmit information *only* through documentation, a limited form of contact which nevertheless may have qualified some institutions in their own eyes to have assumed the sobriquet of partnership. Knowledge of the college course and its expectations should be *actively* acquired and this could best be achieved by encouraging teachers to attend and participate in planning meetings.

The recommendation of CNAA was that teachers should have a part to play in making decisions about the school-based element of the course. There was no suggestion that their responsibilities should go beyond this. Rather the Council implied and also formally emphasized that the task of teachers was to help students to become competent practitioners in the classroom, thereby indicating the desirable limits of their influence. 'Teachers have become concerned that basic aspects of the teacher's task, taught to them during their college days, have been omitted [from training courses] not fully appreciating that it has been agreed that they, as practitioners, are responsible for conveying these crucial elements to students at the chalk face' (p. 27). This was a model of partnership which stressed collaboration by teachers and tutors who nevertheless were to remain experts in their respective areas. It was a partnership of reciprocal interdependence.

A distinction needs to be made between two dimensions of analysis with respect to Circular 3/84. The first of these is the dimension of the elements or components of partnership, that is, the domains in which the training of the student can be shared. These include, for example, the assessment of the student on the professional or methods courses taken by the student in the training institution. It has already been pointed out that in selecting for mention some of these elements of partnership, Circular 3/84 formalized or legitimated partnership structures in the colleges and university departments. The second dimension concerns personnel rather than structure. It raises the question of *who* takes the major responsibility in any one partnership domain. If it is agreed that student assessment, say, is an area in which the two institutions can collaborate, then a further question concerns which party assumes principal responsibility in this area. Two arrangements suggest themselves. There may be a preference for a 'relationship of *equivalence*' with both parties sharing responsibility in all areas. Or the preference may be for a 'relationship of *complementarity*'. In this case, the parties agree to distribute responsibility between them across the areas, but achieving a balance of responsibility overall.

A closer look at Circular 3/84 suggests that the way in which it has interpreted and re-presented current professional practice has resulted in a model of partnership which tends to stress equivalence rather than complementarity. Teacher and tutor *share* responsibility both in the school and in the training institution. This is interesting and significant. The models of partnership (if the recommendations of the UCET Report are accepted as constituting an implicit model) which are proposed by the professionals in the institutions advocate role specialism within a framework of close collaboration. The DES on the other hand equates the roles of teacher and tutor. The bureaucratic and impersonal language in which the Report is written seems to suggest that the teacher and the tutor can each do the work of the other. For example, the Circular informs the reader that 'students should be prepared . . . to teach the full range of pupils', 'Courses should pay attention to other aspects of the teachers work', and so on. *Who* is to 'prepare the students' is not indicated, since the Circular does not specify role responsibilities. Moreover the requirement that tutors should undertake some teaching experience in schools seems to be further evidence of an implicit underlying belief that teacher and tutor can and should readily exchange tasks. One implication of this is that neither party has specific or remarkable skills. By extension, teacher training could be located in the schools with little depletion of quality since the college or department tutor has little that is unique to contribute. While the teacher must be retained, the tutor becomes marginalized if not dispensable. In this way it is suggested that Circular 3/84 presaged the direction of future government policy on teacher training. This is not to suggest that the content of Circular 3/84 was anything other than professional in intent. It aimed to establish in all institutions a minimum level of the partnership training which the professionals themselves had developed. Although its focus was the curriculum, its impact was principally constitutional.

Since the CNAA model of partnership drew on the experience of the Post Graduate Initial Training Board it represented the structuring of existing practices. And since over the years the movement away from theory and distance between the parties and towards practice and partnership has in general been evolutionary, and has consisted of pragmatic adjustments to existing structures rather than any revolutionary reassessment of the school–institution link, the model is principally a structural one. Although it has an interactive emphasis, collaboration between tutor and teacher is presented in terms of roles and role responsibilities. This is also true of Circular 3/84. Nor does Proctor (1984), who rigorously analyses and evaluates government policy on partnership, go beyond this framework. The structural perspective remains unquestioned.

Eggleston (1985) does however introduce a new element into the notion of partnership. Among the necessary conditions for what he calls 'collaborative tutelage' he suggests: 'the division of labour between college tutors and school teachers must be made explicit', 'tutors must understand their own role and that of teachers and vice versa', and 'there must be a large measure of agreement about *intentions*' (p. 183, emphasis added).

The new dimension here is that of professional judgements, dispositions, sentiments, justifications and so on, for it is these which would be evoked if teachers and tutors were called upon to articulate the 'intentions' which lie behind the structure of their practices. Moreover, what is required is '*agreement* about intentions' and, since this cannot be assumed, negotiation and hence prolonged debate and reflection will be required. This is a form of partnership which is very different from that proposed in Circular 3/84. It retains the distinctiveness of the different roles of teacher and tutor but it proposes that they should each have an explicit mutual understanding of the other's work. It is a form of partnership which is based on an appreciation of the other as a discriminating and reflective though 'opposing' colleague, and hence one which attributes high moral/professional value to the teacher. This is entirely coincident with the way in which the training of the student has been moving. Indeed it is a logical necessity that the relationship between school and training institution should be of this sort if the student is to undergo a form of training in which the generation of personal 'theory' through reflection on practice is to predominate. It would after all and in general be difficult for teachers and tutors to encourage students to reflect on their practice if they did not have this skill themselves. Yet it is more than that. If school-based training is to be anything more than a distortion of a more traditional training programme, then the respective contributions to training of tutor and teacher have to be reviewed, negotiated and agreed. This was recognized by the teams which planned the innovative Oxford course. They held 'regular plenary meetings ... to examine, develop and achieve shared understandings of what the new programme was to involve' (McIntyre, 1988, 111). As a consequence a common perspective by the respective partners on both the ends and means of the programme was achieved.

Furthermore this goal of shared understanding and its necessary dependence on articulated justifications applies not only to the teacher–tutor relationship on the Oxford course. It is also a principal aim for the triadic relationship of student, teacher and tutor with respect to the student's own work. The course is based on a model of learning which engages the student in 'an active and rational exploration of the tasks of teaching' (ibid., 108). The student learns to distinguish between different forms of knowledge about teaching, and, since the status of such knowledge can only be provisional, to question and test it critically. But knowledge about teaching comes from a variety of sources having been constructed or deduced according to a variety of criteria. Students can only come to terms with the different perspectives that they will encounter in the school and in the university, and evaluate, use and personally integrate these perspectives, if there is an understanding shared between all the parties concerned not only of the intermediate status of knowledge in their respective areas, but also of the need to respect the criteria and evidence of the other parties.

This very sketchy account of some of the principles on which the Oxford course is based gives an indication of the complexity of the model of partnership which is operating there. In terms of the theory–practice continuum outlined above, these principles place the course well towards the 'radical' pole. There is integration between theory and practice, and 'theory' has more to do with the personal practical principles that the student acquires through the testing of both received and self-generated knowledge than it has to do with 'scientific' theory transmitted didactically. This is not to say that this latter sort of general theory is entirely neglected, but it is subjected to the same review procedures as other forms of knowledge. If this model of training is in the end to train teachers who are confident and self-aware practitioners rather than insecure and hence ineffectual occupants of the teacher role (because knowledge is regarded as provisional) then teacher, tutor and student must share an understanding of the assumptions and beliefs on which the course is constructed.

The model of partnership promoted by the DES in Circular 3/84 is very different. That it does little more than affirm the status quo at the minimum level is to be expected. If 'partnership', which is seen as an important means of improving the quality of training, is to be accepted across the range of institutions, then the model of partnership proposed must in effect be a formalization of current aspirations. Apart from one or two elements such as the requirement of recent and relevant teaching experience for the tutor, this form of partnership required little more from teachers and tutors than that they ensure that the rhetoric and the reality were brought into line. No change of attitude is required. The perception of education studies seems to be that it is still taught in the training institutions and is 'applied' (Annex, para. 11) and it is not until the final sentence of the final section on course structure and content that the theorizing student makes a very brief appearance (para. 12).

Thus by the mid-1980s the situation with respect to partnership in initial training was complex and varied. On the one hand central government had uniquely intervened to enforce a minimum level of partnership. In doing so it endorsed the trend towards closer collaboration between school and training institution, but the model of partnership which it advocated was ill-defined. The survey of initial training undertaken by HMI between 1983 and 1985 seems to imply that partnership practice within the institutions was widely distributed on the continuum of formal theory/unrelated practice: personal theory/integrated practice. Partnership was well developed in some institutions, in others 'hardly embryonic'. The courses at Sussex and Oxford seemed to exemplify the direction in which their aspirations suggested the institutions in general were moving.

THE POLITICAL CONTEXT[1]

The way in which partnership developed in the training institutions has been outlined above. It was suggested that the relationship between theory and practice had evolved in response to critical argument and the testing in practice of that relationship, and that partnership had emerged as a logically and technically justifiable stage in this development. And precisely because the relationship between theory and practice has been subjected to continuous review and analysis the trend has been towards an integrated model of training, as is exemplified in the new course at Oxford. It was also noted that external influences such as the James Report seemed to have further promoted existing professional trends. This third section returns once again to the relationship between the professionally generated model of partnership and external events which have the potential to affect it – the teacher training policies of central government during the

1980s. On this occasion, however, the respective presentations of the theory–practice relationship of the professionals and the government, and hence their respective views on partnership, have diverged rather than coincided over time. This is the substance of the following discussion.

It has already been pointed out that the impact of Circular 3/84 was constitutional rather than professional and that in this latter area its requirements for the institutions were unexceptional, reflecting as they did the more or less minimum standards of partnership already in operation. But more important in the context of the current discussion was the conceptualization in the Circular of the theory–practice relationship: theory was still applied. Although in the training system this may have been, indeed probably was, quite commonly the case, at the level of practice, in analysis and debate, this form of the relationship had been discredited.

The HMI discussion paper *Teaching in Schools: The Content of Initial Training* was published in 1983. As both a comment on current practice and a policy document it recognizes the importance of partnership: 'Partnership between schools and initial training institutions should be strengthened at all levels and in all aspects of the student's training' (HMI, 1983, 17). It is a document that typifies the approach of the Inspectorate. The tone of the text is mild and persuasive ('there is value in . . .' 'much can be gained from . . .') and it encompasses the range of existing acceptable and good practices without appearing to endorse some rather than others. This is the case with respect to the relationship between theory and practice. On the one hand the theory–practice relationship appears to retain its traditional 'disciplines' form. What is learned in the college is applied in the school. Educational and professional studies 'are centred on the students' practical experience of schools and teaching' (ibid., 10). Yet the text also advocates a more radical model of theory *vis-à-vis* practice based on 'experiment rather than on a didactic approach' and on 'a commitment to the practice of self evaluation' (ibid., 13).

Teaching in Schools was a revised version of a discussion paper prepared by the Inspectorate for the Advisory Committee on the Supply and Education of Teachers (ACSET) which prior to the issue of Circular 3/84 was invited to report on the structure and content of initial training to the Secretary of State. Since members of the Inspectorate have first-hand and recent knowledge of events and developments in the training institutions, it is not unreasonable to assume that their views would have been given serious consideration. However, *Teaching Quality* (DES, 1983), the White Paper which preceded Circular 3/84, contains no reference to the latter formulation of the theory–practice relationship. Education studies should be 'closely linked with practical experience in school' (ibid., 19).

A major concern of *Teaching Quality* is with qualifying standards, and to this end it cites the ACSET recommendation that 'a satisfactory level of professional competence, including practical teaching skills should be a necessary condition for the awards of a BEd or a PGCE degree' (ibid., para. 59). But has not this been the case for some time? What is of interest in the context of the present discussion is the emphasis on skills which remain dissociated from theory. And this is also the form which the theory–practice relationship was to take in Circular 3/84 which followed. 'Theory' is still the disciplines of education which are somehow made relevant for the student's work in schools; skills, which are of course acquired through practice in schools, appear to remain atheoretical.

But as long as the gap between theory and practice continues partnership will remain at best at the level of (improved) structural collaboration, and the core of the student learning experience is unaltered. It is not until the theory–practice relationship is reconceptualized that a satisfactory *integrated* model of partnership will evolve. Moreover, certain other consequences follow from a failure to confront the theory–practice dilemma. The first of these is that by representing 'theory' as an area of external knowledge, it becomes possible to exclude it from the training programme. As the importance of practice in school is acknowledged by allocating more student time to it, 'theory' as an item on the timetable can readily be marginalized or even eliminated. Secondly, if practice is viewed as the learning of skills as it is here, rather than as a process of personal and professional development, then there are implied consequences for the assessment of the student. If the form of training the student receives places an emphasis on the progressive acquisition of insight and the generation of some personal practical principles then it is inappropriate to assess this student according to any kind of yes/no schedule. But if training is envisaged principally as the acquisition of skills, whether or not theory is 'applied', then assessment according to competence is not unreasonable. One either has adequate mastery of a skill for the purpose of the moment or one does not. Thus by the middle of the decade a professional concern with standards in teacher training on the part of central government had, if not widened, at least confirmed the gap between theory and practice. In so doing it made possible the elimination of theory and so opened the door to the possibility of apprenticeship training.

Catenote 4, which was issued by the Council for the Accreditation of Teacher Education in 1986 (which body was established by the DES and the members of which were appointees of the Secretary of State), does nothing to reverse this trend, although it specifically focuses on links between training institutions and schools. It is for guidance only and it makes out the case for increasing partnership between the two types of institutions with complete professional conviction. It mentions the importance of sharing aims, approaches and common understandings, and of tutors and teachers holding conferences, and it gives numerous examples of good practice. Yet these recommendations are in the end but extensions of the existing well-established forms of school–college links. School experience is where students 'expect to develop and test the practical classroom skills to which they have been introduced elsewhere in the course. For tutors there are rich opportunities to help students make connection with issues and ideas encountered in books, lectures and seminars' (para. 5). Thus 'theory' is not generated in the classroom or, to put this another way, practice *per se* is devoid of theory. The theory–practice gap remains the gulf it was.

Circular 24/89 (DES, 1989a) *Initial Teacher Training: Approval of Courses* replaced Circular 3/84 and differs from it in a fundamental respect. It is at this point, in the view of the writer, that the curriculum and content of training *per se* are transferred from the professional to the political domain. (It is argued that in issuing Circular 3/84 the Secretary of State was assuming his dormant powers in order to enhance the professional quality of training.) The section 'Co-operation between Institutions, Local Authorities and Schools' clarifies and expands the school–UDE relationship. Teachers are to be given further power: they should now be involved in 'the planning of initial teacher training courses and in their evaluation'. In this, the Circular again reflects what is becoming a regular practice in the institutions (HMI, 1987). However, the directives are now also taken beyond current practice, and so represent an extension of central control. It is, for example, a novel requirement that institutions 'should have a written policy statement which sets out the roles of tutors, headteachers, other teachers employers and students in relation to students' school experience' (para. 2.5). The requirements of Circular 3/84 were within the bounds of current practice, and thus the substantive control that it exercised could be regarded as vicarious. In Circular 24/89, constitutional control continues and substantive control has become direct.

A careful reading of Catenote 4 and Circular 24/89 indicate the way in which power is leaching from the training institution and being credited to the school. 'Partnership' as it is here proposed is becoming as one-sided as it used to be in the post-Robbins era, although now it is the teacher to whom status and authority is being attributed. This is regarded as another indication of the way in which there is slippage from the area of professional discourse to that of political discourse. The concern with partnership is of a *professional* nature; it is proposed and supported because it is perceived as improving the quality of training. By definition it incorporates some notion of equality, and this is true whether the model of partnership is one of equivalence or one of complementarity. But that power is being redistributed in favour of the teacher to an extent over and above that required of partnership is indicated in the way in which the contribution of the tutor is devalued. For example, in the Circular the (potential) contribution of the teacher to student training is given in high profile. The teacher is frequently mentioned by title (Annex B, paras 1–6). Yet the sections concerning the contribution of the training institution tend to be written in the impersonal mode or in terms of the institution. The title of tutor or its equivalent is more difficult to find. The portrait of the methods tutor in Catenote 4 (para. 17) is less than flattering. If the tutor has not recently held a school teaching post, then he or she may lack not only confidence, but credibility also.

The confused presentation of theory in Circular 24/89 seems to confirm this view of the tutor. First, theory plays a traditional role. It should provide students with useful background knowledge about their pupils (Annex A, para. 6.3). But it should 'also enable students to appreciate their task as teachers within ... the values and the economic and other foundations of the free and civilised society in which their pupils are growing up, and the need to prepare pupils for adulthood, citizenship and the world of work' (Annex A, para. 6.1). This awkward sentence seems to imply that education theory contributes to the students' professional development (it 'enables students') in so far as the student is explicitly engaged in a form of social engineering. In a yet further presentation of education and professional studies, the institutions 'should ensure that they are clearly linked to students' school experience, so as to enable them to develop both a full range of competences and the ability to evaluate their own performance' (Annex B, para. 6.1). The latter half of the sentence seems to indicate that reference to theory will help the student to improve his or her classroom practice. This might indicate a nod in the direction of the theorizing teacher, although the way it is expressed seems to make this unlikely. The term 'evaluation' suggests that the function of theory is to permit self-monitoring of the student's performance rather than to encourage reflective growth. This is an interesting difference. By extension it could almost be hinting at a return to the Protestant ethic. The process of training has less to do with the expansion and development of the self than with the internalization of constraints. The tutor is clearly a Jack (or Jill) of all trades but has mastery of none. If she or he is confused about the function of theory, how useful can it be to the student? Merit now lies with the practising teacher who has practical skills and observable competence.

Furthermore, the power and authority of the training institution as an autonomous professional body is now weakened. The role of the local committee is to be revised. It must include representatives of business and other outside interests (para. 8) who 'will now be required to play a more substantial and consistent role in the scrutiny and monitoring of courses' (para. 7). Thus the training institution is to become accountable to local business interests. The appropriateness of such a suggestion is not the issue here, but the terms 'monitoring' and 'scrutiny', rather than, say, 'accountability', are not ones that are usually associated with professionals, to whom is usually ascribed the capacity for self-monitoring. Such a proposition implies a lowering of status, a lack of responsibility. When compared with that of Circular 3/84 the tone is peremptory: 'The *Government* attaches great importance to the role of local committees in fostering partnership between teachers, local education authorities and institutions as well as in the critical *scrutiny* of the courses of the institutions they cover' (DES, 1989a, para. 9) replaces: 'The *committees* should be *encouraged* to discuss all aspects of initial teacher training and should play a particularly important role in *promoting* links between training institutions, schools and the community' (DES, 1984, para. 8, emphasis added).

A consideration of the extent to which the developments outlined above represent some of the principles of the New Conservatism will indicate the way in which teacher training has become infused with the political philosophy of central government. That skills are stressed and theory is either marginalized or discredited echoes the belief that theory is empty argument and that common sense and getting on with the job are what matters (Thatcher, 1989). To locate more of the responsibility for training in the schools with a diminished contribution from tutors (since there is less requirement for theory) and moreover to discredit the tutor or lecturer represents the conviction that power should be returned to the people. There is an expectation that teacher education should be accountable to the world of business. Moreover, the emerging emphasis on 'competence' and exit criteria seem to suggest a tendency to regard teacher education itself as a business rather than a profession. Since a performance is judged either competent or incompetent, the term subsumes both a minimum and a maximum level of attainment. In other words it suggests standardization. But 'standardization' is not a quality either claimed by or attributed to professionals. It is on the other hand of crucial importance in the manufacture of products.

The licensed teacher scheme was proposed in 1988. It is a pragmatic solution to the demographic problem of a declining population and to the socio-economic problem of 'retention' in the teaching force. But it also represents the logical development of the trends that have been outlined above. Trainees would be placed under licence in school for a period of two years. They would learn on the job, where they 'would undertake such training as the employer deemed appropriate' (DES, 1988, para. 14). These proposals support the conclusions above concerning the politicization of teacher education. The language in which they are presented is that of the business world. The new scheme will be 'a simpler and more effective system'; alternative training arrangements are dismissed as not 'cost effective'; there is a concern with efficiency, an emphasis on competence. More particularly, that this scheme is a form of apprenticeship is indicated not only by the neglect of the contribution of the training institution ('In some instances training *might* by arrangement be provided by a body other than the employer such as a local teacher training institution' (para. 27(ii), emphasis added) and the almost complete transfer of responsibility for training to the 'shop floor', but also by the suggestion that it is representatives of 'management' who are 'best equipped to make a judgement on the professional qualities of the persons concerned when the time arrives for a decision on qualified teacher status' (para. 15).

If the licensed teacher scheme were the only recent proposal by the government for the future of teacher training then it might appear that 'partnership' was but a step in the process of bringing teacher training under political influence. But an alternative scheme, that of the 'articled teacher', has also been suggested (DES, 1989b). Perhaps this permits an assumption that the licensed teacher scheme is a temporary measure designed like the postwar emergency scheme to meet a short-term need. It is certainly heavily justified in those terms. Be that as it may, that the government can propose two parallel but very different schemes suggests that the tension between the professional and the political dimensions in teacher training is still very much in evidence.

Although the proposals for the training of articled teachers are very sketchy, they appear to indicate endorsement by the government of the way in which teacher training has been developing in the institutions. Since the proposals are for 'the setting up of some experimental schemes for school-based ITT' the government is not only legitimating the aspirations of the institutions to engage in school-based training, it is providing the wherewithal to put these aspirations into practice. Although articled teachers would receive most of their formal training in school, 'such training would be delivered both by the institution's academic and professional tutors and by selected members of the staff of the school' (para. 3). In addition, there should be some off-the-job training either in the institution or elsewhere. It seems therefore to be a scheme based on partnership between the institutions and the schools, although of what kind it is not possible to tell. The content of training is not specified. Does this mean that the initiative is to be left with the consortia to devise a course within the constraint that at least four-fifths of the course should be spent in school?

CONCLUSION

How should the professional community respond to these recent very diverse proposals of the government? It must surely evaluate them in the light of its commitment to provide the best training that it knows how. Teacher training is never static as consideration of the developments that took place during the 1960s and 1970s demonstrates. It is constantly evolving and redefining itself through the twin processes of rational argument and practical experiment. The current outcome of the integration of these processes is the trend towards school-based training in a context of partnership. This seems to be emerging as a goal for the future although it is difficult to estimate the extent to which the major principle on which this form of training is based – a certain form of the relationship between theory and practice – is being exercised in practice.

There is an irony here. Just as the model of training exemplified in the licensed teacher scheme can be construed as representing the political philosophy of the government, so also does the model of training proposed by the professional community support the principles of the New Conservatism in different ways; and this is quite possible because of the complex, many-layered nature of that Conservatism (Jessop *et al.*, 1988). One of the major concerns of the government is that education should keep abreast of trends in the economy, should in fact service the economy. This suggests a need for teaching to be flexible in both method and content and for teachers to perceive their role as a developmental one. But whereas the characteristic of apprenticeship learning is repetition and not innovation, the theorizing teacher should have acquired the habit of critically evaluating her practices and of modifying and adapting them as the need arises. In addition the model of training within the institutions would seem to favour the development of individual responsibility more readily than an apprenticeship scheme. Furthermore, if a comparison is made between the respective values to any government of the two ways in which its principles are embodied first of all in the licensed teacher scheme and secondly in the theorizing teacher model, then it is the *latter* which is of the greater value to a government determined on introducing and stabilizing political change. This is because the habit of critical assessment and adaptation and also personal responsibility are internalized qualities and therefore far more potent determinants of personal action than for example externally imposed accountability, a fact of which Mrs Thatcher has a sophisticated awareness (Thatcher, 1989).

If there is any substance in the conjecture that the model of training preferred by the institutions supports the political intentions of the government, should it make any difference to the assessment of its worth by the professional community? The answer must surely be that it should not, since the conclusion that this model is the best yet devised must rest on other criteria and on a commitment to professional advancement as an independent aim. Current government action is, however, an important stimulus to those in the training institutions to reassess their own views on training. As such it is a benefit to the professionals for it forces the critical evaluation of their own perspectives and so promotes the further development of their professional goals.

NOTE

(1) The following section hypothesizes a growing parallel between the initial training curriculum and the political philosophy of the government. This is not a novel situation. Research by the author suggests that in the post-Robbins era the teacher training programme similarly reflected the ideology of the government of the day.

REFERENCES

Alexander, R. (1979) 'What is a course? Curriculum models and CNAA validation'. *Journal of Further and Higher Education*, **3** (1), 31–45.
Alexander, R. and Whittaker, J. (1980) *Developments in PGCE Courses*. Guildford: Society for Research into Higher Education.
CATE: Council for the Accreditation of Teacher Education (1986) *Catenote 4. Links between Initial Teacher Training and Schools*. London: CATE.
CNAA: Council for National Academic Awards (1984) *Perspectives on Postgraduate Initial Training: The CNAA Validated PGCE*. London: CNAA.
DES: Department of Education and Science (1972) *Teacher Education and Training* (The James Report). London: HMSO.
DES: Department of Education and Science (1983) *Teaching Quality*. London: HMSO.
DES: Department of Education and Science (1984) *Initial Teacher Training: Approval of Courses* (Circular 3/84). London: DES.

DES: Department of Education and Science (1988) *Qualified Teacher Status. Consultation Document*. London: DES.

DES: Department of Education and Science (1989a) *Initial Teacher Training: Approval of Courses* (Circular 24/89). London: DES.

DES: Department of Education and Science (1989b) *Articled Teacher Pilot Scheme*. London: DES.

Eggleston, J. (1985) 'Subject centred and school based teacher training in the Post Graduate Certificate of Education', in Hopkins, D. and Reid, K. (eds) *Rethinking Teacher Education*. Beckenham: Croom Helm.

Elliott, J. (1976) 'Preparing teachers for classroom accountability'. *Education for Teaching*, **100**, 49–71.

Gorbutt, D. (1975) 'Redesigning teacher education at North East London Polytechnic'. *British Journal of Teacher Education*, **1**(1).

HMI: Her Majesty's Inspectorate (1979) *Developments in the BEd Course: A Study Based on Fifteen Institutions*. London: DES.

HMI: Her Majesty's Inspectorate (1983) *Teaching in Schools: The Content of Initial Training*. London: DES.

HMI: Her Majesty's Inspectorate (1987) *Quality in Schools: The Initial Training of Teachers*. London: DES.

Hirst, P. (1975) 'The graduate Certificate in Education course'. Paper for the Universities Council for the Education of Teachers.

Jessop, B., Bonnett, K., Bromley, S. and Ling, T. (1988) *Thatcherism*. Cambridge: Polity Press.

McCulloch, M. (1979) *School Experience in Initial BEd/BEd Hons Degrees Validated by the CNAA*. London: CNAA.

McIntyre, D. (1988) 'Designing a teacher education curriculum from research and theory on teacher knowledge', in Calderhead, J. (ed.) *Teachers' Professional Learning*. Lewes: Falmer.

Patrick, H., Bernbaum, G. and Reid, K. (1982) *The Structure and Process of Initial Teacher Education within Universities in England and Wales*. Leicester: University of Leicester School of Education.

Proctor, N. (1984) 'Towards a partnership with schools'. *Journal of Education for Teaching*, **10** (3).

Sutton, C. (1975) 'Theory in the classroom'. *British Journal of Teacher Education*, **1** (3).

Thatcher, M. (1989) *Speeches to the Conservative Party Conference, 1975–1988*. London: Conservative Political Centre.

Tickle, L. (1987) *Learning Teaching, Teaching Teaching*. Lewes: Falmer.

Universities Council for the Education of Teachers (1979) *The PGCE Course and the Training of Specialist Teachers for Secondary Schools*. London: UCET.

Webster, J. R. (1975) 'The implementation of an integrated approach to teacher training'. *British Journal of Teacher Education*, **1** (2).

Wilson, P. S. and Pring, R. (1975) Editorial Introduction. *London Educational Review*, **4** (2/3).

Chapter 2

The Two Routes into Teaching

Ted Wragg

Like most professions, teaching has in recent years required would-be practitioners to embark on a properly approved course of training. This is not, however, universally the case, as there are countries where formal training is not compulsory. I was told by the Greek Minister of Education in 1988 that one of his greatest problems was that he had to license as a teacher anyone who had completed a course in higher education and, moreover, had to find each person who so wished a teaching post.

In England and Wales training has been compulsory for all except maths and science graduates since the early 1970s. On the surface, therefore, it seems as if there is a single route into the profession for all except a tiny minority. Yet political and ideological debates in the late 1980s led to a situation where two parallel models were under consideration.

Model A represents an increasingly professional view of teachers, arguing that the job is already extremely demanding and will be even more so as we enter the twenty-first century. According to this notion what is needed is a well trained teaching force, not only on entry, but throughout a teacher's professional career.

Model B is based on the assumption that almost anyone can teach, and that the nineteenth-century model of the apprentice teacher is adequate. All that teachers need, it is argued, when they are in training, is to spend time alongside someone in a school and pick up a few tips. They will soon be operational.

Part of the tension in teacher training at the present time is that both these concepts are endorsed by the government. The twenty-first-century Model A is represented by the establishment and subsequent strengthening of the criteria for initial training courses, applied when the Council for the Accreditation of Teacher Education (CATE) scrutinizes these. The nineteenth-century apprenticeship Model B was most strongly manifested in the Green Paper on Qualified Teacher Status (QTS) published in 1988.

The Model A view of teacher training has been predominant for at least the last eighteen years. In 1971 untrained graduates were no longer permitted to teach in primary schools and after 1973 a similar restriction was placed on intending secondary school teachers with the exception of maths and science graduates. Subsequently Maths and English O level were required for all new recruits to teaching.

The James Report (DES, 1972) proposed a number of reforms aimed at making initial training more rigorous, some of which, like the probationary-year induction programme, were never fully·implemented. During the 1980s the establishment of the Council for Accreditation of Teacher Education produced a long set of criteria about entry requirements, the personal qualities of intending teachers, the content and process of courses, and the involvement of trainers in teaching, all of which were designed to increase rather than decrease the quality of initial training.

During the same period the training of teachers already in post reflected the same trend towards greater rigour. Thousands of non-graduates were released for one-year full-time courses in universities, polytechnics and colleges to enable them to obtain a first degree. The Department of Education and Science put significant sums of money into Joint Regional Courses, often lasting about twenty-one days, which involved teachers in attending study centres, usually in higher education institutions, and pursuing some project in their own school related to the course they were following.

There was, however, a countervailing trend which reflected the growth of Model B. There is some considerable nostalgia within sectors of the government for the nineteenth century, which is seen as a period when enterprise was allowed to flourish away from the constraints of bureaucracy. At that time there was nothing like the elaborate CATE-controlled criteria which govern training in the late twentieth century. Model B is based on an apprenticeship system which, by the end of the nineteenth century, had been thoroughly discredited.

In his history of English education Smith (1931) gives an idealized view of education in the past:

> In the earlier order of things the father educated his son by a varied life out of doors, by growing food and breeding cattle, and the boy acquired his skill at an early age. His object lessons were got from the smithy, the weaver's shed, the mill, and the carpenter's shop, and his imagination was fired by the stories and legends which belonged to the familiar woods and streams and the neighbouring castle and manor.

Unfortunately children were also beaten so viciously that laws had to be passed restricting physical abuse of them, teachers were often charlatans who extracted money from their trusting fellows, barely ahead, in some cases, of the pupils they taught, and training was either non-existent or based on the brief, and in some respects eccentric, methods of Andrew Bell and Joseph Lancaster. At the very end of the eighteenth century Bell had encouraged older children to stay on at school to teach younger pupils, and Lancaster had started the Borough Road School along similar lines, for he had read a pamphlet written by Bell.

By 1820 about 200,000 children were being taught in over 1,500 Bell or Lancaster monitorial schools. The 'course' element was rudimentary. Bell claimed he only needed twenty-four hours and Lancaster gave his novices a few lectures on the 'passions'. In general recruits simply copied what they saw in school.

By the end of the nineteenth century there had been substantial criticism of the crude apprenticeship model. The Newcastle Commission of 1861 expressed several reservations, pressing for much better trained teachers, and was very critical of young recruits who showed 'great meagreness of knowledge, crudeness, and mechanical methods of study, arising largely from neglect of their training by their head teachers'.

Many years later, in 1888, the Cross Commission pinpointed the flaws in the teachers produced by the apprenticeship system with devastating accuracy:

> All they could do was faithfully to transmit the letter of the lesson they had received, for

how should they have received its spirit? Consequently all they were called upon to do was to apply exactly the mechanical processes in which they had been drilled.

These children under this mechanical discipline often mistook and confounded the formulas they were called upon to apply. The only remedy for this was to drive into them by constant repetition the daily course of instruction.

The exception in the nineteenth century to this dreary reinforcement of the status quo was David Stow's Glasgow Normal Seminary which was opened in 1837. It was surprisingly modern in concept. There were adventure playgrounds and methods of lesson analysis well ahead of their time. Trainees had to give a 'gallery lesson', when they taught children to a gallery full of fellow students and tutors. Unfortunately some literally 'played to the gallery' which led to a reappraisal of this approach, but it was not all that different, except for the absence of recording technology like sound and video cassette recorders and certain twentieth-century notions of learning theory, from some of the micro-teaching programmes common in the 1970s. David Stow's programme was the true forerunner of Model A.

Even though the apprentices of the nineteenth century were, in the main, immature adolescents, many of the criticisms of that model can be applied today to the licensed teacher scheme. The first is that training newcomers, however important it may be to the profession as a whole, is not the top priority for a school, which must give higher priority to the teaching of all the children in the school. When we tried to launch an ambitious partnership scheme at Exeter in one particular region, which would have involved teachers more fully in the training process, eight primary heads wrote back independently, but in almost identical terms, saying that teachers had their hands full and could not possibly give more than occasional supervision.

Secondly, there is the problem of new recruits being trained in a single school with little opportunity to review practice elsewhere. In a rapidly changing educational environment, teachers need to be able to change their teaching strategies. Many of the precepts of the General Certificate of Secondary Education, such as the notion of 'investigation' in mathematics or the development of 'communicative competence' in modern languages, presupposed that teachers would have a wide range of teaching strategies in their repertoire. If too many teachers were trained solely in one school under the apprenticeship model they could well emerge with too limited a range of teaching styles to be sufficiently flexible when the need arose. Research evidence from classroom observation studies (Wragg, 1984) has shown that many teachers engage in 1,000 interpersonal exchanges or more in a single day and ask hundreds of questions every week. If, when they are laying down a pattern in their early career, they have only limited experience of what might be done, and imitate, in some cases, a single teacher, they may not develop the full set of professional skills likely to be required in the 1990s and beyond. The proposal to recruit ex-military physical training instructors as licensed teachers with no formal further professional preparation, only on-the-job training, is particularly alarming in this context.

Thirdly, there is the matter of the sheer diversity of people recruited under the licensed teacher apprenticeship scheme. The Department of Education and Science has stated that training would be based on a 'deficit' model, whereby, presumably, trainees are 'topped up' on an individual basis like car battery cells. Under Model A, training institutions are able to group students under subject or other headings and provide suitable and cost-effective preparation. Under Model B a school might find it has one licensed teacher who is bilingual in English and Spanish but is a poor communicator and class manager and a second who is articulate and well organized, with industrial experience, but with huge gaps in his or her knowledge of the 17 National Curriculum 'balanced science' attainment targets. The one needs little or no help with the subject matter but considerable work on professional skills, the other is the exact reverse. The training needs are so disparate they are unlikely to be met, nor will there be suitable courses readily to hand for each trainee to attend.

A fourth reservation about Model B comes from the experience of training recruits from industry at Exeter University. Each year we take between twenty and thirty people, usually from an industrial background and having the equivalent of two years' higher education, often a Higher National Diploma. They are given a two-year full-time shortened undergraduate course at the end of which they are given a BSc degree with qualified teacher status, for they are in the fields of mathematics, science or technology. When the licensed teacher scheme was announced all were asked if they would have preferred to take that route had it been available. Only one said he would, but purely on financial grounds. All members of two-year groups said they wanted to train properly, did not wish to risk failure when making a significant career change in their thirties or forties, and would have been especially anxious about class control had they been immediately school-based. The message they gave was unambiguous: they recognized they were embarking on an exacting professional career and they wanted to get it right.

Despite damning condemnations of the apprenticeship system there is still some support for it, even in its crude form. Professor Anthony O'Hear argues (O'Hear, 1988) that, since many teachers in independent schools were untrained and independent schools obtain better examination scores than maintained schools, all teachers should be allowed direct entry to the classroom. Yet this argument is flawed. First of all it is only some and not all independent schools that obtain better examination results than some maintained schools, and secondly it is not the factor 'independentness' or 'untrainedness' that secures such advantages as occur, but rather the fact that entrants to independent schools are usually from more affluent professional backgrounds and arrive with a more favourable social and sometimes genetic endowment than is the case in a school which recruits from the whole population.

The question therefore arises why a scheme which went out of favour for good reasons decades ago should have found some support. The answer lies not so much in the intellectual appeal of the apprenticeship scheme but in the current dilemma over teacher supply which faces the country over the next ten years.

The rollercoaster graph of births in the United Kingdom since the Second World War produced two peaks in 1945 and 1964. After the mid-1960s the birthrate fell slowly at first and then sharply, leading to a reduction of one-third by 1977. Since that year there has been a steady climb. The consequence is that the over-supply of teachers which characterized the late 1970s and early 1980s and which led to the closure of more than a hundred colleges of education has given way to a rise in demand which cannot, on present predictions, be met by conventional means.

In the late 1980s we have been training some 11,000 new teachers each year. This is in sharp contrast with the 20,000 recruits which will be required in the mid-1990s. At present about one in every twelve graduates is recruited to teaching. With the falling populations of 18–22-year-olds this would need to be one in five or even one in four by the mid-1990s. There is no prospect of such a target being met and so alternative routes are quite rightly being sought: hence the Green Paper of 1988 which proposed the 'licensed teacher' route. In its original form this was seen as a tidying-up operation to clarify several routes into teaching, such as the ones for graduates of countries other than England and Wales and the recognition of non-graduates who had acquired valuable and relevant industrial experience.

There is no doubt that the nonsensical waste of time which occurred when some perfectly competent teacher who had trained in Canada or Australia had to wait months or years for clearance needed to be swept away. However, the small number of unqualified but industrially experienced recruits who were already being recognized by local authorities could easily, at a time of desperate shortage, grow from a trickle into a torrent. Major deficits in maths and science already exist, and with the introduction of the National Curriculum, following the 1988 Education Reform Act, modern linguists and teachers of design and technology are also likely to be in short supply. The temptation to recruit thousands rather than hundreds of licensed teachers will become overwhelming.

It is not only in the field of initial training that the trend towards reductionism has been apparent. Following the James Report (1972), which recommended a sabbatical term for teachers every seven years, some local authorities, such as Leeds, tried to develop a coherent secondment policy. Under the pool system which operated until 1986/7 the application of Model A was simple, and in 1986 and 1987 about 2,000 teachers a year were able to spend their sabbatical leave doing full-time courses at a university. This fell to nearer 600 in 1988 and 400 in 1989.

Instead of significant full-time release to acquire greater expertise in special educational needs, curriculum development or management, teachers had to equip themselves for such major initiatives as the introduction of the General Certificate of Secondary Education in two days, for that was the length of preparatory courses. The same model has been proposed for the implementation of the National Curriculum and National Attainment Tests. Yet the James Report proposals, had they been implemented, would have allowed teachers who taught for, say, forty-two years, and were therefore the backbone of the profession, to have six terms of study leave during a professional career. A typical pattern might have been a one-year secondment to obtain a master's degree, a one-term release for some significant piece of retraining, and numerous single days or shorter courses throughout their professional lives.

It could be argued, of course, that training is not necessary, that teaching embodies the sort of professional skills that should be learned purely by imitation of current practice. That is not a view shared by the medical profession. Doctors would certainly not even contemplate a 'licensed doctors' scheme, whereby post-A-level novices spent a couple of years in the surgery of a GP and then were fully qualified. Mere imitation of current practice would also have produced a profession still committed to the use of leeches.

There is not much empirical evidence for or against the effects of formal training, for in recent years untrained teachers have been a rarity, so there has been no opportunity to compare matched groups. In the 1960s, however, when untrained graduates still entered the profession with some frequency, Mildred Collins conducted a careful study at Leicester University (Collins, 1964). She matched two groups of new teachers, one trained, the other untrained, according to degree class, sex and teaching subject. Her findings were very clear. The teachers in the untrained group were rated lower by heads, were more likely to be absent from school and for longer periods, were more likely to have their probationary period extended or leave the profession altogether, and were less likely to read professional journals or join a professional association. There would, no doubt, have been differences in motivation between the two groups, but when Model A and Model B exist alongside each other in the 1990s it seems highly likely that a similar study would obtain similar results.

Training in itself does not guarantee improved professional skills in trainees. What the twenty-first-century model at its best can offer is several ingredients which do not necessarily accrue through the process of imitation. These include a number of factors which are endorsed by the CATE criteria: that newcomers should show proper mastery of their subject matter; have spent significant periods in school under close supervision; have learned to analyse and improve their own teaching; be familiar with different styles and strategies of teaching and the appropriateness of each; understand children's learning difficulties and how to provide remedial teaching; be able to match the task to the individual pupil; know how to monitor and assess children's progress, and numerous others. Good training courses provide suitable experiences for trainees through a partnership between supervising teachers in school and tutors in training institutions. The experience of the nineteenth century was that a pure apprenticeship scheme leaves too much to chance, and, inevitably, omits a great deal.

There have been substantial improvements in the quality of Model A training in recent years. During the 1960s the closure of many colleges and the reductions in student teacher numbers had a devastating effect, but some of the best institutions did survive, though not all those that closed were inferior. During the late 1970s and the 1980s closer partnerships with schools were developed, the use of video cameras to film and analyse teaching became commonplace and, having lagged behind schools in the previous decade, many institutions caught up and surged ahead. Many of the major curriculum packages developed by bodies such as the Nuffield Foundation, the Schools Council, publishers and other sponsors, had involved staff whose main job was in a teacher training institution.

In their paper *Education Observed No. 7* (DES, 1988) Her Majesty's Inspectorate described their evaluations of training in university departments and schools of education. They commended the quality of much of what went on, saying, 'the increasing integration of educational theory with professional training and practical experience in schools not only makes effective use of the limited time available, but also enables students to relate all aspects of their course to the work in the classroom'.

This observation was based on visits by HMI to thirty-two university departments and schools of education (UDEs) from 1982 to 1987. It was not the only positive statement made by HMI in their report, for they also say, on entry qualifications, that universities recruit well-qualified sixth formers and undergraduates to their bachelor degrees and PGCE courses; that students 'nearly all show signs of becoming competent teachers and some are exceptionally able'; on research, 'the quality of research in UDEs has won national and international recognition, and it enriches the teaching on initial training courses'; on in-service, 'Staff are also substantially involved in a wide range of in-service training, which usefully strengthens their links with practising teachers'; on partnership, 'the growing involvement of practising teachers in initial training is a welcome development'. Many of these observations also occur in HMI reports on the public sector of teacher training. It gives the lie to the assertion by critics of Model A that it is overly theoretical and out of touch with what is happening in schools. Indeed it is notable that two of the most used books on a topic like teacher appraisal are by university-based academics (Day, Whitaker and Wren, 1987; Wragg, 1987).

There are, however, critical points which must be noted. These include the observation that 'much of the teaching in UDEs is of a high standard, but, all too frequently, its strength lies in its individual excellence rather than in its contribution to the quality of the course as a whole'; that better management, co-ordination and monitoring are needed to achieve coherence; that the many demands made on UDE staff and the low prestige accorded to initial training in some institutions can lead to an overuse of occasional and part-time staff; that some tutors rely too heavily on teacher supervision during block practice though less so in the school experience phases; that the role of teachers in the training process needs to be clarified. The argument put forward in this paper, however, is not that Model A is perfect, merely that it is vastly better than the nineteenth-century Model B. The HMI report makes valuable observations which can and must be incorporated into future planning.

The systematic crafting of teachers' professional skills and the development of the person inherent in good Model A practice represents the professionalism of teaching; not the power-laden self-interest of the legal profession, but presenting, enhancing and enabling the best of classroom practice, nurturing critical analysis and inquiry, a certain amount of judicious risk-taking in the interest of improving the quality of teaching and learning, and maintaining and raising professional standards. A significant move towards the nineteenth-century Model B could easily de-professionalize both teaching and teacher training. The pressing need to staff schools in the 1990s with anyone not actually on a life-support machine, the temptation for hard-up governors of locally managed schools to hire someone unqualified and cheap rather than qualified and expensive, the open contempt that some politicians have expressed for both teaching and training, can all work against the best intentions of Model A.

There has been some considerable pressure to adopt Model B, overtly on the grounds that it is efficient and close to grassroots, but covertly because it is thought to be cheaper. It is difficult to support this assertion with the full evidence, because some of it is of a confidential nature. There has been, however, an overstatement of the 'effectiveness' of licensed teacher schemes in the United States. At the American Educational Research Association Annual Conference in San Francisco in April 1989 concern was expressed both informally and during symposium discussions at the so-called 'evaluations' of licensed teacher schemes. In some cases these were being based purely on written tests of 'competence'. It was being asserted by proponents of the licensed teacher schemes that those unqualified teachers who had attended Saturday classes under the licensed teacher scheme were 'as competent' as experienced teachers.

These conclusions were sometimes founded on a single pencil and paper test of what seemed to be 'right' answers. For example, in one of the test papers I was shown on a confidential basis, the respondent was asked to cite the three 'most important' principles of lesson planning. Many of the licensed teachers merely reproduced the ones they had been told about and faithfully written down during a Saturday morning class. These were, of course, deemed to be the 'right' answers, since the organizers of the course had constructed the test. The matched sample of experienced teachers, with no knowledge of the often arbitrary prescriptions peddled in a Saturday morning session, replied in their own manner, often with different, but no doubt equally valid responses.

Such dubious 'evaluations' would have no standing in educational research, based, as they are, not on observation, testing of learning or professional lesson appraisal, but solely on a test requiring the reproduction of arbitrary orthodoxy. A similar attempt to boost the licensed teacher scheme occurred in Britain when, in 1988, Kenneth Baker, then Secretary of State for Education, claimed that the scheme had been found to be a success in the United States. Privately some HMIs were said to be unhappy with the way that a report on the New Jersey scheme was being used, on the grounds that politicians were not bringing out fully the reservations that HMIs had expressed in their evaluation of it.

The pressure on licensed teachers to reproduce prescriptions was all too reminiscent of the nineteenth-century experience with the original Model B, recalling the words of the 1888 Cross Commission that 'All they [the apprentices] could do was faithfully to transmit the letter of the lesson they had received, for how should they have seized its spirit?' At its best Model A, by comparison, allows trainees to study teaching materials and strategies in their own subject alongside their fellows, explore and develop their own styles, analyse lessons in different schools or on videotape, read about and reflect on practice and theory alone or with others. It is a vastly superior model.

The way ahead, I would contend, is for a better development of Model A. There are several ways in which it could be developed further. As Her Majesty's Inspectorate (HMI) comments in reviews of teacher training in institutions of higher education, there are strong links with practising teachers. What is important is for this partnership to be developed even further. At Exeter University under the 'Bournemouth Scheme' some teachers supervising students also take courses at the university leading to awards in further professional studies. Supervision and lesson analysis, therefore, are formally recognized as being a legitimate component for a post-experience award, because they are being done in a systematic and reflective manner as part of a structured course.

Another point made by HMI is the need to improve the internal coherence of courses, not so as to reproduce clones instead of thinking teachers and tutors, but rather to make sure that all are aware of the standards and practices of the best, especially in subject methodology classes, where the range of practices is sometimes wider than can be justified. It would also be valuable if initial training could be given higher recognition by the higher education funding bodies. For universities in particular there has been quite legitimate pressure to improve the quality of research, but this should not be done at the expense of initial training.

It is, in my view, the wrong time in our history to slide back into a rudimentary nineteenth-century apprenticeship model of teacher training. Although the licensed teacher scheme is not likely to be as crude as was first thought, it will, nevertheless, represent an increasingly common route into teaching if the needs of the 1990s are to be met. These needs, however, must be seen in terms much broader than mere numbers and vacancy filling. There are numerous reasons why a twenty-first-century model of training must be allowed not only to survive, but also to remain the predominant form, not the least of which is the substantial demands made of teachers at the present time.

In addition to their role as purveyors of knowledge, teachers are expected to be social workers (notice cases of child abuse, deal with social problems), moral guardians (help reduce the crime rate), jailers (keep in school reluctant pupils who would sooner be out of it), surrogate parents and counsellors (for the many pupils who seek sensible objective advice from a sympathetic adult), managers (of finance and school resources) and public relations experts (with parents and local media). Furthermore, in our rapidly changing society teachers must offer both stability and an adventurous taste for novelty and discovery.

Even in the short term the demands following the 1988 Education Act are exacting. Primary teachers must become equipped to teach science and technology, to give and interpret a wider range of tests than those with which they have been familiar in the past, and to be up to date in several subjects of the curriculum. Secondary school teachers face similar pressures, in addition to the ones they already confronted when they implemented GCSE (General Certificate of Secondary Education), TVEI (Technical and Vocational Education Initiative), CPVE (Certificate of Pre-Vocational Education), and all the other acronyms which fell about their ears in the 1980s.

The National Curriculum alone makes severe demands on teachers' subject knowledge, with seventeen attainment targets in science, fourteen in maths, a huge history syllabus, and a similar volume in the other seven subjects, on their ability to assess and appraise, with national tests at 7, 11, 14 and 16, and on their professional skills. A full repertoire of these skills and competencies will increasingly be required and Model A offers a much better chance of nurturing these in newcomers than Model B, which was much condemned even by the rudimentary standards for rote learning required in Victorian times.

In all areas there is increasing emphasis on education, not only for the young, but for adult and mature learners, seeking to re-equip themselves for the job market or for healthy early retirement. Hence the spread of community education and the opportunities that offers to all who wish to learn at whatever stage of life. None of these demands shows any sign of slackening. Indeed most are accelerating. The result of such pressures in a rapidly changing society is that teachers must be better trained both at the beginning of their careers and subsequently. The notion that teaching is simple and that little time is necessary to acquire the elementary tricks of survival, or the modest knowledge necessary to stay a lesson or two ahead of the class, is as inappropriate as it is outdated.

NOTE

(1)　This chapter is based on two papers given to the College of Preceptors and the annual conference of the Universities' Council for the Education of Teachers.

REFERENCES

Collins, M. (1964) 'Untrained and trained graduate teachers: a comparison of their experiences during the probationary year'. *British Journal of Educational Psychology*, **34**, 75–84.

Day, C., Whitaker, P. and Wren, D. (1987) *Appraisal and Professional Development in Primary Schools*. Milton Keynes: Open University Press.

DES: Department of Education and Science: DES (1972) *Teacher Education and Training* (The James Report). London: HMSO.

DES: Department of Education and Science (1988) *Education Observed*, 7. London: HMSO.

O'Hear, A. (1988) *Who Teaches the Teachers?* London: Social Affairs Unit.

Smith, F. (1931) *A History of English Elementary Education 1760–1902*. London: University of London Press.

Wragg, E. C. (1984) *Teaching Teaching*. Newton Abbot: David & Charles.

Wragg, E. C. (1987) *Teacher Appraisal*. London: Macmillan.

Chapter 3

Partnership: A CNAA Perspective

Len Wharfe and Alison Burrows

INVOLVING TEACHERS

Since its inception in 1964, the Council for National Academic Awards (CNAA) has consistently sought to maintain and enhance the quality of the courses which lead to its awards and it has done this through a concern for teaching and learning, curriculum design, staff development, evaluation and the use of external examiners. In the discharge of this role, it has involved individuals from polytechnics and colleges, universities, the professions, commerce and industry. For teacher educators, this has meant interaction with practising teachers from schools and colleges. Therefrom began the debates which have led to the present dialogue about partnership in the CNAA system.

The practice of involving teachers in CNAA courses, both of initial and of inservice education, owes something to a wider debate taking place in the late 1960s and early 1970s about the nature of courses themselves for it was at this time the CNAA validation of education courses began. There was a growing demand that a student's programme of studies should have coherence and therefore it was not satisfactory to see courses as aggregations of component parts drawn from a wide range of provenances. The nub of coherence in teacher education courses was seen in their professional focus, though the nature of this focus has changed over the years. Since a committee for teacher education was first set up by CNAA in 1967, there has been a continuing expectation of the involvement of practising teachers though the word 'partnership' does not figure regularly in the vocabulary of course validation and review until about 1980.

In the approval of courses, CNAA has not been prescriptive about content and process, allowing scope for institutional initiative, enterprise and individuality. It has believed there should be opportunity to respond to resources and traditions, to local as well as to national needs. Quality, not conformity, has been the touchstone. No particular model of co-operation or partnership has been urged and CNAA has consistently recognized that the task of school teachers, which is teaching children, and the responsibility of college tutors, which is preparing students to enter the profession, are very different. CNAA has brought, within this framework of opportunity, an expectation that institutions would indicate how teachers would be involved in four areas of their operation: in course design; in teaching the students, particularly during school placements; in examining students; and in the validation and periodic appraisal of courses.

THE DEVELOPMENT OF PARTNERSHIP

The Council of CNAA first engaged in a debate about the validation of teacher education courses in 1966, leading to the setting up of a first committee responsible for this area in 1967. In responding to earlier approaches from institutions, this committee identified as the central issue in teacher education course validation the relationship between degree-level studies and professional training. A debate which began with the notion of two separate awards, one a degree, the other a professional certificate, gave way gradually to the concept of a single and coherent degree, the BEd. Nevertheless the early validation of course proposals looked separately at the various components of the award rather than its overall design. So in the first batch of validations in 1968 (Worcester College and Enfield College of Technology), 1970 (Notre Dame College, Glasgow, and Dunfermline College) and 1972 (Ulster College and Sunderland Polytechnic) the process relied heavily on higher education practitioners while practising teachers did not figure significantly in these activities.

The appearance of the James Report (1972) along with the first batch of initial BEd validations at Bulmershe College, Didsbury College and West Midlands College marked a new era for the involvement of the profession. Practising teachers had been consulted in the design of the courses at each of these three institutions and there were practising teachers on the CNAA visiting parties as well as among the college teams justifying their schemes. The James Report also reflected this growing involvement of teachers in its proposals for the probationary year, for teacher tutors and for the place of school experience in enhancing the influence of schools and training.

Co-operation with teachers moved one stage further as CNAA sought to discharge its responsibility for the professional recognition of courses as well as for their academic standards after 1972. Colleges were advised to set up their own advisory professional committees which would involve teachers and employing authorities; these committees would also be expected to contribute to the development and operation of courses. One experience of this real involvement of the profession was that disputes arose from time to time between institutional staff and practitioners as to what best constituted professional preparation. Despite these, and even though CNAA did not prescribe the involvement of teachers or LEA members, this practice developed because the interchange was seen to be broadly beneficial and it continued after 1977 when the professional recognition of courses was transferred from recognized bodies to the Secretary of State.

By the late 1970s the first cycle of teacher education awards approved by CNAA came up for review and renewal and this coincided with a vigorous debate involving institutions and the committee for education about many aspects of school experience. A conference held at York in 1976 was followed by a CNAA-funded research project (McCulloch, 1979) and these contributed to the next stage of thinking about awards for teachers. These had already become firmly established as professional awards seeking their coherence in professional practice. The new wave of course proposals adopted the notion of being school-based or school-focused, while at the same time they responded to a contraction in student numbers, an increasing emphasis on the primary-age phase in the initial BEd degree and the restriction of numbers of subjects which could be taught in the secondary PGCE. This next wave of thinking in which the profession was now more widely consulted and intimately involved, partly as a result of experience, partly as a recognition of the strength that derived from co-operation, saw the emergence of the label 'partnership' to characterize the new mode. This is reflected in two CNAA publications at the time: *Initial BEd Courses for the Early and Middle Years* (1983) and *Perspectives on Postgraduate Initial Training* (1984).

The emergence of partnership was associated with a notion of the co-operation of equals: that is, that both the schools and the training institutions had important and valid contributions to make to the design, teaching, assessment and evaluation of courses. But, though these contributions were equal, they were different because they derived from two different sets of experience and two different sets of central concerns. Partnership was maturing as a concept of complementary equality, not identical equality. Key features of this co-operation, such as the involvement of teachers in the selection of students or in course design, the use of teachers in the appraisal of courses, and deals between schools and institutions to permit the exchange of staff for professional refreshment, were all picked up in the criteria for the accreditation of teacher education courses issued by the Secretary of State in 1984. The ethos of partnership as it grew under CNAA validation was, however, fundamentally different from the ethos of the new accreditation criteria with their greater emphasis on prescription.

Since 1984 the CNAA's committee for teacher education and the institutions teaching courses leading to CNAA awards have recognized partnership as normal in the process of training teachers. In this period the experience of the committee has been significantly augmented by greatly increased involvement in the validation of courses in Scotland where the traditions of partnership have been different. The bringing together of the two sets of experiences and the identification of commonalities and of mutual learning was expressed in a CNAA conference held on partnership at Sheffield in the autumn of 1988.

DIMENSIONS OF PARTNERSHIP

Partnership in CNAA institutions has evolved around four main issues: course design, school placements, student assessment and course appraisal.

Reference has already been made to the debate about the coherence of courses in the early 1970s and to the way course design became an instrument to help ensure quality and academic progression. The well-made course became a hallmark of the new approach (Nokes, 1985) and this was clearly signalled in a conference on course design held at North East London Polytechnic in 1972.

Practising teachers were asked to participate in the design process though meetings were invariably held in colleges or polytechnics rather than in schools, teacher members were inevitably in a minority, and the teachers were being asked to participate in an unfamiliar process. Nevertheless there was a genuine sense in which the voice of the profession was heard. The distribution of school placements was of intense interest to teachers who did not wish to be and had no intention of being undervalued in this debate. The teacher members of the education committee of CNAA at the time firmly articulated these views.

The 1983 CNAA report on the BEd for the early and middle years stated the position that had been clearly established by the end of a decade of operation.

> All (members of the conference from which the report grew) agreed that when changes in school experience were not adequately discussed and negotiated in advance this could produce a lack of understanding in schools inhibiting the satisfactory undertaking of school-based tasks and possibly the student's progress. 'Partnership' was the keyword here.
>
> (p. 13)

By the late 1980s, when fewer new courses of initial training were developed, the evidence suggests reduced involvement with teachers in the design process. The lessons here had perhaps been learned. But teacher involvement has grown significantly in other areas such as interviewing students, helping in the design of course literature and handbooks, developing school placement guidelines, and introducing students more systematically into their placement schools.

Whether this evolving partnership can be described as one of equals is open to question. Maybe in course planning and design it never can be. Maybe it should not be. The same cannot be said, however, of the status of teachers in developing classroom skills among students.

The reality of student experience in schools and among working professionals generated vigorous debates from 1974 onwards between CNAA's validating parties, particularly teacher members, and course teams in colleges and polytechnics. CNAA had encouraged institutions to develop coherent rationales for their courses and then to characterize the sort of teacher a course was designed to educate. It was this that often led to a polarized debate. Teachers who had to work with students in their classrooms looked for basic competencies as the starting point from which to develop a fully effective teacher. The model was one of a competent and confident beginner. Tutors in colleges had an eye for the wider educational requirements of training; the starting point for them was the educated professional. The familiar models here were those of the reflective or reflexive teacher. The relative merits of these or other models is not an issue for discussion here. What has mattered in CNAA has been the constructive dialogue which has ensued, a true hallmark of partnership wherein each group increasingly came to understand and to share the viewpoint of the other. It is perhaps a commentary on the nature of teacher education that this debate, already fully fledged by 1974, is still alive and not fundamentally changed today!

Essential competences among students was however one thing for teachers; the growing idea that the student could be working in the classroom for other ends was a different matter entirely. All concerned in teacher education understood the traditional role of the student; but an individual student from a college observing and appraising, often using criteria generated by tutors, tested partnership much further and it has been a measure of its effectiveness that teachers have been prepared to accommodate these potentially threatening activities. The challenge to partnership has been whether the entire staff of a primary school or of a secondary school department understood and accepted what was happening. This has not merely been a question of extending the dialogue beyond the headteacher; it has also been a question of ensuring an active, even proactive, role for all the teachers involved.

Schools and teachers have long contributed to the assessment of students through reports and profiles returned to colleges after school placements. But partnership here has constantly wrestled with a tension. On the one hand, colleges and polytechnics are seen as having the real expertise and therefore must have not only the responsibility for assessment but the final say. Yet teachers themselves also agree that there should be no one better placed to assess work in schools than teachers themselves. The requirement that higher education institutions should recommend students to CNAA for its awards has tended both to highlight the tension and to reinforce the tradition. This ambivalence has often been in the background, therefore, of CNAA debates, but has never been the focus of specific inquiry or resolution. Never, that is, except in one very important way.

From the first validations in the early 1970s, CNAA has insisted that, for courses of initial training, at least one member of the external examining team should be a practising teacher. Further, it has been expected that this teacher would operate across the whole of the assessments and not be confined, say, to visiting students during final block experience. Members of teams of external examiners can testify to true equality in this aspect of partnership.

Partnership in assessment has generated examiners' reports which reflected on the whole process of teacher preparation, providing regular evidence of course achievements and shortcomings. These reports in turn have become part of the evidence, along with the findings of monitoring and evaluation, on which courses have been synoptically appraised after a period of about five or six years. Such critical appraisal is seen by CNAA as both a criterion and an instrument of quality control.

To provide a balanced commentary, such appraisal requires substantial feedback from schools to set alongside that from colleges. The normal process of receipt of reports on students and of meeting with teachers goes some way to recognize this, but reaching out to schools, involving them in regular and systematic evaluation, imposes a heavy burden on busy practitioners and is one aspect of partnership which, on the evidence of course appraisal received by CNAA, is not yet highly developed.

WORK IN SCHOOLS AND PARTNERSHIP

It has already been indicated that one outcome of partnership in course design has been the influence of teachers on the scale and character of work in schools. In 1981, CNAA reviewed the character of PGCE courses, both primary and secondary, then in approval in order to assess the place of school experience and its relationships with course design and delivery.

The survey (CNAA, 1981) of these twenty-four PGCE courses showed a mean of 78.15 days allocated to school experience; courses allocating more than this were characterized as 'school-located' (44.5%), those below 'college-located' (55.5%). Courses were also grouped by the rationale they claimed to adopt for relating school and college activities. Those which had a defined content which was also responsive to students perceptions, especially as they came from school experience, were characterized as 'responsive courses' (74%). The other category argued that the college theoretical studies grew out of or reflected the experience of students and these were labelled 'reflexive courses' (26%).

Figure 3.1 provides its own commentary. The striking feature is the way all the

Figure 3.1. *Orientation Towards Use of Student Experience*

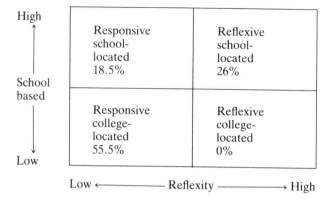

Source: Smith (1982).

reflexive courses had above-average school placement. The implications for partnership are clear: the necessity for effective dialogue for reflexive courses is paramount. The report on the PGCE (CNAA, 1984) relates this to partnership:

> Already there is evidence to suggest that full benefit will not be derived from school-based courses unless the teachers are actively involved in helping to devise the work which is to be done in schools. This implies that they must understand the purpose of the college-based work and be able to influence it. The operation is in danger of becoming pointless without this.
>
> (p. 27)

DEVELOPMENTS DURING THE 1980s

Three separate government initiatives took place during the 1980s which were to influence the debate about partnership in teacher education:

(a) the implementation of DES Circular 3/84 *Initial Teacher Training: Approval of Courses*;
(b) initiation of discussion about a licensed teacher scheme;
(c) changes in the method of funding inservice teacher education.

DES Circular 3/84

As previously indicated, partnership between schools and training institutions in providing the initial education of teachers has been a central issue in the validation of CNAA initial education courses since the early 1970s. The importance of partnership was reinforced in England and Wales by DES Circular 3/84 which detailed the criteria for the professional accreditation of teacher education. The implementation of the criteria in the Circular had an immediate impact on courses which came forward for validation and review from 1984 onwards. Some practices (such as the involvement of teachers in the selection of students and the need for tutors to have recent and relevant teaching experience in schools) which required a partnership between training institutions and schools became essential if professional accreditation was to be achieved.

In Scotland, a document published in 1978 by the Scottish Education Department and the General Teaching Council of Scotland entitled *Learning to Teach* had also emphasized the importance of a partnership in the initial education of teachers, especially in the area of school experience. The impact of this document on courses coming forward for validation from Scotland was also noticeable.

Licensed teachers

In 1988, the government announced its intention to consider the possibility of recruiting teachers in shortage subjects through a system of licensing. The scheme proposed that, under certain carefully controlled circumstances, local education authorities could appoint people without initial teaching qualifications to teach in schools. The local education authority would be required to initiate a training programme for these licensed teachers and, after a two-year period, they would have to be assessed to determine whether qualified teacher status could be awarded.

This proposal was significant because it could mean a shift in the balance of responsibility for the initial teacher education of certain categories of students. Under a licensed teacher scheme, the local education authority and school would have a leading role in determining the balance and pattern of training for the trainee. Training institutions could be contracted by local education authorities to provide college-based tuition, but responsibility for the overall programme of training would remain with the local education authority as the employer of the licensed teacher.

The debate about the balance between college-based tuition and school-based experience (and the relationship between the two) gained an added impetus as a result of this government announcement.

Changes in the method of funding inservice education

The changing relationships between schools, local education authorities and training institutions in the initial education of teachers paralleled changes which were also taking place in inservice education.

Changes in the method of funding inservice education gave local education authorities much more freedom in determining how they spent their grant. One of the results of the changes was a trend away from local education authority support for long award-bearing courses to short courses and in-house training provision. The significance of the change in funding was, therefore, that it made the local education authorities much more significant players in determining the nature of inservice education. Training institutions were still significant providers, but they had to ensure that what they provided met the needs identified by the local education authorities and the schools for which they had responsibility. Failure to be responsive could lead to loss of income which, in turn, could lead to loss of courses and staff.

One significant way training institutions adapted to the new situation was the development of credit accumulation and transfer schemes. These schemes are designed to permit the maximum amount of flexibility in study patterns and teaching and learning methods, including distance learning. They allow teachers to take units at different institutions and accumulate them to gain an award. Credit for employment-based learning is also encouraged in many instances. In some cases, in-house training provided by the LEAs has been validated and can now contribute towards the attainment of an award.

The changes in the funding of inservice education therefore encouraged the development of closer links between training institutions, schools and LEAs and fostered some innovative and collaborative approaches which had potential for initial, as well as inservice education.

It was against this backdrop of ideas and activities that the CNAA Committee for Teacher Education held a conference on partnership in initial education in September 1988.

THE LATE 1980s

The conference had two aims:

(a)   the promotion of partnership as a relationship between equals, each with a significant and complementary part to play in the initial education of teachers;
(b)   the provision of a forum for the exchange of information about current practices.

Significantly, the concept of partnership promoted at the conference included local education authorities as equal partners with the schools and training institutions.

The conference found evidence to suggest that partnership between school and training institutions had grown and improved significantly in recent years. In general, however, the involvement of local education authorities, especially in England and Wales, remained limited.

As well as these positive findings, a number of factors were also identified which could inhibit further development or which might even erode the progress that had already taken place.

One significant factor which it was felt was likely to have an impact on partnership was the financial climate in which the various partners operate. Partnership in initial teacher education makes high demands on resources, particularly in terms of the time of teachers, tutors and local advisers. Teacher involvement in areas such as student selection, course development, and supervision of school experience has traditionally rested almost entirely on goodwill. Teachers frequently contribute to these activities in addition to their school duties, not as a recognized part of them. As resources got tighter and the demands on teachers greater, it seemed possible that schools might find it difficult to justify their involvement in initial teacher education.

There was also felt to be a number of ways in which the introduction of the Education Reform Act could impose a constraint on partnership. The introduction of arrangements for the local management of schools (LMS) will give many headteachers and governors greater financial and managerial control. In weighing the costs and benefits of partnership, there seemed to be a possibility that some of them might feel unable to justify the drain on resources. Would schools that 'opt out' of local education authority control wish to continue to contribute to the partnership? Would governors, with their increased role in the management of schools, have to approve involvement of the school in partnership activities?

In addition to the constraints on partnership which might result from changes in arrangements for funding and managing schools, it was thought possible that there might also be constraints resulting from the introduction of a national curriculum and assessment and testing. Would schools feel that it was inappropriate to permit student teachers to take classes in the year of testing in case it had an adverse effect on pupil attainment?

During the conference it became clear that drawing local education authorities closer into the partnership could be a key factor in ensuring its future success. The continuing involvement of schools in the initial education of teachers may well depend on the preparedness of the local education authority, as employer and policy maker, to encourage and support such activities.

Apart from encouragement and support for teachers in schools, however, there was seen to be another important benefit which could be gained from closer involvement of local education authorities. At present, partnership tends to depend on goodwill, personal connections and geographical proximity. These are not always sufficient means fully to exploit the considerable expertise which exists. There is often a mismatch between the needs of students and the actual practical experience available to them while they are training. There is often no formal or accessible intelligence system on which initial teacher education can draw to improve the match.

One way of tackling this problem is to provide a formal mechanism for bringing the partners in initial teacher education together so that the resources available can be fully exploited and a co-ordinated approach can be implemented in which each partner knows what it can expect of the other and what will be expected in return. One CNAA-validated institution in Scotland has taken major steps in this area by establishing an organization in collaboration with the four adjacent regional councils to oversee all arrangements for school experience for a primary BEd course.

The organization is chaired by the principal of the training institution and includes senior staff associated with the BEd degree as well as primary advisers from each of the four regions. It oversees all aspects of the placement arrangements and the ways in which college-based tuition and placement activities reinforce and sustain each other. It is the machinery for ensuring that the coherence of the degree and the professional collaboration underpinning it are fully realized in practice.

Professional collaboration occurs at three levels. The first concerns the organization itself. It is the forum in which criteria are agreed for placement schools; placement schools are identified; relevant documentation on the course and its assessment for co-operating teachers is agreed; evaluative data on the conduct of placements is considered; and arrangements are made for day-to-day collaboration between staff and co-operating teachers.

The second level of collaboration involves meetings between senior training institution staff and the headteachers and assistant headteachers of participating schools. These meetings are convened in each region by the primary advisory staff and are held in teachers' centres. Their purpose is to discuss with senior school staff the placement arrangements and supporting documentation agreed by the organization.

The third level of collaboration involves bringing together, within the structures created in each region, the lecturing staff and the teachers who will be supervising students. This stage in the process is intended to ensure that there is clear agreement on the nature of the placement, on the particular skills and understandings that the placement is intended to foster, and the means whereby tutors, supervising teachers and students will collaborate in the assessment process.

This example is significant because it demonstrates the commitment of the regional councils to the initial training of teachers and to the principle of partnership; a partnership which goes further than providing supply cover. Advisers contribute towards determining the content of school experience and the criteria by which student performance is assessed. They are responsible, in consultation with the training institution, for determining which schools should be used for certain types of placement.

At present, arrangements such as this are rare in England and Wales. There is perhaps a need to persuade local education authorities that there is a benefit for them in contributing. As the majority of students take up their first posts as teachers in the catchment area of the training institution where they were taught, it is not difficult to see what benefits a local education authority might receive. By working in partnership with the training institutions in their area, they can help to ensure the quality of the teachers they employ.

WHERE NEXT?

Given the developments which have taken place during the last decade, what types of CNAA courses can we anticipate developing in the 1990s?

It seems likely that the BEd and PGCE courses will continue to provide the majority of entrants to the teaching profession and that training institutions will continue to have a leading role in determining the nature of the training that their students receive. However, the trend towards a closer partnership with schools seems likely to continue, with perhaps an increase in the number of courses which are school-based or school-focused. We may also see an increase in local education authority involvement in the development and facilitation of these courses as in the articled teacher schemes.

As the licensed teacher programme gets under way, there may also be some new types of courses developing which cross the boundary between inservice and initial education. Local education authorities are required to provide a training programme for licensed teachers. The training and experience of teaching, taken together, is intended to ensure that licensed teachers achieve the required standard for qualified teacher status.

Given the recent developments in inservice education for credit accumulation and transfer, the recognition of experiential learning, and admission with advanced standing, it seems feasible that we will see some CNAA courses for licensed teachers developed during the 1990s and these will seek to make capital out of the students' antecedent experience, whatever its kind. In relation to these courses, local education authorities and schools are likely to play a leading role in determining the nature of the training received.

REFERENCES

CNAA: Council for National Academic Awards (1981) 'Officer paper: The PGCE' (unpublished). London: CNAA.

CNAA: Council for National Academic Awards (1983) *Initial BEd Degrees for the Early and Middle Years: A Discussion Document.* London: CNAA.

CNAA: Council for National Academic Awards (1984) *Perspectives on Postgraduate Initial Training: The CNAA Validated PGCE.* London: CNAA.

DES: Department of Education and Science (1972) *Teacher Education and Training* (The James Report). London: HMSO.

DES: Department of Education and Science (1984) *Initial Teacher Training: Approval of Courses* (Circular 3/84). London: DES.

McCulloch, M. (1979) 'School experience in initial BEd degrees validated by the CNAA' (unpublished). London: CNAA.

Nokes, A. G. (1985) 'The CNAA and Teacher Education' (unpublished). London: CNAA.

Scottish Education Department/General Teaching Council of Scotland (1978) *Learning to Teach.*

Smith, R. N. (1982) 'Towards an analysis of PGCE courses'. *Journal of Further and Higher Education*, **6**(3).

Chapter 4

Changing Partnership

Gill Crozier, Ian Menter and Andrew Pollard[1]

INTRODUCTION

In many ways, 'partnership' between schools and teacher education institutions is an obvious, necessary and indeed desirable relationship. There has always been a form of 'partnership' but, as we shall suggest later, this has tended to be rather one-sided. The notorious theory/practice divide of teacher training/education was often demonstrated in the gulf between these two 'partners'. The history of this development, however, is not the central concern of this paper. Our concern is more to do with the fact that 'partnership' is very much on the agenda in the 1980s and has been promoted by central government on the one hand and developed unquestioningly on the other by many local education authorities, schools and teacher education institutions. In this paper we raise some questions about the notion of 'partnership', and by looking at its origins and practice we begin to develop a critique.

In doing so, we identify 'partnership' as essentially a functionalist term, implying the 'greater good for all' which would arise from a sinking of differences, a joining of forces and a sharing of expertise, thus claiming the high moral ground. The view that we develop indicates that this is not necessarily a healthy relationship for teachers, teacher educators, students or pupils.

We argue that a number of ideologies are covered by the term 'partnership'. In particular, in the contemporary context, partnership can be seen to represent an ideology which glosses control, with the government hoping that its requirement for more school-based 'training' will ensure that 'theory' is reduced and 'classroom competence' increased. The notion of 'partnership' thus illustrates an uneasy relationship, with the rhetoric and ideologies of both the government and professional groups intermingling in a way which, whilst often using a similar vocabulary, has been underpinned by very different values and has been intended to achieve different goals. We develop this point below, but we also suggest that the self-generated teacher education notion of partnership is itself far from lacking difficulties and internal contradictions.

However, notwithstanding many severe difficulties, we argue in conclusion that 'partnership' needs to be transformed into a dynamic alliance if teacher education is to resist the demise with which it is currently threatened. This, we believe, is crucial to the development of the education system as a whole.

THE ORIGINS OF PARTNERSHIP

The context of partnership in the 1980s

It is arguable that the years of Mrs Thatcher's government have produced a reversal of the normal pattern of education policy-making as pragmatism overlain by ideology. Are we experiencing a new pattern of educational reform in which ideology has initiated and dictated the nature of changes? In this scenario, as applied to partnership in teacher education, pragmatism, derived from a growing shortage of teachers, has acted only as a temporary constraint on the march of ideology.

The power, significance and effectiveness of the years of Conservative government since 1979, leaving oil revenues aside, has been that it has offered a sustained flow of radical policies based around a relatively coherent philosophy – a philosophy which we may dub the ideology of the 'New Right' (Levitas, 1986). This ideology embraces an almost complete trust in market forces as a mechanism of production and distribution but a simultaneous commitment to a moral and social authoritarianism. The latter strand includes, for example, a belief in individuals and families as the only really legitimate units of social organization and regular reference to 'traditional values', 'the transmission of our culture', and to nationalism. This ideology has been deployed to provide a sustained critique of the products of what, in retrospect, we may see as the relative consensus which produced the welfare state. This, together with the professional groups associated with it, is seen as preventing individuals from taking responsibility for their own lives – and thus of being 'free'. Of course, we could mount a critique of this ideology, looking at issues such as power, wealth and the distribution of opportunities to be 'free', but that is not our purpose here. Suffice it to say that in the 1980s a powerful hegemony has been created.

Within education, portents of radical change had been evident through the 1970s and were specifically signalled in the Callaghan speech of 1976 (Whitty and Menter, 1989). The teaching profession and LEAs had enjoyed a growing degree of autonomy since the early 1930s and, in the main, failed to respond to political warnings. Legislators in the 1980s were then able to claim that they must act to break restrictive, irresponsible and 'trendy' practices, the dominance of the unions and the control of LEAs. Education was to be made 'accountable' and 'more efficient' through the introduction of a core curriculum and exposure to market forces. We would argue that the ideology dictated the changes – the place of pragmatism was to condition their pace.

The emergence of 'partnership' in teacher education

In the midst of such momentous innovation, teacher education was offered, and generated, the notion of 'partnership'. On the one hand this was very much self-generated and can be traced through the history of teacher education. It reflects the tension between academic study of education and the development of practical classroom competence. After the establishment of all-graduate entry procedures in the mid-1970s, there was an academic emphasis based on study of the four disciplines of education. By the late 1970s such approaches were being superseded by attempts to link theory and practice through notions of 'practical theorizing' and these, by the mid-1980s, found a new conceptualization in 'reflective teaching' – arguably a new form of professional ideology itself (Menter and Pollard, 1989). The study of the disciplines had fostered a model of 'teaching practice' in which students studied in colleges and practised in schools – a model which was gradually disappearing in the early 1980s, to be replaced by a model featuring notions such as 'school experience', 'school-focused courses' and 'IT-INSET'. Thus, in a very self-directed way, we had teacher education institutions generating their own notions of partnership.

The promotion of 'partnership' through control

This was also the time during which the Thatcherite ideology began to be brought to bear on teacher education (Whitty, Barton and Pollard, 1987). The simultaneous introduction of 'market forces' and of increasingly centralized controls led to major changes. One of the emphases in DES Circular 3/84, which established the Council for the Accreditation of Teacher Education (CATE), was on 'links between initial teacher training institutions and schools'. The Annex to the circular called for various developments:

> Institutions, in co-operation with local education authorities and their advisers, should establish links with a number and variety of schools, and courses should be developed and run in close working partnership with those schools. Experienced teachers from schools sharing responsibility with the training institutions for the planning, supervision and support of students' schools experience and teaching practice should be given an influential role in the assessment of students' practical performance. They should also be involved in the training of the students within the institutions.
>
> (DES, 1984, para. 3)

The Annex went on to detail other matters, such as the need for 'updating' school experience of tutors, the involvement of teachers in student selection and the role of local committees in approving courses. In January 1986, CATE published *Catenote No. 4*, which developed the theme of partnership more fully. Although reference is made to shortcomings of traditional practices there is no consideration given to any practical or ideological difficulties in promoting partnership: 'the most effective partnership arrangements between institutions and schools are often those which have been designed with the needs of students, trainers and teachers *equally* in mind' (CATE, 1986, para. 4, our emphasis). For all parties to benefit 'requires that the relationship between college and school be based on a well developed mutual respect, and maintained at a continuously productive level' (ibid., para. 5).

The IT-INSET project at Leicester, which aims to provide initial and inservice training simultaneously (see Ashton *et al.*, 1983; Everton and Impey, 1989) is cited as an example of 'good practice' and it is said: 'Such schemes enable tutors and teachers to *share common aims, approaches and understandings* in their work with students' (ibid., para. 7, our emphasis).

HMI used very similar language in their 1987 survey of initial training:

The notion of a partnership between teacher training institutions and schools has come to be recognised as one of great importance. It enables the various elements of the teacher training course to be closely linked with practical experience. Practising teachers become actively involved in the process, sharing responsibility for the planning, supervision, and assessment of the students' school-based work and also taking part in the training of the students within the institutions. The partnership also benefits schools themselves, since the experience and knowledge of colleagues from the teacher training institutions become available as a valuable source of support.

(DES, 1987, 22)

In 1988 the CNAA organized a conference on the topic 'Partnership in Teacher Education – Realities and Ideals'. The conference report notes that the conference

concentrated on partnership between schools, local education authorities . . . and training institutions in the development and delivery of initial teacher education courses. . . . [One of the goals of the conference was] the promotion of partnership as a relationship between equals, each with a significant and complementary part to play in the initial education of teachers.

(CNAA, 1988, 1).

The promotion of partnership as an ideal in teacher education is closely linked with the development of increasingly school-focused and school-based approaches. In his speech to the Society of Education officers in January 1989, Kenneth Baker, Secretary of State for Education, picked up the theme of partnership and paid tribute to existing school-based courses:

What I welcome most in these developments is the increased emphasis on work in schools – not just teaching practice, but more formal study too, so that teachers in the schools are more involved in the whole training process. This improves teacher training.

(Baker, 1989, para. 37)

I hope we can build upon this and go further. . . . I want to invite LEAs and teacher training institutions jointly to devise experimental schemes of school based training that would involve the student being given progressively more responsibility during their training.

(ibid., para. 38)

As long ago as 1982 the DES established a research project to look at four school-based PGCE courses. The project's report includes a thoughtful review of the partnership concept, in particular distinguishing between a professional and a political context for the development of the concept:

The motivations behind the political intervention to establish closer partnership between training institutions and schools were clearly very different from those of the profession itself; indeed it is not totally unreasonable to suggest that Government's interest in school-based training may have been in part an attempt to weaken the hold over training by the teacher training profession. Yet . . . to conclude that the current interest in closer partnership with schools was purely or even primarily the result of directives from the centre would be naive.

(Furlong *et al.*, 1988, 13)

We would agree, and, as we have suggested above, what we have been witnessing is the promotion of various understandings and motivations, all of which coalesce, often uneasily, under the umbrella of 'partnership'. This makes clear analysis and debate difficult and certainly, because of the inherent 'goodness' of the term, it has almost become unacceptable to challenge it. In a classic Foucauldian sense (cf. Foucault, 1979), 'partnership' can be seen to represent a discourse which imposes a subtle control mechanism. The overall effect is to reduce the extent to which teacher education and hence education itself can be critical and liberating. In the next section we look at the operation of some of these processes. We should re-emphasize that the profession-generated versions of partnership are not without their internal contradictions.

'PARTNERSHIP' IN PRACTICE

The nature of contemporary 'partnership'

A close relationship with schools has always been a necessity for teacher education. From the days of pupil teachers onwards the placement of trainee teachers within schools has been fundamental. This approach was very much on the lines of an apprenticeship with a 'master'–pupil relationship. Later, with the development of institutionally based training, the teacher receiving students was seen to have a very separate role from that of lecturers within the college. However, with the emergence of 'partnership' there is a clear implication, which is sometimes made explicit (as in the quotation from DES Circular 3/84 above), of equality of power. That is, the two parties should share decision-making, benefits and responsibility. In reality the situation is not straightforward, however. Clearly in many historical instances this has not been the case. The particular nature of the relationship has often been determined at least in part by economic factors. For instance, with regard to teaching practice/block school experience, when students are placed further and further away from the institution and it becomes more difficult for tutors to make regular visits to the students, there is a greater need for teachers to take a central part in the tutoring role.

Relationships with schools, also, have more recently served another purpose of creating and developing a market for INSET courses but with nothing comparable to offer in return except certification. It could thus be said that this notion of 'partnership' has tended to be a one-sided one, although schools might get something out of it in the form of staff development.

As noted above, however, recent government intervention, particularly through CATE, has made 'partnership' between teacher education and schools more wide-ranging and systematic. Teachers are involved in course planning and course writing, interviewing students, secondments to the institutions (ranging from one day a week to one year) and IT-INSET, as well as having an increasingly influential role in school-experience supervision/tutoring. But a more active partnership is not necessarily a more equal one.

With the changing nature of partnership, one could argue, comes also a change in the power relationship. However, who exactly holds the balance of power depends, we suggest, on the particular facet of partnership at a given time. So, for instance, with regard to decisions relating to awarding distinction grades to students for teaching practice/block school experience, student interviews and course planning, teachers and tutors, whilst in theory holding equal decision-making power, in practice do not. Indeed, it is relatively easy to ignore the view of the teachers since, when the ultimate decision is actually taken, it is taken in the institution, quite likely when the teachers are not present and most certainly, if they are present, when they are in a minority.

On the other hand, when the tutor is in school he or she tends to feel unable or less able to challenge what is heard or seen for fear of jeopardizing the partnership. This is perhaps most notable during block school experience when there is a distinctive tendency for tutors to avoid conflict with the teacher, although perhaps sharing a private critique of the teacher's practice with the student (Menter, 1988). Of course, in addition, students may also share a private critique of the tutor with the teacher.

What should have been a natural alliance has been fraught with suspicion and doubt. Teachers, ever conscious of their supposedly inferior status, held little respect for academics. The academic teacher educators, on the other hand, many of whom asserted their allegiance with the classroom and their colleagues therein, none the less held differing perspectives on education *per se* and the process of schooling in particular.

For underlying the question of power distribution within the partnership is a question of values. Even if the partnership is equal, what happens when very different values are espoused by the respective partners? This could be a recipe for conflict. The fact that open conflict rarely occurs (in our experience) is perhaps another indication that there is a certain amount of stage management about the whole 'partnership' notion. But value clashes there often are. Common examples of this range from views on appropriate dress for student teachers, through equal opportunities issues to widely differing expectations of children.

Ideally, close alliances between teacher educators and teachers should provide the opportunity for teacher educators to spread their sphere of influence upon educational practice wider than initial teacher education (ITE), as well as providing the opportunity for the sharing of ideas between teachers and teacher educators. Whilst no doubt this does occur to some extent, it is also true to say that 'partnership' gives rise to conflict and tension between 'college-based' ideas and school-based practice (Beyer, 1988; Ginsburg, 1988). Such tensions are reminiscent of the theory/practice divide of the 1960s and 1970s which we referred to earlier.

A case study of 'partnership'

At this point, two illustrations from a partnership programme at one particular college of higher education will demonstrate the nature of the problem as it arises in the working lives of students, teachers and tutors. The examples are drawn from a course which sought to involve those teachers who were receiving BEd students into their classrooms on a weekly basis with the college-based part of the course (Menter, 1989). The subject matter was English in the primary curriculum.

One college session, involving two tutors, seven teachers and seventeen students, initially focused on the teaching of reading. The session started with lively small-group discussions arising from the students' and teachers' observations of children's language in their schools. Following a brief feedback from these discussions, the tutor who was leading the session said that she wanted to reset the agenda from a narrow focus on reading to cover 'the whole language area'. She referred to the Cox Report (DES, 1988a) and the notion of a distinction between 'contexts' and 'purposes' of English. She then asked teachers and students each to get into a group together, to 'identify questions which you have about where we are going'.

After ten minutes, the tutor went over to join the teachers and her question 'How are you doing?' was met with laughter from several of them. Once this had died down, one teacher started to talk about the students and the ways in which they as teachers were expected to relate to them. The tutor appeared not to want to answer these points but asked them to focus on reading: 'How do you actually organize reading in your classroom?' But the teachers kept bringing the topic back to the students: 'They're only just starting', one of them said.

Back in one of the students' groups, which the second tutor had joined, a student who had looked very bored earlier on, said: 'No one has actually told us how to teach a child to read'. The tutor replied: 'You mean beginning reading'. Another student said: 'What do you say to a child who doesn't know a word?' Presently, the first tutor asked for feedback from the students and teachers which she would write on the chalkboard. She invited students to report first. One of the five mature students in the group said: 'The mechanics of teaching children to read'. The tutor said: 'Can I write "developing literacy"?' A teacher objected: 'Developing literacy sounds too vague'. There were murmurs of support from all around the room.

The tutor then asked for a question from the group of teachers. One offered: 'What to do when recognized approaches don't work'. Another teacher interjected 'Twenty years later we're still asking the same questions'. There then ensued a rapid succession of comments from students and teachers:

> Two students: We don't even know what the stages [of teaching reading] are.
> Another student: Marking and correctness in writing come up.
> Tutor: Can we put 'How do we handle children's writing'?
> Students: How do you teach spelling?
> Teacher: Or should you teach spelling?

Then, as the general hubbub which had developed during this interchange subsided, one of the mature students, who had been relatively quiet, spoke clearly and deliberately. Everyone, apparently, was listening intently:

> Student: We would like to use the resources of all the teachers in teaching reading.

There was a pause and one or two mutterings from teachers and then a teacher said: 'We came out of college feeling exactly the same way. We did history, philosophy and sociology of education. We came out of college feeling absolutely helpless.'

At this point there was 'spontaneous' applause from most of the other teachers. A student then made reference to the National Curriculum and said her concern was 'How do we help children reach the attainment targets?' A teacher pointed out this was 'just coming in now' and the tutor said to the students 'you know as much about this as anyone'. But the students were not satisfied with this, they indicated that they supported the earlier comment about learning from the teachers' experience. A younger student announced: 'What people are saying is a semi-apprenticeship would be quite helpful.'

> Student: Teachers have the experience behind them which we haven't got and so we need help to get [to grips with this].

This session was extremely significant and revealed many interesting factors. A deep cynicism on the part of several teachers about the effectiveness of college courses in training teachers was strongly articulated and was not countered. Students' great desire to be able to teach 'basic literacy' came through very strongly. Alongside this, there was a strong belief in the expertise of serving teachers, as opposed (implicitly at least) to the knowledge of college tutors.

Earlier during this same course, the students had mounted wall displays in some of the teaching rooms at the college to demonstrate their work in schools. One part of a display became the subject of some controversy. In the room where one group was holding its English sessions, as part of the display, were several statements from books, teachers and other sources. One of them read: 'These kids aren't going to get anywhere, we just do the best we can for them while they're here: Mrs X, Headteacher'. The teachers and head concerned read this when they came into the room for an English session on the partnership programme. They were very upset. They felt the remark had been taken out of context and gave a bad impression of the school's commitment to the children. It was eventually removed but not before a number of tutors and students had been involved in discussions about it. The students maintained that the statement was accurate and did reflect the head's views. This was corroborated by a tutor, who was very critical of practice in the school. On the other hand, another tutor was much more praising of the school, saying how caring the head and her staff were.

The first tutor said that he thought the incident demonstrated a contradiction which students were exposed to – on the one hand tutors were encouraging them to develop skills of critical inquiry, incorporating accurate and honest reporting, and on the other hand they were being expected to develop 'professional' relationships. The statement as posted was a clear example of low expectations of children in a school on a large public-sector housing estate. The tutor was striving to encourage students to develop very positive expectations of all the children they had contact with. This argument was symptomatic of very differing views of children and of relationships between teachers and children. But the incident also revealed further differences between tutors.

The outcome of this sort of incident is a strong tendency to reproduce the status quo, at least within schools. Increasingly, however, with the development of partnership, this sits uneasily in tension with parallel developments of reflective pedagogy: if as tutors we are stating one thing to students and yet in practice we are failing to assert it, we are in effect undermining our own credibility. Moreover, as IT-INSET and/or school-based approaches become a more central part of our practice the outcome of this failure to challenge will be to constrain and inevitably control teacher education.

The purpose of 'partnership'

What then is the purpose of the partnership? From the government's point of view the promotion of partnership was initially stated as being to improve the practical aspects of teacher education. However, the recent explicit moves towards school-based 'training', introduced through the 1988 Green Paper (DES, 1988b), may be the first moves to making teacher education based in separate HE institutions almost superfluous. Perhaps partnership for schools will now serve the purpose of providing 'training skills' for classroom teachers so that they will be adequately prepared for apprenticeship training. The closure of teacher education establishments altogether may then follow.

The growing attack on teacher education has come from several sources. In spite of attempts by teacher education establishments to bridge the theory–practice divide, popular mythology would seem to persist. The HMI report on *The New Teacher in School* (DES, 1988c) reported that a significant number of newly qualified teachers were ill-equipped to deal with the classroom situation which they found themselves in. This was widely reported in the press, in spite of the fact that HMI surveys on experienced teachers have come to very similar conclusions. More recently, Michael Durham (1989) wrote in *The Independent* that there is still a widely held view that teacher educators are far removed from the classroom, not having set foot there for years and that the life in teacher education establishments is a soft option from the stresses and strains of school. The criticisms of alleged Marxist bias and irrelevance emanating from the New Right (O'Hear, 1988; Hillgate Group, 1989) add fuel to the 'moral panic' over teacher education.

The reality of teacher education is very different. Most lecturers are regularly spending periods of time teaching in school and opportunities to study Marxism are all but non-existent in most teacher education courses. Certainly it might be hoped that one real benefit of developing relations between teacher education and school teachers might be the correction of press distortions of the nature of contemporary teacher education.

Nevertheless attacks on teacher education prevail, even from those within its ranks. Jumping on the Warnock bandwagon (Warnock, 1988) in support of teaching schools, David Hargreaves is now openly advocating the closure of teacher education institutions as presently constituted. The main argument he offers in favour of teaching schools is that they would allow 'the profession to take responsibility for its new entrants and begin to provide the much needed continuity between initial training and early induction into the profession' (Hargreaves, 1989a). This is a banal argument for such a major recommendation, not least since teacher educators (at least in the polytechnic and college sector) regard themselves as part of 'the profession'. Moreover, Hargreaves gives no consideration of either the theoretical or practical problems involved in such a proposal.

It should be clearer than ever that in order to be effective in producing teachers who are capable of the extended professionalism which HMI, and others seek, partnership must be seen as a dynamic process. It is a process in and through which educational change will occur. A partnership based on simple notions of apprenticeship, of students learning by imitation and direct modelling, is damaging to the development of the teaching profession and therefore against the educational interests of children.

While recent times have seen the emergence of conflicting definitions and understandings of 'partnership' it would be difficult to deny that notions based on the writings of the New Right are in the ascendancy. In documents from the Council for National Academic Awards (CNAA) and to some extent from the Council for the Accreditation of Teacher Education (CATE) the liberal influence of the professionals can be detected but the pronouncements from the Department of Education and Science (DES) and the Secretary of State demonstrate the failure of the professional lobby. One final exposé of the cynicism with which the Secretary of State, the DES and, to some extent, the relevant quangos, promote partnership arises from a consideration of the level of resource allocation which is associated with it. Throughout the development of 'updating school experience' of tutors or of involving school teachers in admissions interviews to initial courses, institutions have had to scrabble around for funding. Genuine attempts at partnership are in fact notable for their high resource implications, either in terms of providing supply cover to release teachers from their classroom commitments or to provide appropriate staff/student ratios for IT-INSET.

From 'partnership' to alliance?

The notion of 'partnership' is, as we have seen, somewhat slippery and imprecise. This renders it vulnerable to multiple interpretation. Thus the intentions, values and practices which professional teacher educators attribute to it seem to us to be significantly different from the images of 'partnership' which are being projected by central government and its agencies.

The fact that 'partnership' in initial teacher education was itself essentially ideological, masking a host of problems and dilemmas facing initial teacher education, institutions and schools, was the essence of this vulnerability to appropriation, reinterpretation and reintroduction in a new ideological guise by a different coalition of influential individuals and social groups. This coalition has comprised ideologues of the New Right such as Oliver Letwin and Anthony O'Hear, together with leading members of the liberal education establishment such as Baroness Warnock (1988), Pauline Perry (1989) and David Hargreaves (1989a, b). They have promoted and exploited a notion of partnership which constitutes a considerable attack on a fully professionalized approach to teacher education, involving higher education of four years' duration at degree level. As the rhetoric has developed, partnership is in danger of becoming synonymous with apprenticeship, and professionalism has begun to be replaced by vocationalism.

It has certainly not been our intention here to deny the importance of links between schools, LEAs and teacher education institutions. Indeed, our commitment to such collaborative work is firm. We believe that the growth of reflective school-focused approaches in initial teacher education has led to genuine advances in the quality of courses, and a real diminution of the theory/practice divide which dogged teacher education for so long, especially in the 1960s and 1970s. However, in trying to move ITE forward to involve the profession, certain vulnerabilities have been exposed and we would suggest that it was exactly the rhetoric of 'partnership', which was generated to mask such genuine problems, which left ITE vulnerable to a critique which was thus also partially self-induced. We were hoist with our own petard as power and autonomy slipped away from ITE during the 1980s and as the initiatives of the New Right began to be felt.

It follows that if generally conservative forces have appropriated the notion of partnership then the time has come either to reappropriate it or to replace it.

We would suggest that it is now essential to promote a number of strategic alliances on the basis of clearly stated educational values.[2] Only if we join together do we stand any chance of moving teacher education institutions from a paranoid and defensive position to one of confidence and strength. So what has to be done? What issues must be resolved?

The basic question which must first be asked is, what is the role of higher education in the world of schooling? If its claim for involvement in the preparation of intending teachers is to be justified then its roles with regard to research, development, advice and support to educationists elsewhere are crucial and should be promoted. What is needed, then, is some redefinition of relationships between these institutions and others.

First, there must be more meaningful contact with the community at large. If teachers have had a bad press over recent years, the coverage of teacher education has been appalling. It is essential that a more positive image be promoted, based on the invaluable work which does go on in the institutions. Governors and parents as well as LEAs must be considered. The commitment will need to be to all sections of the community, with efforts being made to establish links with dispossessed groups, as well as the predominantly white middle-class constituency which many of us find easy to operate in.

Second, there must be closer genuine co-operation with the rest of the profession, especially teachers and advisers, and much of this can be through organizations – unions, subject associations, campaigning groups and so on. For instance, we can speculate that, because the current attack on teacher education is in essence an attack on the professionalism of teachers as a whole, a unity between teachers and teacher educators as partners in the same workforce could lead to some realignment of labour organizations in the next decade.

Third, greater intercollegial activity and organization must be developed. This will be an important component of developing confidence in higher education and the track record is not good. For instance, the response to the initial Education Reform Act proposals in summer 1987 was appallingly damp and there was little effective organization in the opposition to the proposals. Even the trade unions were disorganized in their responses. Other professional bodies may increasingly become forums where intercollegial co-operation can be developed and competition and division, fostered by the market ethos, may be worked against.

Finally, there may be considerable gains to be made from forging closer links with professional educators in other spheres. It is intriguing to observe in nurse education, for example, the move away from a two-tier training system (state enrolled and state registered nurses) at the very same time as we see the introduction of just such a system in teaching.

Our view, then, is that 'partnership' in teacher education is a complex, problematic and heavily ideological phenomenon. As a somewhat coy rallying cry it has been used by the profession to obscure both muddled thinking and an unwillingness to face basic issues such as power and values in the relationship between teacher educators and teachers. This gap, between the easy rhetoric and the genuine problems which had to be faced and worked through, left the notion of partnership extremely vulnerable to appropriation and use in revamped ideological forms by very different social groups. 'Partnership' can thus be taken to denote two quite different sets of values and perspectives on the relationship between ITE institutions and schools. It has itself become a site of ideological struggle.

Of course, in the midst of struggle it is very easy to become distracted and miss the main point. In our view the main issue facing education in the next decade is that only if all those concerned with the education of children – parents, governors, children themselves, teachers, administrators and teacher educators – can unite around a shared set of educational values, that the highest quality of education for the children of the future can be developed. In this context a demystification of notions like 'partnership' is a necessary first step.

NOTES

(1) Our colleague Gill Barrett played an important part in preliminary discussions from which this paper developed.
(2) One of the few coherent attempts to develop a coherent alternative to the dominant market/ authoritarian ideology described early in this paper, is that of the Socialist Teachers' Alliance (1988).

REFERENCES

Ashton, P., Henderson, E., Merritt, J. and Mortimer, D. (1983) *Teacher Education in the Classroom: Initial and In-Service*. Beckenham: Croom Helm.

Baker, K. (1989) Secretary of State's Speech to the SEO, 27 January 1989.

Beyer, L. (1988) *Knowing and Acting: Inquiry, Ideology and Educational Studies*. Lewes: Falmer Press.

CATE: Council for the Accreditation of Teacher Education (1986) *Links between Initial Training Institutions and Schools (Catenote 4)*. London: CATE.

CNAA: Council for National Academic Awards (1988) *Partnership in Teacher Education: Realities and Ideals*. London: CNAA.

DES: Department of Education and Science (1984) *Initial Teacher Training: Approval of Courses* (Circular 3/84). London: DES.

DES: Department of Education and Science (1987) *Quality in Schools: the Initial Training of Teachers, An HMI Survey*. London: HMSO.

DES: Department of Education and Science (1988a) *English 5–11*. London: DES.

DES: Department of Education and Science (1988b) *Qualified Teacher Status Consultation Document*. London: DES.

DES: Department of Education and Science (1988c) *The New Teacher in School*. London: HMSO.

Durham, M. (1989) 'A new school of thought – is teacher training full of hot air?' *The Independent* 4 May.

Everton, T. and Impey, G. (eds) (1989) *IT-INSET Partnership in Training: The Leicestershire Experience*. London: David Fulton.

Foucault, M. (1979) *Discipline and Punish*. Harmondsworth: Penguin.

Furlong, V., Hirst, P., Pocklington, K. and Miles, S. (1988) *Initial Teacher Training and the Role of the School*. Milton Keynes: Open University Press.

Ginsburg, M. (1988) *Contradictions in Teacher Education and Society*. Lewes: Falmer Press.

Hargreaves, D. (1989a) 'Out of BEd and into practice'. *Times Educational Supplement*, 8 September.

Hargreaves, D. (1989b) 'Judge radicals by results'. *Times Educational Supplement*, 6 October.

Hillgate Group (1989) *Learning to Teach*. London: Claridge Press in association with the Educational Research Centre.

Levitas, R. (ed.) (1986) *The Ideology of the New Right*. Cambridge: Polity Press.

Menter, I. (1988) 'Teaching practice stasis: racism, sexism and school experience in initial teacher education', in Terrell, C. and Coles, D. (eds) *Recent Innovations in Initial Teacher Education for Intending Primary School Teachers*. Cheltenham: College of St Paul and St Mary.

Menter, I. (1989) '"Fissures, ruptures and contradictions": a study of "partnership" in teacher education'. Unpublished MEd dissertation, Bristol Polytechnic.

Menter, I. and Pollard, A. (1989) 'The implications of the National Curriculum for reflective practice in initial teacher education'. *Westminster Studies in Education*, **12**, 31–42.

O'Hear, A. (1988) *Who Teaches the Teachers?* London: Social Affairs Unit.

Perry, P. (1988) Concluding Address, *Teacher Education and the 1988 Act*, Conference of The Teacher Education Study Group of the Society for Research in Higher Education, London.

Socialist Teachers' Alliance (1988) 'Draft of an education charter for schools'. *Socialist Teacher*, **40**.

Warnock, M. (1988) *A Common Policy for Education.* Oxford: Oxford University Press.
Whitty, G., Barton, L. and Pollard, A. (1987) 'Ideology and control in teacher education: a review of recent experience in England', in Popkewitz, T. (ed.) *Critical Studies in Teacher Education.* Lewes: Falmer Press.
Whitty, G. and Menter, I. (1989) 'Lessons of Thatcherism: education policy in England and Wales 1979–88', in Gamble, A. and Wells, C. (eds) *Thatcher's Law.* Cardiff: GPC Books.

Section II

The Principles of Partnership

Chapter 5

Partnership in Initial Teacher Education: Confronting the Issues[1]

Robin Alexander

INTRODUCTION

'Partnership' has been on the teacher education agenda a long time. If features in reports as far back as McNair in 1944, and of course has its current celebration in the Council for the Accreditation of Teacher Education (CATE) criteria for course approval (DES, 1989a), with their requirements for local committees and the involvement of serving teachers at each stage of the training process, from course design to final assessment.

Nor does officialdom have a monopoly here. Relationships between training institutions and schools have long been agonized over by the teacher educators themselves, and indeed by many teachers, and the most significant partnership initiatives, far from being forced on reluctant institutions by outside pressure, have usually originated locally and have gone on to provide the models which bodies like the Council for National Academic Awards (CNAA), Department of Education and Science (DES) and CATE have first commended and subsequently prescribed.

However, also prominent in the seemingly interminable discussion of this matter has been a sense of how variable, and in some cases how deficient, have been training institution/school/local education authority (LEA) relationships. In any event, even where all parties are agreed on the need and the procedures, and are generally happy that a satisfactory partnership exists, experience shows how problematic it remains and how rapidly things regress if the relationships between the partners are not nurtured.

The fact that we continue to feel the need to seek ways of securing better partnership in teacher education can be explained in a number of ways. Perhaps we've not tried hard enough in the past; or the procedures have been inappropriate or ill-conceived; or well-conceived but subverted, intentionally or unintentionally, by one or other of the partners; or the particular forms of partnership evolved have not survived the roller coaster of recent educational change; or while some educational wheels do not have to be reinvented, this particular one does.

I suspect that it is a bit of all of these, but I would stress the last point – that we have here a problem which by its nature can never be solved once and for all, because partnership, however institutionalized, ultimately depends on human relationships, and these have to be learned afresh and sustained by individuals.

A framework for discussion

This principle leads me to a distinction, which will be a major strand of what follows, between two overlapping but distinct levels of partnership.

The first is the formal level of structures, designated roles and procedures, which I shall call the *enabling* level of partnership, and it tends to involve staff in schools, training institutions and LEAs who have a managerial or liaison role in relation to initial training – school heads and/or heads of department, training institution course leaders and school experience co-ordinators, and LEA officers and advisers.

The second level of partnership comprises the day-to-day interactions of the various individuals and groups who operate at the cutting edge of the teacher education process: students, tutors, and the teachers and pupils with whom and in whose classrooms students work. This I call the *action* level.

In this connection, and not entirely in parenthesis, we might note two points about the contexts in which discussion of partnership usually takes place. First, it tends to concentrate on the enabling rather than the action level of partnership. Second, though some at least of those involved in such discussions may operate at the action level as well as the enabling level, two of the most important actors from the former, the pupil and the student teacher, are rarely if ever represented. Instead, their perspectives, if considered at all, tend to be delivered by proxy, sometimes generously larded with myth.

These two characteristics of much mainstream debate on partnership have led me to tend to say relatively little in this chapter about the detail of formal structures and procedures, especially as there is no shortage of bodies happy to do so. I also tend to highlight, within the action level, the situation of the student whose progress is our *raison d'être*. And overall, as my subtitle suggests, I go quite deliberately for some of those less comfortable issues in partnership which I believe we have a tendency to avoid in the interests of inter-institutional harmony. I can understand the short-term advantages of this strategy, but long-term we simply exacerbate the problems. Confronting the issues squarely is the only way to begin to resolve them, and it is a mark of genuine partnership if we can honestly and frankly do so.

My framework is a simple and commonsense one. It is the notion that as well as the two *levels* of partnership, *enabling* and *action*, there are – as the other axis of a conceptual matrix if you like, cutting across both levels – four main *dimensions* to the partnership issue. These I term *structural*, *attitudinal*, *personal* and *conceptual*.

STRUCTURAL ISSUES

The most important point here is also the most obvious one. Partnership in teacher education involves encounters between different institutions, each with its own formal purposes, structures, roles and procedures, and each having its own unique and distinctive culture. Schools, polytechnics, colleges, universities and LEAs are engaged in fundamentally different jobs: educating children; training teachers and undertaking educational research; administering local educational provision.

A great deal follows from this insufficiently heeded proposition, and this, in the end, is why partnership in initial teacher education is a perennial challenge; not because of ill-will on anyone's part, but simply because although partnership is in everyone's interests, for only one institution of the three is initial teacher training the primary concern, and the consciousness, commitments and resources of the other two are inevitably and necessarily concentrated elsewhere.

This means not only that partnership cannot be taken for granted, but also that a divergence and perhaps collision of values and perspectives is not unlikely, and it is naive to pretend otherwise.

Moreover, it has to be recognized that at the present time, and for the foreseeable future, the training institution's formal and legal responsibility for the initial training course makes the partnership in certain respects an unequal one. Whatever the rhetoric (or even the reality) of shared values, good relationships and the like, the partnership arrangements between training institution, school and LEA are only viable if they support the former in the discharge of its responsibilities. There are fine lines between consultation, collaboration and advice on the one hand, and intervention or even obstruction on the other.[2]

The point is not intended to be contentious or provocative: realistic, rather. But there's also something here to be exploited, if you happen to believe that differences in perspective are actually productive. School, LEA and training institution see the initial training of teachers differently, and these differences should be made explicit and placed at the heart of the debate about the content and process of initial training. A trainee teacher, then, is a teacher of children and a member of a school's professional community in the making; he or she is also a future employee who will soon be working to a contract and conditions of service; and he or she is a student undertaking higher education, a learner as well as a teacher. Together, these present and future roles add up to a situation, for the student, of complexity, challenge and indeed, frequently, of stress; for the teacher educator, very often, likewise.

A second problem, very different but no less critical, is the contractual and financial basis on which one institutional partner takes on work generated by, and the responsibility of, the other. The most familiar context is school experience, and traditionally schools have become involved in it because they felt it was professionally important for them to do so, and on the basis of goodwill.

Actually, even here, national practice has been variable, with some teachers, particularly in larger schools, having formally designated staff tutor (or equivalent) roles, and time and remuneration to match, while others have simply added involvement in school experience to their other duties. Generally, since during block practice a student's taking over a class or classes releases the teachers concerned to do other things, this has been accepted as a mutually beneficial arrangement.

The 1987 teachers' conditions of service remove the ambiguity about the contractual status of a serving teacher's involvement in school experience. It can now be formally designated as part of the job. But partnership in initial training, for many teachers, increasingly extends beyond the traditional situation of having a student undertaking teaching practice in one's classroom. School staff are now participating in course planning meetings, interviewing course applicants, undertaking criterion-referenced assessment of student progress and performance in school, writing reports, co-tutoring in the training institution, attending course review and validation meetings, and so on.

However, as both Her Majesty's Inspectorate (HMI) and the new CATE criteria acknowledge (DES, 1988, 1989a) teachers may have no training for this activity, though presumably it is grounded in preparatory discussion of some kind. Equally, they may receive no remuneration. In fact, the situation here is variable. Teachers are often paid for a tutoring role in the training institution itself, where they are in effect part-time lecturers, but not for the equally or more demanding school-based tutorial function in relation to school experience, that being definable as within a teacher's conditions of service. In some cases LEAs permit teachers to accept payment for tutorial work which takes place at the training institution, but in others any payment is set against salary and so goes to the LEA. The thinking behind this displays characteristic LEA logic, but is perhaps not calculated to motivate the teachers concerned.

So although on paper the contractual position now looks tidier than previously, the reality is still problematic, and will become even more so as partnership is extended. Moreover, the point about training raised above is not just an aside. Some of the partnership roles currently under discussion are properly and appropriately undertaken by heads and staff on the basis of their professional experience and expertise. But others raise a much more fundamental question: is teaching experience, recent, relevant or otherwise, the sole or key qualification for the teacher trainer? Put another way, does being able to teach 9-year-olds mean that one is automatically able to train teachers of 9-year-olds? Is there really no more to it than that?

We know current government thinking on this, as reflected in the revival of the apprentice model of teacher training through the licensed teacher scheme (DES, 1989b). We also know the teacher educators' fairly predictable response, that although school teaching experience is a vital part of the teacher trainer's apparatus, training teachers and teaching children are not the same, but demand different kinds of professional knowledge and skill.

Predictable the response may be, but it deserves serious consideration, since, self-evidently, the jobs are indeed so very different. For all kinds of reasons, policy makers have chosen to gloss over this issue, preferring instead the simple dogma of 'recent and relevant' and assuming that this takes care of the whole training expertise question. It does not, of course. What it *does* do is prematurely foreclose a profoundly important debate which was opening up in the late 1970s and early 1980s; and, while claiming to do the opposite, it sells short the job of teacher training, and therefore the student and the profession. The new CATE course approval criteria show an important modification of the original line on this issue. Where the original proposals, somewhat oddly, defined the competence of teacher educators largely in terms of their imputed incompetence – a deficit model of professional expertise, if you like – CATE 2 acknowledges that 'there are skills specific to the teaching of young and mature adults at the level of higher education' and that 'serving teachers and newly-appointed tutors may need help in acquiring these skills' (DES, 1989a, 13). At the same time, the licensed teacher proposals might seem to curtail any optimism generated by such statements and in this and other respects the debate about whether a teacher needs more than an on-the-job apprenticeship is still very much with us. (Witness, for example, the controversy generated by Hargreaves' views: Hargreaves, 1989; Caudrey, 1990.)

My final point on structures is rather different. I said earlier that partnership at the formal, institutional or 'enabling' level has little value unless it encourages person-to-person partnership at the 'action' level of the classroom. This is not to say, however, that formal procedures do not matter. On the contrary, given my first point about the parties contractually undertaking different jobs in different places, there is no way that partnership at the action level can ever be achieved without the enabling formal procedures.

But we should also be aware of the dangers of over-formalization of procedures. Elaborate arrangements may look good, and by their visibility satisfy those bodies interested in a letter-of-the-law approach to teacher education, but we all know how they can also stifle creative initiative at the action level, or lead to mindless rule-following.

ATTITUDINAL ISSUES

Institutional affiliation engenders an institutional perspective: by virtue of being a member of a school staff, or of a teacher education institution, or of an LEA advisory team, individuals come to view very differently both their own and each others' situations and tasks. Structures generate versions of reality, then. Equally, they generate solidarities, loyalties and sets of values. Attitudes are formed and consolidated; and one of the reasons they resist challenge and change is that institutional cohesion and individual equanimity may depend on their persistence.

Attitudinal division is, and always has been, a major problem in teacher education, and we would be wise to be scrupulously honest with ourselves about the extent to which we may simultaneously utter sentiments about the desirability of partnership and collaboration in initial training while believing privately that the other partners have got it wrong, are ignorant and prejudiced, or are simply incapable of delivering their end of the partnership agreement.

So it is attitudes, not just procedures, which have to change, and since my point is that structural divides reinforce attitudinal ones, we should be under no illusions about the difficulties involved.

The most intractable such attitudes are those which represent other parties as inadequate to the task *not by virtue of the way they actually undertake it but simply because of the job they do*. Thus, teacher trainers as a profession are all ivory-towered theorists, refugees from the classroom, remote from the chalk-face, incapable of coping with a class themselves though all too ready to tell others how to do so. Or teachers as a profession are parochial, philistine and anti-intellectual, despite their engagement in a job which by definition espouses precisely the opposite values. And as for advisers and HMIs. . . .

Of course, this is often good knockabout stuff that anyone with experience and a bit of insight knows not to be influenced by. And yet such values are peculiarly pervasive, and very resistant, even to the direct knowledge that in many or most particular cases they are grossly stereotypical. They have become part of each group's collective psyche, rather in the way that in their games children persist in portraying teachers, contrary to the evidence of their experience, as begowned and capricious floggers.

I would tend to take a more relaxed view of this problem – that's the way the world is, after all – were it not for the fact that it is the student, rather than the teacher, teacher educator or adviser, who is at the receiving end or intersection of such attitudes, and so often suffers because of them. It really does not matter too much if teachers and teacher trainers rubbish each other since they can look after themselves, but the student is much more vulnerable. 'Forget all that airy-fairy theory they teach you at college – this is what it's all about'/'Take no notice of the staff – most of them are thirty years out of date and just time-serving' are for the student not hoary predictabilities but first-time heard thunderbolts, all the more devastating for being delivered by the two people on whose authority, support and (crucially) valuation the student most keenly depends. What *does* the student do when caught between mutual disparagement, competing messages and conflicting expectations – 'Do it this way . . . no, this . . .no, this . . . There's one right way to do it . . . There's no one right way to do it . . .'.

Usually, of course, the attitudes are expressed more subtly – a telling word, but not personalized, dropped here, arched eyebrows and a pained sigh there. The student, of course, is never fooled: the extent of respect that teacher and teacher educator have for each other becomes apparent very quickly, and the student is either canny enough not to be thrown (or even to turn it to his or her strategic advantage) or becomes more and more insecure.

One could be moralistic about this situation, and say that it is irresponsible for parties engaged in what cannot but be a collaborative activity to behave like this and so exacerbate the already considerable stress placed on the student in training. And if the student's confidence is undermined and his or her professional development is frustrated then a moralistic response is not inappropriate. But of course we need to go further, and seek causes and solutions. Since it is widely accepted that most kinds of prejudice have their roots in ignorance, and since there is plenty of evidence to support the assertion that in the case of teacher education the partners know rather less than they should about each other's professional endeavours, we might consider placing the exchange of understanding high on the agenda of any formal bodies set up in the spirit of partnership. This is something we tend not to do, if only because institutional representatives are busy people and the instrumental task of, say, sorting out school-experience places and arrangements is time-consuming enough. But how much do the teacher educators *really* know about the schools in which they place students – the ideas and values of head and staff, the organizational details, the backgrounds of the pupils, the constraints under which staff and pupils work? And how much do school staff *really* know about the course the student is on, the kinds of understanding and expertise tutors are trying to foster, their justifications for doing so, and the constraints under which they, in their turn, work?

The required knowledge, then, is of each other's practical situation. I stress the word *practical* because one of the obstacles to progress here is the notion that the only true practical arena is the school. But of course teacher training is as practical an activity as teaching in schools. They are different kinds of practice, admittedly, though for both groups the act of teaching itself is a major part of the job. Similarly, the school is not the only 'real world', as any industrialist or social worker, let alone any teacher educator, will attest. The main point, however, is that all professional practice is a complex mix of ideas, ideals, action, opportunities, constraints, compromises and so on. It is essential to a mature and productive relationship between the partners in teacher education that each party recognizes this and understands enough about each other's practical situation – in this more comprehensive usage of 'practical' – to know why things are done as they are done, to presume integrity and expertise unless there is reliable evidence to the contrary, and to steer clear of the superficial or ill-informed judgement.

It is encouraging that the CATE 2 'institutional co-operation' criterion appears to take this longer-term, more fundamental view of partnership.

PERSONAL ISSUES

I distinguished at the outset between the *enabling* and *action* levels of partnership, the former being constituted of institutional roles and procedures and the latter of the interactions of student, teacher, pupils and tutor. It is probably platitudinous to remind ourselves that whatever the quality of the structural arrangements worked out at the enabling level, most hangs, for the student, on the quality of relationships at the action level. Partnership at this level has a very personal aspect.

It's worth noting that two, and sometimes three of the four constituents at this level are frequently underpowered, notwithstanding their importance: the pupil, the student, and sometimes (depending very much on a school's managerial style) the teacher. So it seems appropriate to focus for a moment on the need to respect the situation and needs of each, and to build such respect into partnership arrangements.

Respecting the pupil

Teacher education generates a tension, or even competition, between the learning needs of the student and those of the pupil, for while both are in the classroom for the explicit purpose of learning, the objectives are very different. As far as the school is concerned, there can be no ambivalence here and the judgement has to be in favour of the pupil. Decisions about school-experience placements and programmes must be in the pupils' best interests, and children cannot be made mere guinea pigs. And yet students (and experienced teachers) learn by trial and error as much as by unproblematic success (if such a condition exists), so guinea pigs is what children inevitably are.

The point is made simply to highlight a central dilemma in teacher education. It is always resolved one way or another – it has to be – though it would probably be very uncomfortable indeed if we were to count the cost of some school-experience placements to some pupils. But we should remember that the dilemma is not an occasional one but is inherent in all decisions about placing students (and, for that matter, inexperienced or inadequate teachers), and for that reason needs to be confronted explicitly and openly at both levels of partnership.

Respecting the teacher

The teacher's knowledge, however incomplete, of the particular pupils a student is to work with is greater than that of any of the other partners. And the teacher has of course the day-to-day responsibility for the curriculum of these pupils. It is a *sine qua non*, therefore, that the teacher must be central to all discussions and decisions at the action level about where students are to be placed and what they are to do. And because the teacher perspective is so central it should also be prominent at the enabling level too. Yet how often is it omitted? How often are school-experience decisions taken without reference to the teacher with whom the student will subsequently enter into a close working relationship?

The teacher's day-to-day classroom knowledge is an essential ingredient in initial training and especially in school experience. Equally, there are things about initial training and school experience which the teacher needs to know in order to do the best by the student. It seems painfully obvious, but the teacher needs a clear understanding of the purposes, rationale, content and organization both of the school experience and of the course of which school experience is a part. Yet how often, if we are honest, is it the case that a particular teacher takes a student armed with no more than a memory of his or her own initial training? And, bearing critically on the issue of *attitudes* above, how often then do this memory and its attendant assumptions and attitudes subvert, albeit unintentionally, the student's experience and the training institution's preparation and supervision? The scenario is all too familiar: the student caught between a tutor asserting that the classroom is a place for learning about teaching, and providing carefully structured exploratory and investigative tasks in pursuit of this goal, and the teacher asserting that the classroom is where the student demonstrates how much about teaching he or she has already learned; or between a tutor stressing that he or she is there to help the student and a teacher who insists that the tutor is there to judge, and must therefore be treated, if not as the enemy, then at least with suspicion.

I shall return to this conflict, for such it is, in the next section, but the point at issue here is a simple one. The teacher must know and understand the training course the student is on, otherwise the student can suffer; and in order to gain this knowledge and understanding the teacher needs to be central to partnership discussions and decisions. There's a message here, inevitably, for those who devise procedures at the enabling level of partnership, in both training institutions and schools.

Respecting the student

I made the point earlier that the student has a number of simultaneous roles and that their juxtaposition is one reason why initial training is so demanding for the student and so complex for those who plan and implement it. In particular, it is very easy to forget that students are usually young adults still in the process of establishing their personal identities and independence, frequently insecure and vulnerable, and that in any event they are *learners*, with the needs (and rights) that being learners entails. Together, school and training institution have to foster the emergence of the individual who can think things out and make professional judgements and decisions independently and autonomously; but in doing so they must never cease to be other than wholly dependable themselves.

The student has a right to expect from the school/training institution partnership the following as minimum conditions for successful learning:

(a)   partners pulling in the same direction and delivering, if not identical messages, then at least reconcilable ones;

(b) tutors and teachers who understand and respect each other's roles in the training process;

(c) a professional climate in both training institution and school which is mature and open, and which of itself provides a reasonable model of professional attitudes and relationships for the student.

(d) classroom practice which the student is encouraged to see as having potential for professional learning – which is, therefore, open to analysis and discussion by the student. This indicates, therefore, the need to place students not so much in 'show' schools, and certainly not in schools which insist that their version of practice is the only permissible one and refuse to countenance the possibility of alternatives, as in those schools where staff are convinced and confident about the way they work, yet also happy and able to articulate the thinking that lies behind their practice and willing honestly to discuss some of the difficulties and dilemmas they have to deal with.

'Good practice', then – a notion which features prominently (and rightly so) in any discussion about school experience placements – is, in this particular context, about a classroom's potential for the *student's* as well as the child's learning, even though the latter, as I have stressed at several points, is paramount. It has to be added that while this principle is hinted at in CATE 2's discussion of appropriate school experience placements (DES, 1989a, 15) it does not appear to have been considered in connection with the licensed teacher scheme. There (DES, 1989b, 4) the emphasis is exclusively on the suitability of the licensee: while it is proper that this should be the main emphasis, a sense of the power of the school context to define and influence 'suitability' would have been welcome.

CONCEPTUAL ISSUES

I have argued that the structural divisions between school, training institution and LEA, which are inherent in teacher education as currently organized, engender different perspectives and attitudes which in interaction can be either productive or damaging for the training course and the student, depending on how at the enabling and action levels partnership is tackled. I have also argued that a minimum condition for a viable notion of partnership in such circumstances is the exchange of information about each partner's situation so that as far as possible the training process is conducted on the basis of shared knowledge and understanding rather than supposition or prejudice.

The principle applies across the board: schools, training institutions and LEAs need to know about each other.

There are various categories or levels of information, and circumstances demand selectivity and economy. By and large we are quite good at exchanging information about procedures and arrangements – names, numbers, dates, timetables, reporting mechanisms and so on. However, it must be clear by now that partnership and the problems of partnership, as I have discussed them here, demand in addition something deeper than this. We need to know not only *how* a partner institution operates, but also *why*. Partners need access to each other's thinking and reasoning, to the ideas and justifications in which each other's day-to-day procedures are embedded. Without this *conceptual* exchange, whether it be about a primary school's way of grouping children in the classroom, or the headings on a college's teaching practice report form, partnership will remain cosmetic, misunderstandings will persist, and the student will remain caught between conflicting assumptions and expectations, unvoiced and therefore unresolved.

Since the rationale for all this is the facilitation and improvement of initial training, the one topic which we have no option but to include on the agenda is the training process itself. And since the reality of training is that all partners are in some way directly involved in it, the exchange has to be more than just a unidirectional passing of information, from college to school. It must include debate as well as decisions. And it has to be said that real debate about teacher education between the partners involved in it is all too rare.

Some of the themes for the debate are familiar topics for discussion already, and indeed they also feature in CATE 2: selection of students, assessment and so on. Beyond items like these are three overarching issues of a conceptual kind which perennially generate misunderstanding and difficulty.

School experience

School experience is the component of the course where partnership is most readily accepted as necessary, but also the one where, because it is so complex to organize and administer, we are most likely to concentrate on practical arrangements and neglect underlying purposes. Broadly speaking, although every institution claims that its concept of school experience is unique, most or all are variants or combinations of the three forms of school experience which have been around for about a century.

The first is the 'apprentice' model in which the student acquires most of his or her teaching expertise in the school itself through close association with an experienced practising teacher. The second is the mainstream 'teaching practice' model which most readers of this chapter themselves experienced, where students acquire professional knowledge and skill in the training institution, then apply, demonstrate or 'practise' these during extended periods in school, watched over by the experienced teacher whose class they take over and by a tutor from the training institution. The third, the 'school-based study' model, represents the school and classroom as arenas for the student to observe, study, experiment and learn, as well as to practise; and to this end the actual activities undertaken comprise more than taking the class and include systematic observation, small-scale inquiries, working with individual pupils or small groups, and so on.

There is no necessary connection between a particular conceptual model of school experience and a particular organizational form, though generally teaching practice is undertaken in blocks of several weeks, and school-based study in intermittent or serial school experience.

The idea of apprenticeship deserves a caveat. At one time lampooned by teacher educators as 'sitting by Nellie', apprenticeship is actually implicit in every situation where a student works with an experienced teacher, and is thus an intrinsic condition of school experience, whatever form it takes, and indeed of all human learning dependent on a teacher–learner relationship. The point at issue with the apprentice model, therefore, is not whether it is or should be an element in school experience but which version of apprenticeship is to be adopted. It is true that at one end of the apprentice-ship continuum is the unquestioning imitation of the expert by the novice, but at the other end is the kind of dialogue and collaborative exploration of ideas and practices by student and mentor which characterizes not just apprenticeship but teaching at its best.

It is essential, incidentally, that in the debates about the licensed and articled teacher schemes (DES, 1989b, 1989c) the notion of apprenticeship be opened up in this way; equally, it is important that teacher educators acknowledge the extent to which their own teacher training practice in BEd and PGCE courses may sometimes be grounded in versions of apprenticeship no less unquestioning than those they accuse such schemes of endorsing. The matter is not at all clear-cut.

Though the three models above are simplified characterizations, it will be clear that the assumptions about the nature of professional learning, as well as the school-experience procedures themselves, are nevertheless critically different in each case. Most of us are aware that current practice favours various combinations of school-based study and teaching practice in a much more flexible and eclectic mix than the fairly rigid structures of two decades ago, and that the emphasis is on continuity of contact through a mixture of days, half-days and short blocks rather than infrequent but lengthy block practices. It will also be recognized that the apprentice model is currently enjoying official endorsement, at least as implied in the licensed teacher scheme; though I fear that the version of apprenticeship envisaged is imitation rather than exploration. And although nobody likes to be pigeon-holed, I think it will be accepted that most school-experience schemes, including ostensibly revolutionary ideas like IT-INSET, can be characterized in terms of their particular adaptation of one or more of the three basic models. All of them, incidentally, have been around a long time. The McNair Report for example (Board of Education, 1944, paras 260, 261) contrasts versions of my second and third models above in terms which would not look out of place in a 1990s course document.

I don't want to discuss their relative merits, but instead would make one very basic point in the context of partnership: it is essential that all parties understand precisely what concept of school experience is in operation within the course with which they are associated. A statement of the obvious again, perhaps, but a mismatch of perceptions here between college and school is more frequent than we would care to admit. Moreover, the mismatch underscores my repeated point about pursuing partnership at both the enabling (institutional) and action (classroom) level, since it is currently all too common for a school-based study model to be hammered out between course officers and head while the teacher with whom a student is placed acts on the assumption that the student is on a traditional sink-or-swim block practice.

The precise nature of the student–serving teacher relationship, the version of apprenticeship to be adopted, is rarely discussed in sufficient depth, or made suffi-ciently explicit to the parties involved.

Theory and practice

The second perennial conceptual issue is theory/practice. Again there are competing versions, and the matter is philosophically more complex than space permits, but the essence is somewhat as follows.[3]

The traditional analysis is that theory and practice are two totally different entities or worlds, and that in teacher education this is reinforced by their physically occupying different buildings (a somewhat bizarre notion admittedly, expressed like that, but widely subscribed to). Theory, in this view, is generated by teacher educators and researchers, and is purveyed as specific bodies of knowledge in colleges and universities, while practice takes place in the 'real world' of classroom and school and is what teachers do with, for and to pupils. The so-called 'theory–practice' problem then centres on the mismatch between the two worlds, the claimed irrelevance of much 'theory' to 'practice' and the need to devise ways of integrating them meaningfully. Coupled with this analysis, of course, is all that tedious attendant rhetoric of ivory towers, chalk-face, airy-fairy nonsense and the real world, which sits rather paradoxically with a positivistic tendency for those who knock academic theory to nevertheless need it to legitimate their ideas and practices: 'Research has proved that . . .'.

So theory, by this popular view, excludes practice and practitioners, and practice in turn excludes theory and theorists. That being so, it is hardly surprising that some teachers who take this line so resent teacher educators and researchers, and that the teacher educators who hold similar perceptions find the 'integration' of theory and practice, so defined, well-nigh impossible.

For the theory–practice 'problem', it is at last now beginning to be accepted, is not only procedural, organizational and curricular but also *conceptual*. It continues to be vexatious, in part at least, because the analysis underlying the conventional characterization is faulty. For a start, a theory is only a species of idea and everyone has ideas. Teacher educators and researchers therefore don't have a monopoly of theory; indeed, teachers have theories – that is to say, ideas, assumptions, frameworks in which their classroom activity is grounded. Teachers, then, are theorists too, so the gulf is not so much between theory and practice as between theory and theory – the theory grounded in, for example, conceptual analysis and funded research on the one hand, and the theory grounded in classroom experience on the other. Value judgements, and empiricism, are features of both.

Similarly, teachers in classrooms do not have a monopoly of practice. Teacher educators too are practitioners; and planning, discussing, evaluating, thinking or arguing ideas through and making decisions are all necessary aspects of the practice of teaching, as 'practical' as trimming card with a guillotine. To assert otherwise is to characterize teaching as essentially mindless.

Those who take the line that the practice of teaching is irreducibly impregnated with theory, and that theorizing is a practical activity, then find themselves having to rethink, in effect, their whole approach to teacher training, and – critically for our current theme – the roles and relationships of student, teacher and tutor. For it becomes axiomatic that theory loses its almost inviolable or sacred character as high-status knowledge owned and distributed by an academic priesthood, and becomes instead common property and a universal process, something all can create and participate in.

The emphasis on process is important, for the other part of the package is that theory, in this alternative analysis, is something one does rather than something one is told, and for this reason perhaps the participle 'theorizing', which I introduced above, rather than the noun 'theory', is more appropriate. Theorizing – reflecting on, generating, using, testing and reformulating ideas about teaching and learning – becomes a capacity that is necessary for intelligent teaching, and has important implications for teaching and learning methods in the teacher education course itself, with an active student role being central.

Equally, theory and theorizing require *dialogue*, since the student needs to hear, explore and compare theories from various sources – research, conceptual analysis, tutors, teachers, other students . . . and this is the point at which a commitment to partnership becomes critically important at the action level. Its essence is an open exploration between student and teacher, student and tutor, and, ideally, all three together, of the central challenges and issues concerning everyday classroom practice.

For some, this will seem like a rather abstract version of what common sense has always dictated; for others with a vested interest in preserving the authority and mystique of the lecturer or teacher as fount of jealously guarded knowledge it may constitute a professional threat.

But in any event, the basic point here is that there are more radical ways of dealing with the perennial 'theory–practice problem' than the usual one of trying to make academic theory more 'relevant', and that the whole issue is one of central concern in a partnership context. I suspect, however, that little progress will be made in teacher education until we can break out of the dualist, polarizing straitjacket of theory *versus* practice (one among many such needless dichotomies) and initiate an alternative vocabulary and mode of discourse in which the teacher's job is characterized as a range of capacities and processes in all of which action and thought are firmly intertwined, as are values, ideas, knowledge, understanding and skill.

Good Practice

This is the last in this trio of overarching conceptual problems. I made the point earlier that in selecting schools and classrooms for students to work in we should consider extending our view of 'good practice' to include a school's potential contribution to the learning of the *student* as well as its actual contribution to the learning of the *child*. But the point at issue in this section is rather different, and even more basic. It is the question of how 'good practice' is identified, by reference to what criteria, and by whom.

Usually, of course, these questions, and therefore the answers too, stay in the realm of the tacit. Course tutors may ask advisers to recommend schools, but are less likely to discuss criteria, preferring to assume that their judgements are reliable. Or tutors will hear about schools on their grapevine, or of course have their own network of contacts.

It will be readily accepted that 'good practice' is not an absolute, since the adjective implies an ethical judgement, so the notion of identifying good practice on the basis of second-hand recommendations is, strictly speaking, rather suspect, particularly if neither the criteria nor the evidence are made explicit. On the other hand, while accepting the philosophical point we may argue pragmatically that if such sources produce school placements which in turn deliver productive school experience for the student then it doesn't really matter. (Incidentally, some claim to resolve the philosophical problem by talking not of 'good' but of 'effective' or 'useful' or 'efficient' practice. This is no solution at all: criterial and evidential questions are still begged.)

But there are senses in which it does matter a great deal how we come to define good practice in this context.

For a start, bearing in mind our concern with partnership between schools, training institutions and LEAs, it is a somewhat unequal relationship, to say the least, if just one of the partners is the definer or arbiter of good practice. Pragmatic it may be, but it also implies that the validity of the judgement depends less on its criterial and evidential claims than on the power and status of the judge. By extension, this line also devalues the judgements of the other two partners, including of course the teacher educators themselves. And it also raises ethical questions about the position of the school which is judged unsuitable for placing students yet (a) is unaware that it has been so labelled and (b) has no opportunity to put its own case.

So, stripped down to its essentials, 'good practice' in this context has come to mean merely what those with power endorse, and the chances are that this denotes those schools which happen to reflect and reinforce the currently favoured local orthodoxies. (On the way notions of 'good practice' relate to professional hierarchies, see Alexander, 1989.)

So a minimum condition of partnership, I would suggest, has to be not that one partner takes another's recommendations on trust but that the partners each make explicit and argue their particular versions of good practice through to the point of consensus or its nearest approximation. As well as more truly signalling a partnership of equals, this procedure also minimizes difficulties later on.

But there is another context in which our way of tackling the good-practice question matters a great deal, and that is the professional development of the student, the very purpose that such judgements, and the whole apparatus of partnership, are intended to support. For exploring the nature of professional practice, and identifying and assessing the many alternative criteria by which practice can be judged effective or good, are of course activities in which students themselves must be involved, if professional development is not to mean little more than mindless imitation of another's behaviour. We do the student's development a considerable disservice if we duck this issue.

I raised the 'good-practice' problem initially in the context of partnership, thinking about the way school-experience places are selected and allocated, but it will be appreciated that we are now talking of something more general and fundamental to both initial training and the professional culture of schools, training institutions and LEAs. One of the most pervasive features of some such institutions is their failure to address the value issues at the heart of education. Thus, whole schools, even whole LEAs, may overtly espouse a particular view of education, never putting it to conceptual or empirical test. Similarly, many initial training courses convey the same kind of message, presenting plenty of prescriptions but offering rather fewer justifications or opportunities for analysis or critique.

The stance is at best dishonest, at worst repressive, if not in intention (which is of course usually benign) then in outcome. And of course the student's capacity for self-evaluation, a cornerstone of professional development, is unlikely to flower if evaluation is the one activity everyone else studiously avoids.

So I would suggest that the question of what constitutes good practice should be both a focal activity for the teacher in training and a key agenda item for partnership. To promote the collaborative, mutual exploration of practice, juxtaposing the differing perspectives and criteria of teacher, head, adviser, administrator, tutor, researcher, HMI and student, will not only make for a better system of teacher training, but will also enhance the quality of education in schools. Good practice is identified and achieved dialectically and empirically, not by decree.

CONCLUSION

This paper's discussion is framed in terms of two levels of partnership – *enabling* and *action* – and four dimensions: *structural, attitudinal, personal* and *conceptual.* There are probably more, but for present purposes these serve well enough to highlight some of the central challenges of bringing together separate institutions and people in pursuit of a common goal, that of training tomorrow's teachers as effectively as possible.

I have not ventured into detail about procedures at the enabling level. This is not because of inability or cowardice but because I wanted to provide a counterbalance to the general thrust of recent debate. Formal procedures are immensely important, and my choice of the word 'enabling' underlines this: without them we get nowhere. But to enable partnership outside the classroom is not the same as delivering it within: hence my emphasis on the students, teachers and pupils at the action level. In any event, there can be little support now for more of the kinds of cosmetic exercise we have witnessed in the past – heightening the rhetoric, increasing the number of meetings, taking the refreshments up-market, tidying up the arrangements and then claiming to CATE, the local committee and ourselves that we have thereby achieved partnership – if such junketings so manifestly have little impact on the ways students, teachers and tutors view each other and interact in the classroom.

NOTES

(1)   This chapter is based on a paper given to a conference on partnership in teacher education organized jointly by HMI and Bradford and Ilkley Community College, and attended by representatives from LEAs and initial training institutions in Yorkshire.

(2)   (This is a point of general importance, with ramifications in other areas as well as initial training. For example, the devolution of control of INSET through GRIST and its successor LEATGS, raises serious questions about the autonomy of schools on the one hand and colleges/universities on the other, *vis-à-vis* LEAs and the DES).

(3)   For a fuller discussion, see Alexander, 1984a, 142–50; 1984b, ch. 6.

REFERENCES

Alexander, R. J. (1984a) 'Innovation and continuity in the initial teacher education curriculum', in Alexander, R. J., Craft, M. and Lynch, J. (eds) *Change in Teacher Education: Context and Provision since Robbins.* London: Holt, Rinehart and Winston.

Alexander, R. J. (1984b) *Primary Teaching.* London: Cassell.

Alexander, R. J. (1989) 'Core subjects and autumn leaves: the National Curriculum and the languages of primary education'. *Education 3–13,* **17**(1).

Board of Education (1944) *Teachers and Youth Leaders.* London: HMSO.

Caudrey, A. (1990) 'Learning on the job: progress or corner-cutting?' *Times Educational Supplement,* 26 January.

DES: Department of Education and Science (1988) *Education Observed 7: Initial Teacher Training in Universities in England, Northern Ireland and Wales.* London: HMSO.

DES: Department of Education and Science (1989a) *Initial Teacher Training: Approval of Courses* (Circular 24/89). London: DES.

DES: Department of Education and Science (1989b) *The Education (Teachers) Regulations 1989* (Circular 18/89). London: DES.

DES: Department of Education and Science (1989c) *Articled Teacher Pilot Scheme: Invitation to Bid for Funding* (Circular letter, 27.6.89). London: DES.

Hargreaves, D. H. (1989) 'Out of BEd and into practice'. *Times Educational Supplement,* 8 September.

Chapter 6

The Theory–Practice Relationship in Teacher Training

Paul H. Hirst

In a general platitudinous sense all human action is necessarily 'theory laden'. What makes any event an action is that what is occurring is understood by the agent in some way and is the outcome of a resulting judgement. In this sense all actions are intelligible as actions only to the extent that the events concerned are dependent on how situations are understood by the agent, however partial and inadequate that understanding might be. Such understanding however is in a general sense a matter of 'theory', for it involves concepts, beliefs and general rules or principles. Change these concepts, beliefs or principles and the action that results is thereby different. What matters then in assessing human action or the activities or practices they comprise is not whether or not they are informed by 'theory' in this general sense, but whether that 'theory' is any good. Are its concepts adequate to capture the complexities of the situations concerned? Is what is believed about these situations true? Are the judgements that are made justifiable on rational grounds?

From these elementary considerations it is then but a simple step to recognizing that the professional activities that any teacher engages in are what they are by virtue of the 'theory' that informs them, by virtue of the concepts, beliefs and principles that the teacher employs. And whether that teacher is indeed acting professionally turns on whether that 'theory' is rationally defensible in terms of the best knowledge and understanding of such situations and of what ought to be done in such circumstances. But, if all that is true, what kind of 'theory' is it that properly determines what teachers do, how do we know it is rationally defensible and how exactly is it employed in the immediacies of day-to-day practice? If we can answer these questions on the place of theory in the business of professionally competent teaching, then there is some hope that we can begin to sort out the place and relationship of theoretical studies and practical activities in teacher training. We might then also be able to begin to see who best can do the training job and how they should set about it. It is to these difficult questions that this chapter is addressed in the hope that some light can be shed on how they are to be answered.

There are two approaches to these questions that have dominated teacher training until relatively recently. The first, which for convenience can be labelled the 'traditionalist' approach, has seen the activities of teaching as developing directly through practice. Practical 'common sense', by the process of trial and error, has in a developing tradition found the best ways to teach children, how to organize them for this purpose, what methods and materials to use and so on. Progressively more careful and sophisticated experiments have developed new and better practices. But, eventually, it is through involvement in the activities of teaching themselves that what is going on is both understood and developed to be more adequate. Nowadays the professional tasks of teaching largely take place within institutions having rules, principles, attitudes and practices which have grown up over a long period. And these institutions are themselves located in the institutions, practices and traditions of wider society which constantly influence what schools seek to do and how they do it. In this situation the 'theory' that informs any professionally competent teaching is necessarily the product of the world of teaching itself. The concepts, beliefs and principles employed are inextricably linked with what is going on. They are embedded in knowing how to do things and the teacher may never consciously directly attend to this 'theory' even though it is being employed in conscious decisions. The 'theory' is indeed partly constitutive of the practice but the teacher need not therefore be involved in the analysis or rational consideration of what it involves or entails. In all this the activities of teaching are seen as 'theoretical' in much the same sense as, say, cake-making is 'theoretical'. What is required in the practice is an understanding of what one is about, what is being aimed at and adherence to the general rules or principles of acting successfully. Of course when it comes to the activities of teaching, human development and relationships are involved and the complexities and unpredictabilities that result must be fully recognized. The social circumstances of schools may also change, making new demands on teaching in ways that have little significant parallel in a practice like cake-making. But these features only serve to make the business of teaching all the more one that can be understood, mastered and developed only in the doing.

What cake-making requires of an individual practitioner by way of theory is simply an understanding of what to do to achieve success. It is the recipes that matter. Any conscious reflection on the terms and principles involved in these does not seem to be required, let alone any knowledge of how these are justified from past experience. As for any understanding of food chemistry, such theory would seem to be quite irrelevant to the successful conduct of the practice. Just so with teaching, it is claimed. But though the individual cook need not stand back and reflect on the terms of successful practice, even in such a relatively simple practice successful recipes or principles exist only by virtue of reflection and critical discrimination that has progressively picked out the features of successful practice. The very existence of the recipes has depended on distinguishing both successful cakes from unsuccessful and the procedures that lead to the successful. All the more so in the complex world of teaching. But the successful practice of an individual requires simply the development in practice itself of an understanding of and adherence to the principles that map out successful procedures.

An individual teacher's practice is thus acceptable professionally only if it is informed by 'theory' – that is, understanding and principles – that is justifiable in the light of wide-ranging practical experience. Not merely that individual teacher's personal experience, for indeed that experience is likely to be far too limited to provide adequate justification. The experience of professionals as a whole in similar situations is what is wanted, for the most adequately justified principles will be generalizations from a great deal of experiment in practice. The generation of such understanding and principles for the individual teacher's use is however to be understood as of its very essence practical in character. The concepts, beliefs and principles of this 'theory' have their proper meaning and validity only as used in concrete actions and activities. The discourse of practice in which this 'theory' is articulated is thus necessarily rich in implicit, tacit, presuppositions that do not begin to be explicitly indicated by the discourse itself. What the concepts, beliefs and principles pick out is accurately discerned only to the extent that those implicit tacit elements in the practices are understood. Successful teaching then turns on the availability of such practical 'theory' and its use in practice, not on any capacity to master that 'theory' in any self-conscious critical way, let alone the mastery of its justification in past practice or any fundamental academic theory that might relate to it.

From the 'traditionalist' point of view teaching as a professional activity can be mastered only by immediate involvement in the job itself under the direction of someone truly proficient in its successful practice. It means students in training must come to use the relevant concepts, beliefs and principles by acquiring them in developing the actual conduct of those practices themselves. 'Apprenticeship' is the name of the game. Of course if the initiation into the 'theory' and the practices in proper relation to each other is to be successfully done, the 'master' in charge of the process will need to have an explicit grasp of the elements of the 'theory'. Without that it is hard to see what training the 'master' can possibly provide beyond simply being a model to copy. But once a student has 'mastered' the best available practices, true professionalism will require two other things. First, it must be recognized that new and more successful practices can be expected to emerge in the light of new circumstances and demands and in the light of the continuing experience and experiment of professionals. Training must therefore introduce students to their need for continuous attention to developments in professional practice in the search for new and more successful ways for carrying out their individual responsibilities. Secondly, true professionals will recognize the responsibility of professionals collectively, if not individually, to engage in experiments in practice to promote the development of more rationally defensible forms of 'theory' and practice. In this respect, too, students in training need introducing to the proper foundations of the activities they engage in and the proper relationship of what they do in relation to others working in the same field. What, on this approach, is not considered of any necessary concern by teachers or students is engagement in any detached, academic study of education, interesting and legitimate though that may be in itself.

Convincing though this approach may seem it has come to be questioned in perhaps its most fundamental tenet. That all practical activities must indeed be mastered exclusively in the very doing of them, rather than in any mere understanding of them, can be readily granted. But is justifiable practice in teaching something that can be developed internally within the practice of teaching itself? Is the analogy with a practice like cake-making tenable? In such practices physical events or states that are causally produced by the activities of the agent are aimed at. Success is a matter of direct observation. The concepts, beliefs and principles of successful practice are thus generated under stable, objectively given material circumstances that are not themselves humanly determined. In teaching the situation is radically different for psychological and social states are aimed at, states which are achievable by rational and social, not merely causal, procedures. Success or failure is then more often than not only indirectly observable, demanding careful and sophisticated interpretation of observable evidence. And the notion of success only then makes sense in terms of personal and social value judgements of far-reaching significance. The emergence of successful practice by trial and error in such a situation is a highly complex matter and the success of practices of teaching that may exist in schools is therefore a very controversial matter. Indeed it is not at all obvious that 'theory' in such a practice, even if it operates in a manner not dissimilar from that of a practice like cake-making, can be justified in a similar trial-and-error process. Indeed a glance at the history of many social practices, including teaching, readily reveals that for all the trial-and-error evolution they may have been subjected to, they have later come to be firmly rejected on quite other grounds. For though the self-correcting process of trial and error is in one sense capable of producing successful practices it does so necessarily only within certain wideranging beliefs about human beings, their capacities, their social relations and moral values. Locked into such an array of presupposed fundamental beliefs, the process may refine for success practices that in a more basic sense are in say psychological, sociological or philosophical terms grossly mistaken. So much has the notion of self-correcting social practices come under criticism that in the 1960s a quite different view of the nature of educational theory and its significance for practice emerged.

If educational practice is locked into fundamental and far-reaching beliefs about men and women, society and human good, then rationally defensible practice is surely only going to be possible if built on rationally justifiable claims at this basic level. Without this guarantee we are, in the end, as liable to be in error as to be on rationally justifiable grounds. The 'common sense' of teachers as developed in practice that never calls basic beliefs into question is thus to be seen as riddled with unexamined premises which are not to be trusted. Instead what is needed is the explicit examination of the basic beliefs on which practice is to be built and the determination of what is to be done on a set of rationally defensible premises. On this view professional practice must stem from the relevant achievements of philosophy, psychology, sociology and other appropriate disciplines being derived from these in a logically defensible manner. It being an impossibility to bring these individual disciplines to bear directly on every particular practical situation, the disciplines are to be seen as the justifying grounds for a body of general practical principles which set out what is to be done in situations which share certain specific characteristics. In the light of these principles rational judgements can be made for appropriate action in individual cases. It is of the essence of this second 'rationalist' approach to theory and practice that practice is seen as properly derived from theory that is quite independently developed. Theoretical beliefs justified in academic disciplines using the canons of these disciplines alone are the proper basis for the formation of the 'theory' teachers must use. In so far as practices themselves can generate the principles of such 'theory' it can only be via the investigation of practices within the terms of the disciplines. The generation and justification of principles can properly owe nothing to the trial-and-error procedures of an evolving tradition of practice if it is to escape the contamination of imported unexamined premises.

On this view, the immediate 'theory' that informs the practice of an individual teacher is a set of concepts, beliefs and principles that have been developed independently of practice itself. It has been generated by a multidisciplinary understanding of human nature and society including a justifiable set of values. The general principles of such 'theory' will lead to a pattern of justifiable practices for which the teacher must have developed the necessary practical skills. In so far as the 'theory' informs the practices it is because the practices are built to embody what has been independently determined. This 'rationalist' view then sees a number of different levels of educational theory which progressively approach specific practices. There is first the level of academic research in the disciplines, research which can be either wideranging in its concern for fundamental beliefs and values or more specific in relation to educational ideas and practices. There is the second level of theory, a form of 'practical theory' which, drawing on first-level work, formulates general practical principles for practices appropriate to types of circumstances. Thirdly, there is the level of the application of 'practical theory' in which the individual teacher, using principles justified at the second level, determines what to do in any given situation. Fourthly, there is that level in which the teacher settles to a pattern of justifiable practice that is not determined by any direct employment of principles. The complex demands of teaching necessitate such settled procedures, but faced even daily with new circumstances and new demands relevant principles must be called into play however immediate the use of them has to be. Remaining professionally alert therefore means that teachers must at least be able to be flexible in applying justifiable principles operating at the third level. They will further need to attend to the demands of new or revised principles that are generated by educational studies at the second level. And if they are not to have a limited and mistaken view of the proper status and justification of what they do, they will at least need to appreciate the ultimate dependency of principles on understanding in the fundamental disciplines.

Professional training on this view has a number of quite distinct elements. First, it requires a mastery of the most up-to-date body of concepts, beliefs and practical principles relevant to the work for which students are training. What is more, as that theoretical knowledge alone is the basis for the determining of professional practice in particular circumstances, the grasp of 'theory' must be explicit rather than merely implicit and embedded in a set of practices. It must too be so mastered that defensible rational judgements can be made in different unique particular circumstances. To then effectively implement such judgements in practice demands of students a second form of mastery, that of a body of executive skills to bring about what 'theory' determines. Thirdly, if they are not to be left simply to implement the practical principles first delivered to them by others, students must also understand the need to be always open to a new and more adequately researched 'theory' to which their practice should conform. And only if they have some grasp of the generation and justification of such principles by the foundation disciplines in 'practical theory' will they be in a position to begin to assess for themselves new practices advocated by those working in educational studies.

But such a training cannot be given unless a body of adequately justified practical principles is available and that in turn requires relevant developments within the foundation disciplines. Until then teacher trainers can only act in the light of those principles they judge most defensible and encourage students to be alert to considerations in the disciplines likely to lead to more adequate principles. With all these limitations recognized, the 1960s and 1970s saw the serious attempt to introduce the 'rationalist' approach into initial training. Because of the as yet undeveloped nature of the disciplines, however, work on teaching methods remained largely traditionalist in character and studies in the foundation disciplines were developed alongside. Not surprisingly, the suspicion thus created of the 'traditionalist' approach which dominated the practical parts of the course created considerable tension. And such tensions only increased with the continuing failure of the disciplines to actually generate useful practical principles. But the longer it took even to begin to deliver such principles the more the study of the disciplines seemed an irrelevance in training. For some time the immaturity of the disciplines and their methodological difficulties served as an adequate explanation. Scepticism about the ambitions of the disciplines began to grow, however, and in due course the 'rationalist' approach itself was called into question.

The idea of the disciplines ever providing a comprehensive basis of knowledge and understanding necessary for the derivation of practical principles began to look more and more preposterous. The disciplines in themselves had great difficulties in developing academically rigorous work for even very limited aspects of practice. At best they seemed unlikely, in the foreseeable future, to be able to provide more than certain limited theoretical beliefs to be taken seriously in the formation of practical principles, but quite inadequate for the task as a whole. Even more serious than the existing state of the disciplines, however, was the growing conviction that the very idea of delivering practical principles from bodies of knowledge and understanding achieved in the distinct theoretical systems of the disciplines might be mistaken. How conceivable is it that the conceptual apparatus of such diverse abstract theoretical studies can adequately embrace the complexities of a social practice like teaching? Does the logic of practical reason enable us to formally build together such discrete elements to provide justifiable conclusions? Is not the whole idea itself in the end not only practically but logically mistaken? What began to emerge was the recognition that, in seeking to make social practices subject to fundamental criticism from work in the disciplines, the rationalist approach had in fact radically reconstructed the very notion of rational practice. In this new notion, the legitimacy of practical experience in the generation of concepts, beliefs and justifiable principles of practice was being denied. As a result, instead of subjecting 'theory' generated within the context of practice to fundamental criticism, the 'theory' of practice was being made the product of fundamental disciplines alone. In rejecting the rationalist approach, then, it does not follow that some other way might not be found for realizing the original intention. What is needed is a more careful approach that does justice to both the traditionalist emphasis on practical experience in the generation and justification of practices and to the rationalist demand for their more fundamental examination in the light of the disciplines.

In developing a more adequate picture of the nature of social practices such as teaching maybe progress can be made if we look first with care at what exactly goes on in the contemporary development of successful technical and technological practices. On a strictly traditionalist account, simple practical developments like cake-making or more sophisticated achievements as in, say, aeronautical engineering are pictured as the outcome of self-correcting practice. Trial and error alone is the key. In the case of simple practices like cake-making this view is very plausible. The criteria for the achievements sought are indeed simple and the knowledge and control of the causal processes of the physical world necessary for meeting those criteria are again simple. Informal processes are alone adequate for the necessary knowledge and understanding for successful practice to be generated in the trial-and-error procedures of practice itself. They are adequate even for the generation of new possible practices in terms of new ends that can be pursued by new means, for example, new kinds of cakes made from new materials in new processes of baking. Again, in such simple cases the principles of successful practice can readily be articulated directly from the conditions for successful practice itself. These principles, justified by the experience of practice, then provide general guidelines indicating to others how best success can be achieved.

But in the case of more sophisticated and complex technological practices, such an account is quite inadequate. Successful practice has here depended crucially on work in certain basic sciences. Not as in the strictly rationalist picture. That suggests that the successful development of aircraft, for instance, was, and is, dependent upon exhaustive academic research in basic sciences from which practical principles for aircraft design are derived prior to the building of planes which are inevitably successful. It is rather that academic research has made possible tight control of practical experiments in design and has provided suggestions for new forms of design that could be practically tested. It is not that the achievements of basic disciplines have removed the need for practical experience in achieving practical success. Rather these disciplines have revealed certain fundamental characteristics of the physical world to which technological practices must necessarily conform. The disciplines are able to establish certain features that are given to us on which alone successful practice can develop. To the extent that we are ignorant of these, merely trial-and-error experiments in practice are 'blind'. We lack understanding of what constitutes success in practice and are ignorant of the mechanisms on which the process of trial and error actually operates. Successful practice is indeed developed in practice itself, but that process requires a match between the level of an insight into what we wish to achieve and our understanding and control of the circumstances for achieving it. Though informal knowledge of the everyday world may be adequate to satisfy these conditions for the generation of numerous simple technical practices of great value in daily life, including cake-making, only with the achievements of certain basic sciences have more sophisticated modern technological developments been possible.

These considerations suggest that the establishment of successful practices in relation to the physical world is marked by the following features. First, there has to be generated knowledge and understanding in terms of which we formulate what is being sought; that is, there must be criteria for what counts as a successful practice. Secondly, sufficient knowledge and control of the causal processes of the physical world must be achieved for those criteria for success to be met. Thirdly, how those criteria are best met can be discovered only in practical experiment in which by trial and error those procedures that achieve success can be selected. Fourthly, from successful experiment in practice, it is possible to set out certain practical principles which distinguish the features of successful rather than unsuccessful procedures. These principles are thus generalizations that can provide guidance to others seeking to act successfully. They pick out only certain features, though, and are necessarily partial abstractions from complex characteristics. Their significance may therefore be tied closely to the circumstances of the practices from which they are derived, and their value as generalizations relatively limited. Successful practices are established in procedures that must themselves be handed on, many of whose characteristics are implicit in the circumstances and not articulated in the discourse in which practices are communicated to others. Fifthly, the basic scientific disciplines have enriched the whole of this process by injecting into it knowledge and understanding to sophisticate it at every stage. Much fuller understanding has become available of just what is actually involved in forms of practical success that we seek so that the criteria for sucess are much more adequately articulated. We have new knowledge of the causal relations of the physical world. As a result practical experiment seeking successful processes by trial and error can be more sharply and systematically focused. New possibilities for practical achievements can be more readily engendered. The general principles of practice can also be much more carefully articulated and therefore more adequately communicated to others. Indeed the whole 'theory' of practice becomes much more elaborated and developed into what may be described as the 'practical theory' which we have in such areas as aeronautical engineering. In such areas of practices the basic sciences have led to extensive experimental achievements and sophisticated bodies of 'practical theory' that express the practical understanding and principles of these achievements.

It is perhaps unfortunate that the term 'applied sciences' for such bodies of theory is not infrequently taken to suggest too rationalistic a foundation for their claims. It also frequently serves to suggest, mistakenly, that the dependence of such 'applied sciences' or experiments in practice parallels exactly the basic sciences' dependence on experiment. What we have above all in such 'practical theories' are bodies of general practical principles for the determination of successful practice in particular cases. Principles which articulate the justification of particular practices and which are themselves justified as generalizations from successful practice, not by direct appeal to the basic sciences. The basis that the sciences have provided for technology is knowledge and understanding without which its sophisticated successful practices could not have been adequately formulated or developed.

But in the light of these comments what of the generation and justification of successful social practices such as teaching? How far can we pursue parallels with technology by virtue of both areas being areas of human practices? Though we must proceed with caution if we are not to slip into serious error, certain very important points can I think be made. To begin with I suggest the overall pattern of approach is similar. Successful practice and its 'theory' are surely necessarily generated in practice itself no matter what area we are concerned with. Criteria of success must necessarily be developed in this process and knowledge and control of human and social affairs are of the essence of successful social practices. It is by practical experiment that procedures achieving success in social practices can be selected and it is from these alone that the principles of such practices can be determined. Again the basic disciplines relevant to social practices can provide knowledge and understanding crucial to sophisticating this process at every stage.

But when it comes to more detailed characterization of how that sophistication takes place a number of important differences between kinds of practices must be taken into account. First it must be recognized that although in technological practice the idea of successful practice does contain an important valuational element that may be social or moral in its import, in most such practices the achievements concerned are forms of mastery of the physical world which are generally accepted as morally and socially desirable. In the case of social practices, moral and social values are at the very centre of what constitutes a successful practice. In some cases the achievements sought and the means to these may be such that they are universally acceptable. But the ends and means of most social practices are so complex and wideranging in their significance that controversy and diversity of judgement about what constitutes success is commonplace. What are judged successful social practices are always developed and justified against a background of moral and social values. And what on one set of values may be considered successful may on other grounds be judged merely effective. Secondly, it must be recognized that social practices operate in much more flexible and open-ended ways than those of technology. The world of physical causation constrains technological practices in a deterministic form. How far these are equivalent, objectively given constraints on social practices is certainly at present a matter of fundamental dispute. In general, freedom of choice is seen as a part of social relations and the notion of fundamentally different patterns of social living that constitute alternative forms of human good is at the very least considered seriously defensible. Thirdly, social practices are frequently so closely interrelated that changes and developments in one area may have major implications for developments in other areas. What is considered success in any one area must therefore be judged in relation to what is considered success in parallel or wider ranging practices.

Because of these particular features of social practices the role of the relevant basic disciplines in the development and justification of these practices understandably differs from their role where technological practices are concerned. Their contribution to elucidating and critically influencing the criteria of success employed in developing practices in, say, teaching is likely to be crucial. Without their aid implicit controversial moral and social values are liable to go undetected and unexamined and the wider social implications of accepting such criteria of success may well be ignored. In the absence of a framework of causal mechanisms, the importance of the basic disciplines in enabling us to understand and operate within the procedures of a given social framework is crucial for working at all systematically in experimental practice. To leave the development of social practices to trial-and-error experiment in a framework unexamined by the basic disciplines is to treat them as if they were operating in a framework of causal mechanisms. In fact that means simply that the disputable social and moral values of their social framework are being uncritically assumed. Elucidating the principles of successful practices is equally likely to require understanding from the disciplines. In fact those disciplines will be our only hope if the practices of, say, teaching are to be both effective and defensible in relation to an existing social framework and to more fundamental social and moral considerations. Where social practices are concerned then the basic disciplines are more fundamental to their experimental development than in the case of technological practices. If in the latter case they have been the key to sophisticated developments, in the former case they are also crucial if practices are to begin to have fundamental and not merely pragmatic defence.

What then of the professional practice of teaching? If the above characterization of successful social practices in general is correct, successful practices in teaching will indeed develop in practice itself. They will be progressively established within a given institutional and social framework that significantly determines what counts as success. The criteria of success at any given time may be determined by the members of the profession itself to only a limited extent. But within that domain of professional freedom, it is by practical experiment in teaching, by trial and error, that the specific ends and means of successful practice are generated. Not that it is acceptable for individual teachers on their own to work out from scratch what to do. The pursuit of successful practice can only hope to get anywhere by the collective attempts of those engaged in similar tasks to achieve success within the given framework, systematically building practices on the trial and error of experience. The establishment of successful practices is thus a matter of experimentally developing a tradition of practices, a procedure which necessitates the progressive articulation of the 'theory' of those practices as they develop. But that tradition of practices, if it is to be anything other than inadequately conceived, understood, focused, tested, and articulated in principles, must be developed by making maximum use of the understanding and rational criticism that basic disciplines can provide at every stage of the process. Professional practices need to be developed in a way that parallels the development of technological practices, their structuring by means of informally conceived 'theory' giving place to structuring in systematically developed practical theory that is defensible by reference to experiments in practice informed by the basic disciplines.

In relatively few areas of teaching is it as yet possible to point to the existence of practices which have been established on adequate practical experiment in the light of the best available work in relevant disciplines. Many practices of teaching have become established with little or no experimental justification even of an informal kind, let alone any more fundamental examination of their elements. But the need for the evaluation of practices is becoming much more widely recognized and the desire to establish well-articulated principles of successful practice is revealing the need for more critical work in the basic disciplines. Indeed if teaching is ever to become a truly professional business there would seem to be no escape from much fuller attention to the development of the necessary body of practices informed by and justified by a defensible domain of practical theory. The growth of what may be called 'education studies' that seek the development of such successful educational practices and their practical theory is a matter of very considerable urgency. It clearly depends on the work of experienced teachers with wideranging mastery of some area of professional practice experimenting in ways informed by relevant work in the basic disciplines. It requires the critical elucidation of present practices, the generation of new kinds of successful practice and the articulation of these practices in principles that make the crucial features of those practices available to others. This is obviously a difficult and complex collaborative exercise in which teachers well versed in current practices and their practical theory engage in experiment whilst working closely with experts in the disciplines. At present much of the relevant expertise that exists is dispersed amongst theoretically minded experienced teachers and lecturers in teaching methods and the foundation disciplines of education. Sustained collaboration between these parties for the development of professional practices that are experimentally and fundamentally justifiable is long overdue.

Given such a body of defensible practices, individual teachers, as in the traditionalist approach, first need to be 'master' of those practices and their use in particular situations. That mastery necessitates acquiring the concepts, beliefs and principles of these practices, that enable the teacher to interpret particular situations and to act justifiably. But the body of defensible practices is constantly developing as new and more successful practices emerge in the kind of complex discipline-informed practical experimentation I have been considering. Individual teachers must therefore constantly reflect critically on their personal practices and their justification in comparison with other and newer practices and their claims. That reflection will cover the teachers' immediate responsibilities of course but must recognize the relationship of what is done there to other more wideranging concerns. Such critical reflection on their own practices requires of teachers self-conscious analysis in terms of the 'theory' that informs them. It demands, too, attention to the practices and practical theory emerging experimentally in educational studies. How detailed that attention should be beyond a knowledge of the current achievements of educational studies is of course not specifiable. Clearly an understanding of the experimental inquiry and fundamental disciplinary work underlying current achievements enables teachers to appreciate much more fully their nature and significance. But it is surely inappropriate to expect all teachers to be able to engage in creative work in educational studies as part of their basic professionalism or even to be able to appreciate fully the detailed justification of current achievements.

The significance of seeing such critical reflection and its resulting change in teachers' practices as part of their basic professionalism is heightened in so far as the criteria for what constitutes their success in teaching, as well as the achievements of success itself, are considered their own responsibility individually or collectively. The extent of teachers' freedom to change their own practices depends very much on the formal and informal constraints within which they work. But to the extent that they have formal responsibility to take decisions over what counts as successful teaching, they have responsibility to reflect critically on the general character and justification of these practices. And in an open and democratic society, where there can justifiably be considerable diversity of opinion as to what constitutes successful practice, teachers need to undertake quite wideranging reflection so as to be able to justify adequately the judgements they make. In the absence of sophisticated work in educational studies to support them, their situation can at times create quite acute dilemmas. To the extent that teachers' practices are not left to their own determination, it nevertheless remains part of their professionalism, collectively or individually according to context, at least to contribute to the determination of what they should do. They possess intimate knowledge that others do not have of the area of practice with which they are concerned and of its personal and social significance for both pupils and teachers. Whatever their prescribed framework for their professional activities individual teachers thus have responsibility to understand the significance and possibilities of the freedoms they enjoy, the limits of these and alternative possibilities for their freedom in areas where they are able to contribute to the critical examination of that framework. To this end teachers need to be aware not only of the current state of developing educational studies but of the nature, significance and limits of that work in the proper determination of their practices. They thus need to be aware of the essentially practical justification of practices, their relationship to wider personal, social and moral concerns and the significance throughout of work in the basic disciplines.

What is being suggested in this approach to the professional activities of teaching is that they involve the teachers' mastery of a body of established and developing practices as in the traditionalist approach. But unlike the traditionalist approach, because of the nature and justification of those practices the individual teacher is seen to need an explicit understanding of the practices and the practical theory that informs them so as to be able to reflect critically on their significance for his or her own practice. What is more, that reflection is seen as requiring of the teacher a grasp of the justification that different practices have in experimental practice. But to see practices as adequately justified merely in such a 'traditionalist' way is considered mistaken. What is also needed is that teachers appreciate the need for those practices to be developed in the light of understanding achieved in the basic disciplines. Without that grasp, the significance of different practices is constantly in danger of being seriously misjudged. The 'rationalist' approach was therefore right in insisting on teachers' need to understand theoretically the practices they are engaged in. It was right, too, in insisting on a crucial role for work in the disciplines in the development of any adequate practical theory. It was, however, mistaken in its basic notion of the nature of practical theory and its relationship to practice and the place of the disciplines in its justification.

If the professional practice of teaching involves the mastery of this kind of reflective practice with its complex interrelation of practical and theoretical elements, what crucial demands does it make on initial teacher training? First and foremost it clearly requires the mastery in practice itself of the most defensible practices currently available in the areas of teaching for which training is being given. This involves developing the 'theory' of those practices in exercising judgement and skill in particular actions and activities. It involves taking on board many attitudes, habits of mind and patterns of behaviour. It involves thoughtful, intelligent practice in a complex structure that is given to the student but within which the uniqueness of the student's own personal qualities and abilities is a significant, if limited, determinant of that student's practice.

The development of the consistent practice that is being sought requires critical reflection by students on their particular actions and activities. It is by learning to judge accurately themselves their success and failure and by modification of their practice in the light of the characteristics of successful practice that they personally develop the necessary capacities. But secondly, students need to understand, from the inside as far as possible, other forms of successful practice which are currently being advocated. Such practices may in significant ways be more successful than their own or genuinely alternative approaches concerned with different but comparable achievements. The point of this study is to extend the range of practice available to students and to promote the continuous development of their own, particularly in relation to new circumstances they will meet and the emergence of successful new practices elsewhere. Such personal development, however, requires critical reflection on one's own and alternative practices. Students therefore need as a third area of work to undertake serious comparative study of such practices, examining their 'theory', their criteria of success, the activities involved, their principles, implications and justification. This engagement in educational studies of a very particular kind demands an analytical examination of practices and their related practical theory. But if such work is to become the vehicle for personal professional development it must be continuously related to students' own practices. It will therefore focus primarily on the significance of such educational studies for work within a given institutional and social framework. But beyond that lie questions of the relationship of such practices to other human, social and moral concerns and their more fundamental justification in relation to work in the basic disciplines. There is thus a further area of study that students need to undertake if they are to understand fully the nature of their professional responsibilities. Critical reflection on practices and their theory at this fundamental level is complex, wideranging and difficult, embracing as it does achievement in a number of different disciplines. It is therefore doubtful if initial training can do more than introduce students to its character and significance. To leave them unaware of the crucial role of the disciplines in the generation and justification of professional practices would however be to leave them with a distorted understanding of their own activities. Such work again needs to be linked to their own practices so that they recognize that all that they do involves presuppositions which are properly subject to critical examination in the disciplines. At least some introduction to this fundamental level of critical reflection on their own practices is a vital part of training.

I have sought to outline the relationship between theory and practice in teacher training on the basis of an account of the nature and significance of theory in practice that can truly claim to be rationally defensible and thereby professional. Individual practice, I have argued, requires the mastery of practices that have been justified in practical experiment that is informed by the achievements of relevant basic disciplines. Such mastery, I have suggested, requires that students be introduced to a range of practices and that they reflect critically on these in a number of different ways. At first that reflection is directed to personal performance in terms of given criteria. It is later more wideranging, comparative and rooted in a particular form of the study of educational practices and their practical theory. Still later it is directed to the examination of these practices and their practical theory in the light of basic disciplines. What I have not discussed is how such training can successfully be built into specific courses. Clearly that is a practical question which must be answered in terms of where the contexts for such training are to be found, who has the necessary expertise for the task, how best the work is sequenced and how best conducted. That at the first stage practising teachers alone are in a position to train students in their mastery of initial practical procedures there can be no doubt. Similarly only specialist tutors in higher education can be expected to be knowledgeable enough about the latest work in educational studies and relevant work in basic disciplines for the later stages of work in critical reflection. And if training is throughout to be concerned with students developing critical reflection on their own practice it is hard to see how it can be undertaken responsibly without detailed collaboration between teachers and tutors, schools and training institutions. But in keeping with my argument, how that is best done is a matter to be determined in practical experiment. For what practical experiment would seem to suggest I can here only refer to what has been written elsewhere (see Furlong *et al.*, 1988, especially Chapters 6–8). In this chapter I have been concerned primarily with a consideration of certain philosophical issues which with work in that basic discipline can contribute to the development of justifiable training practices: the nature of practice, its theory and the relationship between the two. Without greater clarity on that the practice of training is, I fear, likely to remain as 'informal' a practice as much current teaching in schools.

REFERENCE

Furlong, V. J., Hirst, P. H., Pocklington, K. and Miles, S. (1988) *Initial Teacher Training and the Role of the School.* Milton Keynes: Open University Press.

Chapter 7

School-Based Training: The Students' Views[1]

John Furlong

The past few years have seen an unprecedented number of attempts to find new ways of training teachers, both in the sense of reforming existing routes and in developing new ones. Accompanying these reforms there has been a vigorous public debate concerning the value and relevance of teacher education. Some of the most vocal critics have been those of the New Right (O'Hear, 1988; Hillgate Group, 1989; Lawlor, 1990), who argue that training courses place too much emphasis on theory which is at best unnecessary and at worst subversive. This has led some of these critics to press for a licensed teacher or apprenticeship scheme where heads and governors decide what training, if any, their teachers need.

Others of a more liberal persuasion have come to somewhat similar conclusions. For many years Warnock (1985; 1988) has been advocating the introduction of 'teaching schools' which, like teaching hospitals, would take full responsibility for the training of new teachers. This idea has also been taken up by Hargreaves (1989), who asserts that teaching schools are an attractive alternative to conventional forms of training, because under such an arrangement the profession would be taking responsibility for its own new entrants. Teaching schools would also, he suggests, provide much-needed continuity between initial training and early induction into the profession.

Although such views may have had some influence on official policy, to date a notion of a training 'partnership' between schools, LEAs and training institutions remains the dominant professional and political orthodoxy (HMI, 1987; Secretary of State, 1989; DES, 1989; Booth *et al.*, 1989; Labour Party, 1989).

What is interesting about this debate on the future of teacher education is that much of it has been conducted with comparatively little reference to any systematic evidence as to how students or probationers view their training. Commentary on what students 'want' and 'need' is plentiful, but with the exception of two HMI surveys (1982; 1988) systematic research is extremely limited. Moreover, valuable though they are, the HMI surveys were conducted before the Council for the Accreditation for Teacher Education (CATE) had begun to make its influence felt on the structure and content of initial training courses. Most of the probationers they surveyed would therefore have experienced quite traditional courses – few would have been built on the principles of partnership that are now the centre of policy concern.

Yet the views of participants can be illuminating in exploring the 'best' way to train teachers. Clearly students' views do not provide the whole answer, nevertheless they are an important dimension in the debate and provide clues to issues that are perhaps too often overlooked in other forms of analysis or argument. It is therefore useful to be able to consider evidence from one particular study which systematically explores the views of students on school-based courses that are built on principles of partnership; this is the purpose of this chapter.

BACKGROUND TO THE STUDY

The evidence to be presented arises from a DES-funded evaluation of four school-based PGCE courses. (Full details of the project, including the methodology used, have been published elsewhere: see Furlong *et al.*, 1988.) Two of the courses were for primary students, two for secondary, both university and public-sector courses being represented.

The precise nature of the school-based training to be established was not specified by the DES; the courses therefore varied considerably in their philosophy and practice. In each case, however, it was envisaged that in comparison with traditional courses an increased proportion of the overall training would take place in school rather than in the training establishment and that practising teachers would be more centrally involved in both the planning and delivery of the training.

Towards the end of 1982 the University of Cambridge Department of Education was invited by the DES to conduct an evaluation of these four experimental programmes using a 'case-study' methodology. Seventy-five students participating in the four courses (between fifteen and twenty students from each) were to be monitored (five of this number withdrew during the year). In addition, those among this monitored group who obtained teaching posts the following year (fifty-nine in all) were to be followed up at various stages during their probationary year (1984/5).

In line with the principles of case-study research, data were gathered by a variety of means. In both parts of the project (the study of the courses and the probationary-year study) the research design involved a questionnaire survey of the whole cohort together with an in-depth examination of the experiences of a sub-sample of students or probationers using more 'qualitative' techniques. For the general survey, four major questionnaires were administered; one at both the beginning and end of the training course, another after half a term's full-time teaching and a final questionnaire at the end of the probationary year.

From the wealth of evidence collected, this chapter considers the students' views of their training, focusing in particular on three issues: practice, reflection and theory. What emerges is that students have an equally strong concern with all three dimensions of professional preparation and clear ideas as to how these dimensions should be interrelated in their training. The evidence also shows that they consider that lecturers and teachers each have a vital, though perhaps different, contribution to make to their professional development.

PRACTICE

> Generally the course has kept me aware of the practicalities of teaching and has made me feel as though the majority of the work has a direct practical use.

The first point to note is that all of the students valued the fact that their training was 'school-based'. In the end-of-course questionnaire, 100% of respondents ($n=66$) said that in retrospect they would still select a school-based type of course. And from their responses to an open-ended question on the advantages of their training it is clear that what they had valued most was the involvement with school which their courses had afforded them. Over three-quarters of all the advantages listed related directly to practical training – e.g. 'familiarity with the school', 'establishing relationships in school', 'realistic experience', 'regular contact with school' and, most frequent of all and mentioned by one-third of all students, 'the extent of practical experience'.

As we will see below, students were not only concerned with practice – they also had a strong interest in reflection and theory. But these courses which emphasized involvement with schools had clearly got it right as far as the students were concerned. Eighty per cent of them said that they felt that the balance between school and college work had been correct. Only five out of the sixty-six students felt that more time should have been spent in school, another five wanting more time in college.

In terms of the broad structure of their courses, therefore, most students were well satisfied. However, this does not mean that they did not find things to criticize and many of their criticisms highlight their concern with practice. In the questionnaire at the end of their probationary year, the students (now fully qualified teachers) were asked to reflect on what they still considered to be the major weaknesses of their training. Two-thirds of all their criticisms related to what they saw as specific weaknesses in the practical training that was given – e.g. 'lack of work on special needs', 'poor preparation for the variety of teaching situations experienced', 'specific areas of curriculum weaknesses (such as the diagnosis of reading difficulties)' and 'poor preparation for mixed ability teaching'. Wherever there were weaknesses in the practical training given, probationers felt that they were still struggling to fill in the gaps a year after their course had finished.

Student concern with practical training is perhaps unsurprising. As many of them noted, the practical business of teaching is an overwhelming and demanding experience. As such it tended to dominate their subjective view of their courses. But what exactly did these students want from practical training and who should provide it?

One of the interesting things to emerge from our data was that despite the students' appreciation of their close involvement with school, they still saw lecturers as having a major role in their practical training. In the end-of-course questionnaire we asked the students to rate on a 1–5 scale how well prepared they felt they were on thirty different aspects of professional practice (see Table 7.1). We also asked students to report who had significantly contributed to their training in each area – lecturers and/or teachers. As has already been noted, the four courses varied considerably in their aims and organization, one significant difference being the degree to which training was intended to be delegated to teachers. But as Table 7.1 demonstrates, lecturers as well as teachers were seen as being extremely significant in virtually all the areas where the majority of students felt well or quite well prepared. On items where the majority of students did not see themselves as being so well prepared, lecturers were seen as having made a less significant contribution. This correlation between students' self-assessment as being adequately prepared and the involvement of lecturers appeared for each of the four courses, even those courses that deliberately delegated much of the practical training to schools.

Table 7.1.   *End-of-Course Self-Assessments by Students*

Aspect being self-assessed	%	Teachers	Lecturers
	Percentage of students feeling well/quite well prepared	Students' assessments of main contributors to their training	
To teach their subject specialism (secondary only)	84	*	*
To teach across the secondary age range (secondary only)	78	*	*
To prepare lessons and teaching materials	74	*	*
To teach number (primary only)	73		*
To understand the importance of language across the curriculum (secondary only)	72		*
To understand the importance of language and learning (primary only)	70		*
To organize the classroom	67	*	
To employ a range of different teaching approaches	63	*	*
To explain effectively	63	*	*
To teach pupils with different cultural backgrounds	61		*
To prepare schemes of work for an extended period	61	*	*
To question effectively	61	*	*
To initiate and develop discussion amongst pupils	57		*
To understand the place of your subject in the whole curriculum (secondary only)	56		*
To discipline and control effectively	55	*	
To motivate pupils	55	*	*
To mark pupils' work (secondary only)	53	*	
To undertake pastoral duties (secondary only)	53	*	
To teach less able pupils	49	*	
To teach mixed ability groups	44	*	
To teach reading (primary only)	44		*
To appraise the effectiveness of your teaching	40	*	*
To assess pupils' progress	35	*	
To teach pupils with special educational needs	26	*	*
To teach more able pupils	26	*	
To develop appropriate learning strategies having assessed the level of pupils' attainment	23	*	
To teach within an integrated programme (secondary only)	16	*	*
To offer specialist advice to colleagues on an area of the curriculum (primary only)	15		*
To liaise effectively with support services	14	*	
To liaise effectively with parents	14	*	

Given that these were innovative courses where more responsibility had been delegated to teachers it is interesting to consider what the students expected of teachers. What emerged was a concern with both the content and the style of supervision.

In their end-of-course questionnaire, students were asked to rate the teachers they had come into contact with most during their training on four criteria – whether the teachers were able to articulate the basis of their own practice; whether they were able to provide critical though constructive comment; whether they were able to be helpful without being over-prescriptive; whether they were able to relate practice to wider educational principles. On the first three of these the overwhelming majority of students (approximately 70%) rated their teachers as 'able' or 'very able'. It was only on the last criterion – relating practice to wider educational principles – that most students (approximately 60%) rated their teachers as merely 'able' or 'unable'.

However, despite this apparent weakness, when we asked students to identify key areas of inservice training that teachers who supervise students might need, not one mention was made of the need for training in theory or principles. Over three-quarters of the suggestions made related to the *style* of supervision offered and in particular to teachers' interpersonal skills – for example, 'awareness of students needs', 'empathy', 'training in how to criticize positively'. Other comments related to the need for teachers to have more detailed knowledge of the course and to have their responsibilities in training more carefully specified.

The *content* of what students wanted from teachers was captured in a number of tape recordings we made of teachers and students working together; for the most part what they wanted was concrete advice. The teacher who gave the following feedback was considered 'very helpful':

> The next thing then is that on the tables you didn't wait for silence before you started. You didn't actually get complete silence when you called for it and you should have had a pause there to wait for complete silence, OK?

But despite this interest in being given concrete advice, teachers also had to take care not to be over-prescriptive; this was considered just as much of a problem as neglect. One primary student explained her difficulties like this:

> It depends on the teacher. The first teaching practice teacher was over-prescriptive while the second one left me a great deal to myself to work out my own difficulties when I could have done with some more critical comment.

From their comments it is therefore apparent that students did not expect or seem to want teachers to spend time considering wider educational principles or theory. What teachers needed to be was highly competent and reflective practitioners with the interpersonal skills to work supportively with students; a mixture nicely captured in this comment from one student:

> . . . it is vital that they should have a self-appraising attitude and be in the habit of analysing their own teaching methods so that their teaching is good and they can pick out specific areas. This will also enable them to look objectively at students' teaching and suggest improvements.

As has already been noted, lecturers were also seen as having an important role in practical training. Interestingly, however, whether classroom supervision was to be undertaken by teachers or lecturers, similar criteria were applied. The content of supervision had to involve concrete advice while the style had to be positive without being over-prescriptive. As one maths student commented: 'I don't think that I want to be told [by the lecturer] actually what to teach on the topic of "area" but just to make me think about how it might be taught – the approaches and so on.'

When discussing the practical dimensions of training, most of the students' comments related to their time spent in school. However, they realized that practical work could go on in the training institution too. Even formal lectures could be 'practical' if handled in an appropriate way. For example, one short course was highly commended by large numbers of students precisely because it was 'bursting with practical ideas' and 'while you wouldn't use all the ideas now you can use them in the future'. The strongest criticisms were reserved for lectures which students felt should be practical but turned out not to be.

What comes through from both the questionnaires and the interviews therefore is that students saw the heart of their training as the practice of teaching. They wanted practical suggestions from their lecturers and detailed and supportive criticism from their teachers; at the same time, though, they wanted the opportunity to explore and experiment for themselves. However it would be quite wrong to think that these students thought that practical training was enough. It was certainly seen as being central but virtually no student felt that practice in itself, however well supervised, was sufficient. As one student commented:

> A day in school seems so much more valuable than a day spent in lectures, however, although we are learning the practical side we don't always understand *why* things are as they are – it's not always clear what the teacher is getting at even when she tries to explain or why she has done what she has done.

Helping them understand 'why things are as they are' was largely seen as the responsibility of the training institution. As one student commented: 'It's college that provides the thinking behind the teaching.'

'TALKING IT OUT OF THEIR SYSTEM' – REFLECTION AND DISCUSSION

Moving students beyond the level of practice was considered a vitally important aim by course leaders in all four training institutions. And despite their variations in organization, all courses saw discussion and reflection on practice as one important strategy in achieving this aim. One course leader described the purpose of discussion and reflection in the following terms:

> So it's a question of over the next couple of sessions [after teaching practice] almost of just talking it out of their system – getting them to see similarities and differences between the kinds of experiences that are deeper than superficial differences. . . . I think the students do get quite blinkered and see everything as being absolutely locked into that context instead of seeing that they are in that context to develop a generalizable competence that they can take out and sell and operate in a whole range of institutions.

Certainly the students agreed that discussion and reflection were essential for their own professional development, though due to the pressure of work on their courses, that concern was more readily apparent from negative rather than positive comments. For example, in the open-ended question on the disadvantages of their courses, a quarter of all primary students mentioned the lack of time for reflection. In another question we asked students how satisfied they were with the proportion of time spent in college and in school discussing a range of issues – their own teaching, others' teaching, teaching methods and wider professional issues. Important differences emerged between the primary and secondary students here. On all of these items, both in school and in college, approximately 70% of the primary students said that too little time had been available. Secondary students were by and large more satisfied with the time available for discussion in school, except that over half said there was not enough discussion of wider professional issues. In college, though, more than a third considered that too little time had been devoted to discussing teaching – theirs and others'.

Not all discussion had to be led by lecturers. For many students peers provided 'the greatest source of support and encouragement'. A concern with discussion and reflection was carried over into the probationary year too. A third of our sample reported that they had had no formal induction in school at all and over half rated their school induction as seriously inadequate. However, in an open-ended question about the most valuable aspect of their first year in school, approximately a third mentioned the importance of professional discourse among colleagues. Of those who experienced some form of induction almost three-quarters said that the most valuable part of it was the informal contact and discussion with colleagues.

Discussion and reflection were therefore seen as very important by these students. 'Talking it out of their system' helped them to get their own experience in perspective, learn from others and start to explore the more generalizable significance of what they saw and did in school. It also had personal benefits as well. As one primary student explained: 'I think a lot of the emphasis on a PGCE course should be in the development of the person as a confident and capable adult. Discussion would help to develop attitudes and build up confidence.' Reflection and discussion were therefore seen as essential, but for many students they were not enough. If they really were to understand 'why things are as they are' many students believed that some consideration of educational theory was also necessary.

THEORY

It is clear that the course is too short – the school side didn't suffer but theory side did. Ideally a two-year course is needed.

The fact that these four courses were school-based does not mean that course leaders and lecturers devalued the role of educational theory. Far from it: almost all of them thought that it was a central part of professional preparation. Nevertheless, in order to achieve the extra time in school, the amount of time traditionally devoted to educational theory had been reduced in all four courses; many students recognized this fact and felt that it was a disadvantage.

In the end-of-course questionnaire we asked students to list the disadvantages of their courses. Half of all primary students and a third of all secondary students mentioned the lack of time for educational theory. A year later, at the end of the probationary year, a quarter of all primary students still said that lack of work on theory had been a serious weakness in their training.

Not all comments were negative, however. In an open-ended question, over 20% of the students mentioned the ability 'to relate theory to practice' as one of the major advantages of school-based training. This process was facilitated by the fact that much of the training was 'concurrent'; students moved back and forth between their training institution and schools. As a consequence students reported that they were able to relate their 'experiences in school to the theory in university' and 'bring areas of personal experience into the seminars and discussions'. However, concurrent training brought its own problems too. Many of the students had regular teaching commitments in schools for much of the year; as a consequence, if they were to survive they had to prioritize their work. For most of them, preparing lessons became the first priority; reflection and particularly reading were squeezed out unless there was a formal assignment to complete.

The fact that many students missed out on educational theory is further demonstrated in Table 7.2. In the end-of-course questionnaire we asked them to assess how well they had been prepared to understand a number of basic professional issues that are frequently addressed in education courses. Although there are one or two interesting differences between the primary and the secondary students, overall what is demonstrated is that this group of students did not feel particularly well prepared on most of these basic issues.

Table 7.2.   *Students' Assessments of How Well Prepared They Are to Understand a Range of Professional Issues Traditionally Covered in Education Courses*

	Well/quite well prepared (%)		Not well/badly prepared (%)	
	Primary	Secondary	Primary	Secondary
The way pupils learn	41	44	59	56
The principles of motivation	32	28	68	72
The impact of teacher expectations	44	56	56	44
The nature of intelligence	15	9	85	91
Language development	50	19	50	81
The relationship between language and learning	47	28	53	72
Pupils' personal and social development	41	43	59	57
The arguments behind different forms of educational grouping (streaming, banding, mixed ability)	38	78	62	22
The principles that should underline the school curriculum	68	70	32	30
The effect of inequality on educational achievement (race, class, gender)	100	75	0	25
The organization and structure of the current British educational system	17	65	83	35
The history of the British educational system	20	44	80	56
The relationship between school and society	41	63	59	37

Primary students *n* = 34.   Secondary students *n* = 32.

It is interesting to speculate as to whether a group of students undergoing a more traditional course would rate themselves any better – perhaps not. And to be fair to these four courses, none of them was designed formally to cover the full range of these issues. Nevertheless, the lack of time for theory was something that was widely recognized as a weakness of the training offered.

To recognize a weakness is of course not the same thing as to say it is important and a significant minority of students accepted that less time devoted to formal educational theory was a reasonable price to pay for more time in school. As one student wrote: 'Although I would have liked more theoretical training and intellectual consideration of wider issues, I realize that within the time constraints of a one-year course, practical considerations have to take precedence.' But the majority disagreed:

> I have not personally been affected by the lack of or poor quality of psychology, philosophy, history or sociology of education as due to my previous education and life experiences I brought an understanding of these issues to the course when I came. However I feel the course to be particularly lacking in these areas for someone with no background in them.

Others commented on the need to 'systematize the theory side of the course' while a vociferous minority were even more critical still, suggesting that the training was 'too shallow' or that it was a 'PGCE in teaching not in education'.

Not all of the courses attracted equal criticism on this point. The critical comments recorded here relate to two courses in particular. What is interesting is that as part of their strategy to raise more fundamental issues, these two courses did in fact retain some formal teaching of theoretical issues, but it was these elements that attracted the most hostile comment. For example, one course retained a small number of formal lectures in psychology and sociology; almost all of the students were highly critical of these. The other course ran a series of whole-day sessions or 'mini-conferences' on major educational issues such as multicultural education, or special needs; these, too, attracted very severe comments.

Students were often critical of different aspects of their courses but we saw no evidence that these particular sessions were any worse (or any better) than the rest. Why therefore should they be singled out for such strong criticism and how are these criticisms to be understood in the light of complaints about lack of time for theory? A closer examination of student comments seems to suggest that their criticisms were not about the theoretical content *per se*. Rather the problem lay in the teaching methods employed and the fact that the content was detached from the students' own concerns as teachers.

> Certain areas were imposed on us via plenary sessions which were often a waste of time. I don't think that lectures to the whole course are a good way of dealing with important fields of study.

> I think in the application of those sorts of theories you've got to have the situation there in front of you first and then look outside to references or whatever. It's no good just sitting down and learning it because that's pretty pointless and it's the application that matters.

The other two courses were apparently more successful on this issue. Theoretical issues were introduced in a systematic way without attracting hostile comment. What was different was the teaching strategy and the way in which the content was related to the students' own professional concerns in the schools where they worked.

In one course students had to use part of their time in school to undertake a series of investigations – examining the curriculum, exploring the relationship between the school and its local community. On returning to college their findings were systematically shared with other students in discussion. The lecturer was then able to use this experience to raise more theoretically informed questions arising from the practice they had witnessed. The other course achieved a similar result by running a series of school-based seminars in which teachers and lecturers participated. The topics covered – e.g. the role of language in the classroom, and pastoral care – were entirely professionally oriented. Teachers contributed by describing practice in their school or their own classroom and lecturers were then in a position to use these examples of practice as a basis for raising more theoretically informed questions.

Our evidence therefore suggests that, contrary to popular belief, the majority of students did want some formal training in educational theory but they wanted it in a way that related to their own professional concerns and interests. But exactly what purpose does educational theory serve? How did students see it helping them in their professional development?

At the lowest level, theoretical knowledge was seen as part of what it meant to be a professional. One student complained that she was 'completely stumped' at a job interview when she was asked about the work of Piaget; it was only at this point that she realized that she had missed out on something which other teachers took for granted.

Educational theory was seen as serving more important purposes too. Some was seen as being of direct practical value in the planning of teaching and learning, as is illustrated in this comment from a primary student:

> We were badly prepared in terms of the study of child psychology. Hence any understanding of the stages different children have reached in different types of development had to come from personal trial and error. Psychological insights are of vital importance in preparing any programme of lessons and when I changed schools I found pitching the level for a different age group very difficult indeed.

Sociologically informed work could also be of practical value. An ex-student (interviewed when she was a probationer) commented how useful her education seminars had been in helping her to understand how her school functioned as an organization.

A number of students also talked about the value of 'looking in depth' at educational issues and even 'taking a sideways look' at practice. Educational theory was seen as an important tool in this questioning process; it helped to challenge assumptions and probe beneath the surface. Many of the teachers who took part in investigations and discussions with students also commented that engaging with theory for the first time since they themselves were students had 'brought them up with a jolt' and 'made them much more introspective'.

But what exactly did students discover when they 'probed beneath the surface' of educational practice? Sometimes what they learned were theoretical justifications of current practice – the work of Hirst in relation to the curriculum, or the work of Ball, Lacey and Hargreaves on the impact of school organization on pupils. Equally important, though, was the opportunity that theoretical work gave students to sort out their own fundamental values:

> I think where it succeeded was that it gave us a coherent and very acceptable philosophy of teaching so that you have a focal point that you can always go back to when you're wondering what your objectives are and how you're trying to achieve them. Why you're teaching. You're not left floundering or in doubt because you can assess quite carefully where you stand.

In all of these different ways the majority of students valued the role of theory; it helped them ask the question 'why?' Sometimes it provided them with concrete answers; sometimes it helped them to sort out their own values; sometimes it made them realize that there were no answers.

CONCLUSION

The purpose of this paper has been to explore students' views of training when it is based on a close partnership between training institutions and schools. What is interesting about those views is how closely they correspond to the 'ideal' aims of school-based training that we identified in our main study. One of the purposes of our research was to use case studies of these four courses in order to clarify the essential nature of school-based training. To this end we suggested that it was possible to distinguish a number of different dimensions or 'levels' of professional preparation. These were:

Level (a) Direct practice – practical training through direct experience in schools and classrooms;
Level (b) Indirect practice – 'detached' training in practical matters usually conducted in classes or workshops within training institutions;
Level (c) Practical principles – critical study of the principles of practice and their use;
Level (d) Disciplinary theory – critical study of practice and its principles in the light of fundamental theory and research.

(Furlong *et al.*, 1988, 132)

We argued that these different levels of training appear in almost any course. What we saw as distinctive about school-based training was how these different levels were linked or integrated. We suggested that, ideally at least, a school-based course would place students' direct practical experience – Level (a) – at the heart of the training programme. Such a course would then try to establish a course structure, content and pedagogy so that students could readily integrate their practical work in schools with other levels of training.

Interestingly it is precisely this pattern of work that is identifiable in the students' comments on their own training. It is clearly evident that what they wanted was a training that was strongly practical in its orientation; for them, practical work, whether it took place in the school (Level (a)) or the training institution (Level (b)), was at the heart of their professional development. Yet to say that practice was seen as central does not mean that that in itself was sufficient. Far from it. Students also wanted the opportunity to understand their teaching experience by reflecting on it and discussing it with those around them. It was only by going through this process of shared discussion and reflection that they could start to understand those practical experiences in a more generalized way at the level of principle. This was part of what we characterized as Level (c) – the beginnings of critical professional development. But for most students even this was not sufficient. They also wanted to explore certain issues in more fundamental ways by reference to educational research and theory – Level (d). Like so many other students, they were critical of theory that was taught in an abstract way. What they were seeking at this level was the opportunity to explore issues that were of direct personal and professional relevance to them. For the most part this meant that theory, if it was to be valued, had to be directly related to their practical experience of schools and teaching.

None of these four courses lived up to this idea. If they had, the students may have been less critical than they were. Yet despite their many criticisms, the overall evaluation made by the students was overwhelmingly positive. As was noted at the beginning, every one of them would have elected to undertake a school-based course if they had to choose again. By the end of their courses, most of them recognized that they still had a great deal to learn, but that within the constraints of a one-year programme they had been well prepared for the probationary year ahead. One student captured the general feeling at the end of the course when she wrote: 'Overall, a very good preparation for teaching. I'm now much wiser and quite exhausted.'

NOTE

1   The evidence on which this paper is based was collected by Keith Pocklington and Sheila
    Miles; I am indebted both to them and to Joan Whithead who gave assistance with statistical
    analysis. I am also indebted to Sheila Miles, Martin Booth, Margaret Wilkin and Paul Hirst
    for their comments on earlier drafts of the paper.

REFERENCES

Booth, M., Furlong, V. J., Hargreaves, D. H., Reiss, M. and Ruthven, K. (1989) *Teacher Supply
    and Teacher Quality; Solving the Coming Crisis* (Cambridge Papers in Education No. 1).
    Cambridge: University of Cambridge Department of Education.
DES: Department of Education and Science (1989) *Future Arrangements for the Accreditation of
    Teacher Training: A Consultation Document*. London: DES.
Furlong, V. J., Hirst, P. H., Pocklington, K. and Miles, S. (1988) *Initial Teacher Training and the
    Role of the School*. Milton Keynes: Open University Press.
Hargreaves, D. H. (1989) 'Out of BEd and into Practice'. *Times Educational Supplement*, 8
    September.
HMI: Her Majesty's Inspectorate (1982) *The New Teacher in School*. London: HMSO.
HMI: Her Majesty's Inspectorate (1987) *Quality in Schools*. London: HMSO.
HMI: Her Majesty's Inspectorate (1988) *The New Teacher in School*. London: HMSO.
Hillgate Group (1989) *Learning to Teach*. London: Claridge Press.
Labour Party (1989) *Children First*. London: Labour Party.
O'Hear, A. (1988) *Who Teaches the Teachers?*. London: Social Affairs Unit.
Secretary of State for Education (1989) *Speech to Society of Education Officers*, 27 January.
Warnock, M. (1985) *Teacher Teach Thyself*. London: BBC Publications.
Warnock, M. (1988) *A Common Policy for Education*. Oxford: Oxford University Press.

Chapter 8

Partnership and the Training of Student History Teachers

Martin Booth, Gwenifer Shawyer and Richard Brown

INTRODUCTION

DES Circular 3/84, *Initial Teacher Training: Approval of Courses*, clearly sets out the policy that all courses of initial teacher training should be developed and conducted on the basis of full collaboration between the training institutions and schools. Within the courses themselves the closest co-operation between lecturers in training institutions and teachers in schools is envisaged, with teachers taking a major part in both the school-based work of the students and work based in the training institution. Yet there is evidence (Proctor, 1984) to indicate that there is considerable uncertainty as to the nature, operation and effectiveness of such a partnership, particularly in the most central element of training, the school-based work.

THE RESEARCH PROJECT

A research project recently undertaken within the University of Cambridge Department of Education added weight to this contention and confirmed observations increasingly being made in North America and Europe that the effective supervision of student teachers is a highly skilled activity demanding areas of knowledge and skills over and above those currently possessed by many practising school teachers. The research, which was funded for the period January 1986 to December 1987 by the Economic and Social Research Council, investigated two interrelated areas within the context of the one-year Postgraduate Certification in Education course for history graduates. First, it examined the attitudes, assumptions and practices of the training institutions and their students towards the teaching, learning and assessment of history. What was the conceptual understanding of the discipline of history which PGCE students brought to the institutions? How far did training institutions consider the structure of the subject and link it with a theory of pupils' understanding of concepts in history? What were the styles of teaching best suited to develop such understanding? Secondly, the research looked closely at the school-based experience and training that students received in history teaching methods. How far did this link with and progressively build on the institution-based part of the course? To what extent did the teachers involved with the students understand their role? In brief, how far and in what ways was partnership between training institutions and schools being implemented as far as the training of secondary history specialists was concerned?

Given the need for close and sustained observation and only a small research team, it was decided to make detailed studies of two training institutions only. Two case studies therefore were undertaken of the 'methods of history teaching' courses at the University of London Institute of Education and the Manchester Polytechnic School of Education. These courses were for graduate historians intending to become secondary school history specialists and formed the major element in the Postgraduate Certificate in Education. Of the forty-three history students who started at London in September 1986, twelve were followed in detail; of the nineteen at Manchester, eleven were followed in detail. Data were collected from both courses through semi-structured interviews and observation. Interviews were conducted with tutors in the training institution and with heads of history departments in twenty-three teaching practice schools. Extensive visits were made to the training institutions to observe seminars and lectures on the theory and practice of history teaching. Nine days were monitored when students were in schools with tutors for one day a week during the first two terms of the course, and each student was visited once during each block practice with the exception of one student who was visited on the second practice only. Full accounts were kept of all observed sessions.

These detailed investigations were set in the context of a questionnaire survey of all students who started secondary school PGCE history courses in 1986 in England, Wales and Northern Ireland. Two questionnaires were used, the first in September 1986, the second in April 1987. Many of the questions called for responses on a five-point Likert scale (in which the subject chooses one of five possible answers ranging from complete agreement to complete disagreement with a statement). They focused on the ways in which students had been taught history as secondary school pupils; their expectations of the course and how far these had been fulfilled; the supervision they received on teaching practice; their confidence and anxiety as they looked ahead to teaching. The responses from the 171 students (out of a possible 358) who replied to both questionnaires were analysed statistically.

London and Manchester students also completed a short annexe to the first questionnaire and additional questionnaires in December 1986 and March 1987 after each period of teaching practice.

The critical focus of the research was the ways in which student teachers acquire the knowledge and skills to make them effective in the classroom. Educationists from Dewey onwards have been concerned with this issue. Current work by Lee Shulman and his associates at Stanford University, California, continues with this concern but focuses particularly on how teachers can reflect critically on their teaching and thus develop new knowledge and skills. Their research provided the basis for a model for the evaluation of the two courses.

Shulman and his associates in their preliminary findings (Wilson, Shulman and Richert, 1987) have developed a model of pedagogical reasoning which includes comprehension (what teachers need to know), transformation (how they make subject matter accessible to pupils) and evaluation and reflection (how teachers evaluate and reflect on their classroom practice in order to create new comprehension). It is possible to use the major sections of their model to indicate the kinds of knowledge and practice which postgraduate history students need to develop.

A MODEL FOR THE EVALUATION OF THE TWO COURSES

(a)   Comprehension

Teaching requires knowledge and understanding of five categories:

  (i)   subject content;
 (ii)   the concepts and procedures of the subject (what Bruner calls the 'structure');
(iii)   a range of possible teaching strategies;
 (iv)   the teaching and learning with which the pupils are already familiar;
  (v)   the knowledge base and existing conceptions of the pupils.

(b)   Transformation

Teaching requires expertise in four categories:

  (i)   matching teaching strategies to objectives;
 (ii)   assessing pupil learning;
(iii)   communication;
 (iv)   classroom management.

(c)   Evaluation and Reflection

Teaching requires critical evaluation and reflection:

  (i)   evaluation of classroom teaching and learning;
 (ii)   reflection on that evaluation, leading to new knowledge and understanding and thus improving practice.

The three sections of this model are closely interdependent. Knowledge is transformed into action; professional progress and the development of new knowledge can occur only through critical evaluation and reflection.

THE AIMS AND STRUCTURE OF THE TWO COURSES

Before the data collected from the research are evaluated against the model, a brief indication must be given of the aims and structure of the two courses.

The aims of the London course were expressed in a handout given to students on their first day: 'The fundamental aim is to enable students to develop into effective history students, progressively improving the quality of their preparation, evaluation and classroom practice.' Work in the Institute aimed to provide a conceptual and theoretical framework for reflecting on the range of experiences which students gained in schools. After a two-week observation period, students came to the training institution and for the first six weeks spent one day in the institute on 'methods' work and one day in schools with their history tutor. The other three days focused on broader professional concerns. Then followed the first block of practice of five weeks with Fridays spent back at the Institute. At the beginning of the second term there was a further five weeks in the Institute with one day a week 'methods' work in schools; this was followed by the second block of eight weeks' teaching at the same school as in the first term. The students spent five days a week in the school. The third term was institution-based with two days a week devoted to history methods.

Manchester also aimed to produce competent and confident teachers who would continue to reflect and to innovate after their initial training. The course too had two blocks of practice – six weeks at the end of the first term, seven weeks towards the end of the second term but in a different school from term one. On both practices, Fridays were spent back in the training institution. There was also school experience during the first four weeks of the course, with visits to a primary school and one day a week spent in comprehensive schools on what was described as a 'feet-wetting' exercise. Each block of practice was preceded by a week's observation.

THE EFFECTIVENESS OF THE COURSES

The model described above was used to evaluate the effectiveness of the two courses with supporting data drawn from the National Survey. We considered first how far the students had sufficient knowledge and understanding of their subject area. Clearly, a thirty-six-week PGCE course cannot hope to add to the students' knowledge of subject content. The research sample comprised graduates who were presumed to be competent to acquire the additional knowledge which they might require for teaching practice. Of the London students, nine were history graduates, one was an economics graduate and two had combined degrees which included history. Eleven had honours degrees, eight upper seconds, two lower seconds and one third. In Manchester, two students were history graduates and the others had combined degrees which included history. Five had upper seconds and six had lower seconds. Yet only half felt confident at the beginning of the course that their knowledge of history would be adequate for teaching 11–16-year-olds, a proportion in line with the results of a national questionnaire. In London, tutors strongly encouraged their students to share their subject expertise for planning lessons.

It was also assumed that students understood the concepts and procedures involved in history, although tutors recognized that students varied considerably in their degree of sophistication. Such understanding was, however, addressed within the PGCE courses. Concepts such as evidence and empathy were included in the programme of institution-based work but the focus was on the approaches for teaching (in Manchester) or on what children were able to achieve (in London). Nevertheless, in considering possibilities for teaching and learning, students found their own conceptions challenged.

With the first two categories of knowledge the students needed for effective teaching, there was, therefore, a not insurmountable problem for the tutors; the students at least had some understanding. When it came to knowledge of a range of teaching strategies, however, the students were in alien territory. What emerged clearly from London and Manchester and from the national survey was that for the overwhelming majority of students their own school history had been didactic, limited in its learning demands and overwhelmingly geared towards examination success. When on teaching practice in schools, however, they hoped to adopt very different strategies. They were concerned with introducing source materials such as primary written documents, pictures and artefacts. They wanted to develop their pupils' empathetic and conceptual understanding of the past through pupil-based learning. It was vital therefore that they were taught about suitable teaching strategies.

Lesson plans or teaching materials were considered in the training institutions, sometimes with videos of children using the materials. In the structured environment of serial practice (one day a week in schools) students observed experienced teachers, and within a team led by their tutor planned and evaluated their own lessons. In preparation for block teaching practice Manchester students spent two weeks observing in schools and London students spent a varied amount of time observing at the beginning of teaching practice.

The remaining two categories under the heading of comprehension (knowledge of the teaching and learning procedures with which the pupils were already familiar and familiarity with the knowledge base and existing conceptions of the pupils) are of course situation-specific. The former can to a certain extent be gained by observation, the latter by diagnostic assessment exercises. London students were given examples of such diagnostic approaches early in their course. In Manchester, as part of their work on assessment, students were shown how to differentiate between levels of response which their pupils might make to any given task.

How successful were the students in these areas? Certainly the seminars, workshops and lectures which they attended in order to obtain the knowledge essential for successful history teaching were, for the most part, carefully prepared, lively and interesting; but the real test of the extent of the comprehension was in the classroom. Here the skills of transforming this knowledge into the hard currency of classroom practice were called into play.

Not surprisingly, students displayed very varied abilities in this area, particularly in connection with classroom management and control. This was certainly the matter about which a considerable majority of students both at London and Manchester and in the national survey showed greatest concern at the start of the course. They were asked to complete the following sentence: 'When I look ahead to teaching history on teaching practice I am least confident about . . .'. Table 8.1 shows the percentage returns of the nine most frequently mentioned categories of concern. Three-quarters of all students both nationally and at the two case-study institutions were concerned that their general teaching skills of management and control (categories 1 and 3) might in some ways prove deficient; 54% of the students were concerned about their lack of historical knowledge and of knowledge of appropriate and varied teaching skills (categories 2 and 4).

Inevitably therefore a majority of the students would start their block teaching practice with the issue of classroom management and control high on the agenda. Clearly initial success in the classroom varied considerably according to the extent of the student's knowledge and the skills of control, management and communication that

Table 8.1   *Matters of Concern as Students Looked Ahead to Teaching Practice (percentages to nearest whole number)*

Category	%
1 Teaching uninterested/disaffected pupils; discipline	53
2 Making subject interesting, variety of approaches	32
3 Classroom management	22
4 Teaching unfamiliar periods/topics	22
5 Slow learners/pitching lessons at right level	11
6 Stamina/workload	11
7 Communicating with clarity	11
8 Mixed ability	8
9 Relationships with teachers/tutors	4

the student possessed. What the research showed clearly, however, was that progress in these matters was dependent upon the quality of a student's evaluation and reflection.

There were of course certain opportunities for evaluation and reflection built into the courses. The importance of reflection was stressed in the aims of the London course and in the structure of the Manchester course. Reflection was meant to permeate the London course whereas in Manchester it formed the third element of the year (following introduction and consolidation). Tutors and students spent time evaluating lessons which they had planned and taught together during the school experience visits in the first term and there were written assignments and teaching-practice files which asked for lesson evaluation. But at the heart of it all was the evaluation and reflection which stemmed from the experiences gained on the block practices. For these provided the acid test for judging the quality of the students' evaluation and reflection in terms of whether it led to a refinement of their teaching. It was failure, in varying degrees, to evaluate and reflect which for many students led to an increasing inability to profit from the course and to develop professionally.

The major reason for this breakdown was that the students required constant assistance (particularly in introducing strategies which they had not experienced as pupils) but this was rarely provided. The focus of their evaluation and reflection needed to be not only subject-specific but situation-specific. As Shulman's analysis stresses, their professional development could occur only as a result of continual, focused 'reflection-in-action'. This was not, however, a practice which students could develop on their own and here the role of the teacher supervisor was of crucial importance. Yet it was precisely at this point that the greatest weakness of the PGCE history courses was shown; so much depended on the part played by the teacher supervisors but this was ill-defined, largely unexplored and essentially voluntary.

Interviews with the heads of school history departments involved in supervising students showed a wide variation in the degree of understanding that they had of the institution-based part of the course and their practice in supervising students. Overwhelmingly, however, the teachers saw their role in limited terms. They were essentially there to provide practical, 'chalk-face' advice; their concerns and the concerns of their students were with the day-to-day management of the classroom, with 'action teaching'. Theory was seen as something separate, the concern principally of the training institution; by implication the theoretical perspective was down-graded and a sense of superiority and worth attached to the task of 'real teaching' rather than thinking and talking about teaching. The following comments make the point clearly:

> I feel that the theory and philosophy of history teaching can be quite well dealt with by the people at the Institute. Having been to the Institute I'm quite certain – unless it has radically changed – that that is the emphasis of their teaching. I expect it is much less so now but it used to be theory, theory, theory. I tend to play the practical teacher role, and emphasize classroom management, preparation, marking, the day-to-day life of the classroom.

> . . . it used to be said some years ago that many people who worked in colleges couldn't get out of the classroom quite enough and so they became college lecturers where they could talk all day about educational theory. I think this is less true than it was. . . . What they [students] do with the children should work and the children should have got something from it and their books should have been marked. The children will think they have done some proper work. . . . It should appear to the children that they have had a proper teacher and not someone who can't do anything . . . practical . . . [Students] have to know what to do if a pupil threatens to throw a chair at you or something like that.

> I would see my role as essentially practical, that I would be able to help with the practicalities of life in the classroom – on a very simple level like the tricks you pick up, helping with resources, showing how to work a slide projector – very simple practical things – because I think they tend to be the things which can wreck a lesson and very simple techniques can improve.

There is of course a sense in which the teacher supervisors' comments are not only understandable but justifiable. Surely no student can make progress or develop professionally until he or she has mastered the techniques of classroom management and control; children's skills, concepts and knowledge can never develop unless there is an ordered learning environment. This is to presuppose that the teacher learns the first before going on to the second whereas the research indicates that the two are intimately entwined; to suppose otherwise is to make a false distinction between teaching means and learning ends. It also presupposes that the supervisor will move on to a consideration of the children's learning once the basic management skills have been mastered. The research showed clearly that although the students' preoccupation with management and control had diminished considerably by the end of the block practices, the school supervisors in the main were still concerned with matters of management and control. Table 8.2 gives percentages of students expressing lack of confidence on

Table 8.2 *Matters of Concern as Students Looked Ahead to Full-Time Teaching (percentages to the nearest whole number)*

Category	%
1 Stamina/workload	22
2 Teaching unfamiliar periods/topics	21
3 Teaching uninterested, disaffected pupils/discipline	21
4 Making subject interesting/variety of approaches	19
5 Classroom management	15
6 Mixed-ability teaching	12
7 Relationships with teachers/tutors	7
8 Slow learners/pitching at right level	5
9 Communicating with clarity	1

particular teaching issues as they looked ahead towards the end of the course to full-time teaching.

Whereas in October at the start of the course 75% of students were concerned about classroom management and discipline, the figure had dropped to 36% by May (categories 3 and 5). Worries now focused on matters of work load, content and teaching methods.

Yet the learning ends of teaching were not what teacher supervisors in the main discussed with their students. The research asked the students to indicate how far general issues such as classroom management and disciplining disruptive pupils featured in their discussions with their teacher supervisors as against subject-specific issues such as using and evaluating historical sources, devising empathy exercises and developing a sense of time. It was the former which were the most frequent topics for discussion. More than this, a majority of teacher supervisors ($c.$ 55%) never held regular meetings with their students but relied on casual meetings, for example during break. A majority of tutors from the training institutions ($c.$ 54%) visited their students less frequently than once a fortnight; and though they were more likely than the teacher supervisors to discuss subject-specific issues, their main concerns, like the teachers', were the matters of classroom control and management.

Teaching-practice supervision for the majority of students was therefore limited, erratic and concerned mainly with the immediate and general issues of classroom management and control. Their professional development was largely dependent on their own efforts which, unaided, were insufficient to refine practice. The case of one student graphically illustrates this point.

The student was a highly competent and well-qualified historian; with pupils she was self-confident. Her block practices were undertaken in a school where the history department was in sympathy with the aims of the training institution's history-methods course. The teachers were very supportive in their attitude towards the student; but they provided almost no formal supervision involving observation and regular meetings. The student lacked the experience to evaluate her lessons on her own; her practice proceeded on a trial-and-error basis. By the end of the practices she was certainly an assured and competent controller of the classroom but her professional development as a teacher of history seemed to have come to an end as she felt that she knew all that was needed as far as the teaching of history was concerned. It was an attitude which was a direct consequence of the fact that no one had helped her to reflect systematically on her practice.

CONCLUSIONS AND RECOMMENDATIONS

The research showed that the progressive development of the students' professional competence was dependent on the extent and effectiveness of the reflection and evaluation of classroom practice undertaken or observed. But such reflection and evaluation must deal equally with both the immediate practicalities of the situation and with learning ends and their theoretical underpinning if professional growth is to take place; theory and practice must be interdependent. For this to take place there must be a close relationship between the school-based and the training institution-based parts of the course. Such a relationship has to be built on a clear understanding and agreement by both tutors and school supervisors of the nature of the pupils' historical concepts and the ways in which these can be developed; there has to be agreement about the roles of tutors and supervisors and the styles and agendas for supervision which will allow the student to develop professionally. Neither the case studies which formed the bulk of the research nor the national survey suggest that at present such a relationship is the norm. Though the training institutions seemed clear about their aims for the institution-based part of the course, the schools were far from clear and the school supervisors (who were largely responsible for the students during at least one-third of the course) not only found it difficult to articulate their own practice in terms of teaching means and learning ends but were also very uncertain as to how they could best help the students to develop professionally. For many, supervision of students consisted of hurried occasional meetings in which the main topics for discussion were matters of classroom management and control. Time for evaluation and reflection on the pupils' learning was conspicuous by its absence. The links therefore between the school-based experience and training and learning of history which it was the main aim of the research to identify were shown to be either very tenuous or non-existent.

That such effective links do not, for the most part, occur is no criticism of either the training institutions or the schools; the training institutions have little or no authority to implement such a partnership and neither they nor the schools have the resources to provide the joint planning and training required. The research points strongly therefore to the need for the Department of Education and Science and local education authorities to make resources and time available to allow for a genuine partnership to be effected.

Such a partnership, it was felt, would be concerned with two main issues: joint planning of courses and exploration of the nature and styles of supervision. Courses should be planned by tutors and teachers together so that agreement can be reached about the knowledge and understanding that students need to operate effectively in the classroom. If the principle that theory – whether it be about subject-specific matters, matters of general classroom management or broader professional responsibilities such as the pastoral curriculum – can best be addressed within the context of actual practice then it may well be that the focus of initial teacher training must be school-based, rather than divided up into large blocks of school-based and institution-based work. Indeed, the research indicated that a powerful deterrent to real partnership lay in the model of training which over 44% of the students experienced: a single block of practice preceded and followed by a term in the training institution. However hard the notion of 'reflection-in-action' is pressed, the teachers and students will perceive the training institutions as in the business of giving the theory which is then applied in the schools. Even the split practice of two blocks (which accounted for the experience of the majority of students in the survey) does little to alter this perception. Admittedly the time at the training institution is increasingly concerning itself with school-experience visits. Tutors will take students into school to undertake some group teaching: students may spend a morning discussing the theory and practice of the pastoral care system with the year heads and form tutors. Seventy-three per cent of the students in the research survey indicated that this sort of activity took place during the institution-based part of the course. But a course planned on the basis of a genuine partnership in which the partners are equals will tend not to make any clear distinction between institution and school, between theory and practice; all parties will be concerned with effective professional development and the creation of opportunities for guiding the students in the evaluation and reflection of their work.

Joint planning along the lines indicated above must be accompanied by joint training so that both school supervisors and training-institution tutors are clear about their roles and have the necessary knowledge and skills to encourage the progressive transformation of the students' knowledge into effective classroom teaching. Such training should focus on three areas. First, there must be agreement about the agendas with which the supervision of students must be concerned. Such agendas will be concerned both with the subject-specific issues such as historical source-based work as well as the more general issues such as classroom management and control. The former will be seen as the heart of the agenda, the end to which the other skills must lead. Secondly, there must be agreement about how and in what manner the school can arrange opportunities for the student to approach the items on the agreed agenda. How much observation should there be? How much team teaching or small group work? When should full class teaching be introduced? With which classes should role play be attempted? All the evidence from the research indicates that there is no simple or single answer to these questions, for each student will have different needs, different strengths and weaknesses. Discussion in this area will also be concerned with the nature and frequency of formal supervisions. That supervisions should take place on a regular, weekly basis if the student is to develop professionally is beyond question; the research showed that in the minority of cases where students did have regular meetings of a formal nature with the teacher supervisor they were twice as likely to discuss subject-specific issues such as evidence-based and empathy exercises. Thirdly, the training must be concerned with exploring the styles of supervision. It goes without saying that a supervisor should be supportive (one student in the research described his supervisor's comments as 'trite and destructive'). But styles of supervision must go beyond this and tutors and teacher supervisors need to debate the most effective ways of enabling students to become reflective practitioners. Will the emphasis be on clinical supervision with the implicit assumption that the student suffers from poor teaching and needs to be cured? Will the emphasis be on counselling or will it simply aim at getting the student to articulate reasons for actions taken? Again, the evidence from the research would suggest that there is no one route to be taken and it may well be that a supervisor adopts aspects of all these approaches at some time. A disastrous lesson may well be followed by supervision in which the teacher supervisor takes a positive lead in suggesting an alternative approach. In other circumstances, a more questioning approach may be called for. Whatever the line adopted, it is essential for the supervisor to remain positive and to have evidence taken from the lesson observed with which to substantiate points made.

A partnership between training institutions and schools which is concerned with joint planning of the knowledge and understanding needed by student teachers and the reciprocal relationship of this to the expertise of teaching will need to go far beyond the occasional meeting for the exchange of information. What is required is a course which enables training institution tutors and teacher supervisors both to explore the particular nature of their subject area and its relationship to classroom teaching and to develop the skills of supervision in order to make effective the relationship between the different elements of an initial training course.

A number of schools and training institutions are now jointly engaged in mounting such courses; for example, the University of Cambridge Department of Education has run training of this kind for the past three years (see Chapter 11 in this volume). But such local initiatives are not enough, given the pressures to move towards a far greater degree of school-based training and the need therefore for a reappraisal of the relationship between school and training institution. Nationally, there must be a fundamental change in attitude as well as in course structures by the training institutions. Training cannot now be their exclusive preserve – partnership and school-based training courses demand, at the least, equality and a sharing of functions and responsibilities. Schools must accept that they have a fundamental part to play in the new approach to initial training and that this may involve the learning of new knowledge and the acquisition of new skills. The most recent criteria issued by the Department of Education and Science for the approval of initial teacher training courses (DES, 1989) put particular emphasis on the need for schools to be involved in the planning and delivery of courses and the selection of students. Lecturers must regularly spend time teaching in schools; where necessary teachers may have to undertake training to prepare them for their new responsibilities. Such requirements may do much to put the issue of the roles and responsibilities of training institutions and schools to the forefront of the debate on partnership.

REFERENCES

DES: Department of Education and Science (1984) *Initial Teacher Training: Approval of Courses* (Circular 3/84). London: DES.
DES: Department of Education and Science (1989) *Initial Teacher Training: Approval of Courses* (Circular 24/89). London: DES.
Proctor, N. (1984) 'Towards a partnership with schools', *Journal of Education for Teaching*, **10** (3), 219–32.
Wilson, S. M., Shulman, L. S. and Richert, A. E. (1987) '150 different ways of knowing: knowledge in teaching', in Calderhead, J. (ed.) *Exploring Teachers' Thinking*. London: Cassell.

Chapter 9

The Oxford Internship Scheme and the Cambridge Analytical Framework: Models of Partnership in Initial Teacher Education

Donald McIntyre

Two recent attempts to theorize about initial teacher education, especially with regard to collaboration between colleges or universities and schools for this purpose, have respectively been undertaken at Cambridge and Oxford Universities.

These two initiatives have been very different in kind. The Cambridge initiative was a research project, which was commissioned by the Department of Education and Science in 1983 to monitor and evaluate four examples of initial teacher training programmes of a 'school-based' kind, and reported in Furlong *et al.*, 1988. The Oxford 'internship' initiative (McIntyre, 1988; Benton, 1990) was the development of a new initial teacher education programme involving a very close university–schools partnership. The joint planning for this new programme started in 1985 and implementation of the programme started in September 1987. The Cambridge group's theorizing was thus undertaken in the context of a research and evaluation enterprise, while the theorizing for the Oxford initiative has been in the development, and testing in practice, of the rationale for a new programme.

Although contemporaneous, these two initiatives have been conducted quite independently of each other, with no cross-fertilization of ideas. The purpose of this chapter is to attempt such a cross-fertilization by comparing the two initiatives so that each may be critically examined in terms of the concerns, the concepts and the criteria of the other.

This chapter comprises two main sections. In the first, the analytical framework developed by the Cambridge group, and the major problems which they encountered in their four case studies, will be used to interrogate the Oxford internship scheme: how adequately has the Oxford scheme anticipated the concerns and problems identified in the Cambridge evaluation? In the second main section, roles are reversed, and the Oxford model is used to interrogate the Cambridge analytical framework: how adequately does this framework conceptualize the problems and opportunities involved, and the tasks which need to be undertaken, in initial teacher education?

OXFORD'S INTERNSHIP SCHEME EXAMINED IN RELATION TO THE
CAMBRIDGE ANALYTICAL FRAMEWORK

In this section, the theoretical framework developed by the Cambridge team will be summarized, and the Oxford scheme will then, so far as possible, be outlined in terms of this theoretical framework. Consideration will be given to how effectively the Oxford scheme is calculated to avoid or to overcome the major problems which were identified by the Cambridge researchers in other school-based schemes.

The Analytical Framework

The Cambridge group present their analytical framework as based on their examination of two of their case studies of school-based training, and as drawing especially on the work of three authors: Schön (1983), Bernstein (1971) and Hirst (1983).

Schön's main thesis is that professional activity involves not the application of scientific generalizations or rules based on them, through the recognition of specific instances, but rather the interpretation of unique situations through analogy or metaphor, often through the use of unarticulated knowledge, through exploratory action, and especially through 'reflection-in-action'. The Cambridge group accept the validity of this thesis and furthermore believe that this 'characterization of professional activity as reflection-in-action ... has important implications for our understanding of the nature of professional training' (Furlong *et al.*, 123).

The ideas drawn from Bernstein are those of *classification* and *framing* and the related contrasting of *integrated* and *collection* curriculum codes. Bernstein describes the extent to which areas of knowledge are demarcated and separated in a curriculum as the strength of classification of the curriculum; and he describes the extent to which teachers maintain control over the knowledge accepted as relevant in a given teaching context as the strength of framing. Collection codes are those in which classification and framing are strong and where, in Bernstein's view, the underlying theory of learning is likely to be didactic, while integrated codes are those in which classification and framing are weak, with a more self- or group-regulated theory of learning, and also with a different idea of what is to count as knowledge.

The Cambridge group see traditional programmes of initial teacher education as generally having strong classification, especially in the divisions made between theoretical college-based courses and school teaching practice; and also strong framing, in that lecturers exert strong control over the knowledge to be taught, at least in the university context. 'By contrast, it would seem to us that a curriculum appropriate to the epistemology of professional practice put forward by Schön would be more likely to approximate to an integrated code' (ibid., 125). This is so because

> the recognition that teaching is an interactive process whereby one draws on one's past experiences and understandings to experimentally impose meanings on a situation applies equally to the novice as to the experienced practitioner.

Important commitments underlying the Cambridge team's evaluation are expressed in terms of Schön's and Bernstein's ideas. For beginning teachers to learn to engage in the kind of professional activity which Schön describes (and prescribes) would seem to necessitate, first, that practical activity is placed at the very heart of training. Moreover, if the main purpose of other elements of the PGCE is indeed to help students sophisticate their skills, knowledge and understandings in relation to such practical work, then this will also demand weaker forms of classification and framing. Weaker classification will mean that education studies and curriculum studies will be more closely related to each other and most particularly to work undertaken in school. A pedagogy derived from weaker framing in which students have greater control over selection, pacing and organization of knowledge would also seem more appropriate . . . lecturers will be more concerned to emphasize how knowledge is created.

(ibid., 125–6)

The third author on whose work the Cambridge group drew especially was Hirst (1983).

For Hirst, the teacher's professional common sense refined both by practice and by the disciplines [is] the basis of 'practical principles', suggesting a logic and rationality that is missing from more mundane 'common sense'. The disciplines of education, although not exactly marginal, since their role is to refine practical principles, are nevertheless relegated to a secondary position.

(ibid., 8–9)

Noting that Schön is not helpful in describing the kinds of knowledge and skills which teachers use to define the situations with which they deal, the Cambridge group relied heavily on Hirst's thinking to articulate different 'levels of professional training' which might be used in initial teacher education. Four such levels are distinguished, and they have been set out on p. 97 of this book.

The main purpose of the Cambridge group was to discover the extent to which, and the means by which, the programmes of initial teacher education that they were studying had adopted integrated code curricula. They were concerned with both the selection and weighting of topics and the 'levels of training' used, and with the integration both of different topics and different levels. They concluded that in exploring these issues, the two factors of greatest importance were the *personnel* involved and the *structure* of courses. With regard to personnel, they noted that it was only teachers regularly working within a specific school context who could effectively undertake training at Level a, while, in contrast, the conditions of work of college lecturers generally enabled them to offer training more effectively at the other three levels. With regard to structure, they were concerned with the relative weighting of different elements and with the way they were patterned, concurrent arrangements of university courses and school experience being seen as having more potential for integration. The range of schools involved and the physical location for different elements were also seen as important.

Finally, in considering the *pedagogy* of initial teacher education, the Cambridge group turned again to Schön for a conceptual framework from which they derived evaluative criteria. As noted, they suggest that the underlying pedagogy of the college components of traditional PGCE courses has been consistently didactic, while that of traditional teaching practice has been a combination of imitating role models and trial-and-error learning, all of this being derived from a conception of professional activity as a technical following of rules. However, 'the recognition that teaching is not a technical activity but an interactive process, where one draws on one's past experiences and understandings *experimentally* to impose meaning on a situation would appear to demand a different pedagogy' (ibid., 137).

From this starting point, three questions emerged as important in relation to the strength of the framing within classes in teacher education courses. Are student teachers expected to play *active* or *passive* roles in these classes? To what extent is the *choice of agenda* given to the students or made open to negotiation? To what extent do students have control over *what is seen as appropriate knowledge* for them to learn in these classes? In the context of direct practical experience in schools, the prior question was whether or not there was active tutoring at all, but if so, then the above questions would apply to this component of courses also.

The Oxford Internship Scheme

It is appropriate first to outline the organizational framework of the PGCE programme for intending secondary school teachers at Oxford, commonly referred to as the internship scheme. The scheme is based on a partnership of the University Department of Educational Studies, Oxfordshire Local Education Authority, and all those Oxfordshire secondary schools which wish to be involved. At any one time, fifteen to seventeen secondary schools are actively involved, with ten student teachers, or 'interns', on average attached to each of them. This attachment extends throughout most of the year, from mid-October until the end of June, interns being in the schools for two days a week for most of the year (joint or J-weeks) and full-time in the schools for ten to twelve weeks from February until May (school or S-weeks).

The course has two main components, a curriculum programme concerned with all aspects of classroom teaching, and a general programme concerned with other aspects of schooling, including personal and social education, whole-school and cross-curricular issues. The curriculum programme is operated entirely on a subject basis, separate programmes being planned according to common principles in the several subject areas. Within each subject area, school-based work is primarily the responsibility of experienced subject teachers known as *mentors*, each mentor working throughout the year with a pair of interns attached to his or her school subject department. University-based curriculum studies, and co-ordination of the whole subject curriculum programme, are the responsibility of *curriculum tutors* for that subject.

Each school has a *professional tutor*, a member of the school staff who has overall responsibility for the school's part in the scheme. Each school also has associated with it a different member of the university staff, the *general tutor* for that school. The general programme is the responsibility of professional tutors and general tutors. During J-weeks, part of the programme, largely the same for all interns, is provided in the university by general tutors; and the complementary school-based part of the programme is provided jointly in the schools by professional tutors and general tutors throughout both J-weeks and S-weeks, this part of the programme being planned separately for each school.

Several schools not actively involved in the scheme initially have since expressed a wish for such involvement. To facilitate this, the head teachers of the schools currently involved have agreed to drop out of active involvement for a year by rotation. Increased student numbers have also facilitated the involvement of more schools.

The active involvement of as many schools as possible in the county is a major consideration because of the part played in the scheme by Oxfordshire LEA. Because the LEA recognizes the advantages of the scheme for the professional development of teachers in the participating schools (McIntyre, 1989), it has consistently provided substantial financial support from its inservice budget to give mentors and professional tutors extra non-teaching time.

There are many respects in which the premises on which the internship scheme is based are closely similar to those of the Cambridge analytical framework. Two of these may be highlighted initially. First, there is a shared belief that no satisfactory initial teacher education course is possible without much closer and more effective integration of school-based and university-based elements of the course than has been common: leaving the task of integrating 'theory' and 'practice' to student teachers has demonstrably and not surprisingly been quite inadequate. Second, there is a shared recognition of the different contributions which practising school teachers and university lecturers are each well placed to make: only practising teachers can directly introduce interns to the practice of teaching, and especially to the use of the contextualized knowledge (of individual pupils, of established relationships with classes, of resources and their availability, and of school customs and procedures) which is such a crucial element of professional teaching; and on the other hand, the conditions of university lecturers' work enable and oblige them, much more than is generally possible for practising teachers, to know about alternative teaching approaches being used elsewhere, to study relevant research and theoretical literature, and to explicate and critically examine the principles which should or could inform the practice of teaching. In terms of the Cambridge framework, school teachers are best placed to conduct professional training at Level (a), while university lecturers are best placed to contribute at the other three levels.

It is towards the achievement of the effective integration seen by the Cambridge group as of paramount importance that much of the planning of the internship scheme has been directed; and much of this planning can be understood in terms of the Cambridge group's key concepts of *personnel* and *structure*.

In relation to personnel, integration within the scheme is sought through a close and effective *partnership* between school and university staff. This partnership is facilitated by a number of planned characteristics of the programme:

(a)   *clarity about, and valuing of, the complementary contributions to be made:* the respective contributions which university and school staff are best placed to make are made explicit, the value of each is emphasized, and a consistent policy based on this division of labour is adopted. Thus, for example, the assessment of interns' practical teaching competence is primarily a responsibility of mentors, with curriculum tutors having a moderating role. Help of any kind for the interns from any source is of course welcomed, but the scheme would not be seen to be operating effectively if a curriculum tutor gave significant amounts of time to talking about, or demonstrating, his or her own classroom teaching strategies, or if a professional tutor gave the interns in his or her school lectures, or workshops, on general curriculum theory (rather than 'what we do here and why we do it that way'). Fortunately most participants find it rewarding that the expertise they are well placed to provide is valued, and are reassured to know that they need not pretend to kinds of expertise they are not well placed to offer.

(b)   *concentration of the scheme within a relatively small number of schools quite close to the university:* for each school and each professional tutor to accept responsibility for around ten interns, and for each mentor to accept responsibility for two interns, throughout the year, requires much more than the traditional marginal commitment of schools to initial teacher education; and together with this greater commitment by school personnel goes greater power in the planning and implementation of programmes. Both in their involvement and in their influence, individual school staff therefore move closer to equality with university staff. Perhaps more important in practice is the opportunity that the scheme provides for establishing quite small and stable teams within the several subject areas to plan and implement the curriculum programmes. These teams of curriculum tutors and mentors in each subject area meet regularly, generally about twice each term, to plan and review the university and school components of their programmes. The complete team of professional tutors and general tutors is a rather larger body which meets usually once per term; but of course the professional tutor and the general tutor in each school meet together weekly throughout the year, and they also meet with the school's mentors for school internship team meetings about twice each term.

(c) *integration within the university element:* the problems of integrating school and university elements of the course are greatly simplified by the division of the university element only into general and curriculum programmes, concerned with different aspects of school activity, not into programmes concerned with different kinds of knowledge relevant to the same aspect of practice. Thus the curriculum programme in each subject area incorporates all the kinds of knowledge considered relevant to subject teaching and classroom practice, curriculum tutors being responsible for integrating in their university-based work Levels (b), (c) and (d) of professional training in terms of the Cambridge framework. The same is true for the general programme, but for each of the themes of this programme a different tutor takes responsibility for preparing seminar, workshop and reading materials, and in some cases for giving an introductory lecture. The loose coupling which is planned between curriculum and general programmes to connect whole-school and classroom issues is greatly facilitated by the fact that virtually all curriculum tutors are also general tutors.

(d) *investment:* the close and effective partnership between university and school staff which is basic to the integrated nature of internship would not be possible without the investment of a great deal of time and energy by school and university staff. Mentors in particular tend to invest a great deal of energy into this extra work; when asked why, their explanations emphasize the importance of the task, their valuing of the scheme, and the satisfaction which the work gives them. The partnership would not, however, work if university tutors were themselves withdrawing from the school-based element and leaving it to school staff. Curriculum tutors probably spend more time in schools than they did before internship was introduced, but that time is used much more for talking with mentors, interns and other teachers, and for engaging in collaborative teaching, and much less for observation alone, than it used to be. This investment of time is essential to maintain an ongoing integration of the contributions of curriculum tutor and mentor, and also of the different elements of the course for individual interns. Furlong *et al.* suggest that:

the most important and distinctive training contribution of lecturers at Level (a) is to integrate or link this work to other levels of training. In this work it is usually lecturers alone who have expertise ... But such 'supervision', that integrates critical reflection by the student into an analysis of his or her own practice, is a rare phenomenon in most courses. We saw only occasional examples if only because the conditions for it existed so rarely.

(1988, 171)

Each mentor and pair of interns can normally expect their curriculum tutor to visit them for half a day once every four weeks during J-weeks and once every fortnight during S-weeks. General tutors are normally in schools for half a day each week throughout the year. As noted earlier, the LEA also invests substantially in the scheme because of its professional development advantages for established staff; and the value of that investment necessarily leads university tutors constantly to try to ensure that these professional development benefits are realized.

In relation to *structure*, the organization of school-based and university-based studies as *concurrent* throughout most of the year is, as the Cambridge group suggested, of fundamental importance to the achievement of integration. Obviously enough, however, integration is only made possible, certainly not ensured, by a concurrent organization. Equally important, therefore, has been the *use* of this opportunity to plan for integration. All curriculum programmes are planned so that the university and school staff involved agree on:

(i)   a *general progression* through which interns' responsibilities in schools are gradually increased over several months towards regular whole-class teaching, with complementary preparatory work being undertaken at each stage in the university;

(ii) the *selection of topics* for the programme, all of these having a direct relevance to teachers' work in schools and being dealt with in both contexts;

(iii) the *timing* of the programme, to ensure that interns are exploring topics in the university and in the schools at agreed and closely related times;

(iv) the *main ideas* to be explored in relation to each topic; and

(v)   the *activities* relevant to each topic to be undertaken in the university and in the schools (e.g. seminars, reading, workshops, observation, small group teaching, interviewing teachers, investigations of pupils' work). Furlong *et al.* note that courses

can influence their students' practical development much more systematically if they provide them with specific activities to engage in in schools and by structuring these developmentally both in observation and in teaching exercises ... when jointly constructed by teachers and lecturers working together in the course, and used under adequate guidance of teachers who appreciate its analytical rather than didactic purpose in professional training as a whole, such structured work can become a powerful training vehicle.

(1988, 174–5)

Similarly, the general programme is planned in outline by all general and professional tutors, while each pair of general and professional tutors plans appropriate seminars, workshops and investigations for their school-based programme. Over the year as a whole roughly equal time, and certainly equal importance, is given to school-based and university-based study and experience or, in the Cambridge group's terms, to Level (a) and to the other three levels. Within university-based study, Level (d) is involved because of the need for practical principles to be critically examined in terms of their implicit educational values, their conceptual clarity, and the soundness of their basis in social scientific theory and research, but because of the criterion that all topics should be directly relevant to teachers' work, Levels (b) and (c) tend to predominate.

Much of the Level (b) work in curriculum programmes involves drawing on the experiences of interns, in relation to the same issues, from different schools. The value of this work is greatly enhanced by the tutors' intimate knowledge of the school departments concerned, and their close partnership with the mentors, as well as by its relationship to the direct experience of individual interns. Level (b) work drawing on other sources is of course necessary where none of the schools involved adopt approaches about which interns need to be informed. There is some confidence that the internship programme provides, in general, a satisfactory resolution of a problem noted by Furlong and his colleagues:

> The dilemma is whether to emphasize broad and systematic preparation for class teaching within the training institution, with all the inadequacies of detached knowledge that that involves, or to opt for more realistic but necessarily narrow, school-based preparation. We were not convinced that any of our four courses had got right the fine balance that is necessary in this area.
>
> (1988, 179)

One respect in which the structure of the internship scheme falls short of the Cambridge group's specifications is that interns spend most of the year in one school, not in the range of schools said to be desirable. Certainly, each intern spends a preliminary orientation period of two weeks in a different secondary school, but it cannot be claimed that this provides diversity of teaching experience. Initial concern that this was a weakness of the scheme has, however, given way to a confidence that the benefits of spending the year in one school greatly outweigh the disadvantages: among the important things which this arrangement helps interns to learn are what it is important to learn about a new school, and how these things may be learned. None the less, it is recognized that the lack of experience of inner-city schools for interns is a disadvantage, and the possibility of some such experience towards the end of the year is being explored.

The *pedagogy* of the internship course, like its curriculum, can usefully be presented in terms of the Cambridge group's concepts. In relation to the first of these, the seminar and workshop approaches favoured in the university-based parts of the course mean that interns learn mostly through *active* involvement. It is noteworthy that the Cambridge group's concern in relation to school-based elements was about the level of activity of *tutoring* in the schools: the very active role adopted by mentors, backed up by an intensive involvement also of curriculum tutors, ensures that there is indeed active tutoring as well as active roles for interns in the school-based work.

As the Cambridge group rightly suggest, two much more fundamental questions concern the extent to which student-teachers have control over the *agenda* of topics to be studied and the extent to which they determine *what is appropriate knowledge* for them to learn in relation to given topics. Two fundamental premises of the internship scheme relate directly to these questions. First, it is taken for granted that from the time they start the course interns will have agendas of their own, that these may often be very different from any official agenda, and that the most significant learning will be that derived from interns' individual agendas. Second, it is also assumed that there is no established body of knowledge, whether explicitly formulated or implicit in practice, which would be adequate to guide interns' teaching or their learning to teach, even if it could be effectively communicated to them.

These two premises might seem to imply a learner-controlled pedagogy, or at least a heavily process-oriented pedagogy of the kind which the Cambridge group would appear to favour. Yet the primary obligation of any initial teacher education pro-gramme must be to prepare people to cope competently as classroom teachers; and for many of those who begin PGCE programmes this is a demanding target, not likely to be attained unless their efforts are quite efficiently directed towards it. The pedagogy of internship therefore requires some carefully considered compromises.

In relation to *agenda*, integration of school-based and university-based elements depends, as already explained, on careful advance planning by school and university staff of what will be studied, and when; but within this framework, interns are encouraged to explore whatever ideas on the given topics are important to them. Also, in both general and curriculum programmes, times are laid aside for interns to discuss unscheduled issues which have arisen for them in the context of their school-based experiences. Thirdly, during the course of the PGCE year there is a shift in emphasis towards autonomy for interns, so that for example two major assignments for the year, completed in the summer term, are focused on aspects chosen by the intern of, respectively, his or her own teaching and schooling more generally.

With regard to *criteria of appropriate knowledge*, the emphasis in all written work set for interns is on process criteria, and in particular on the articulation and evaluation of educational beliefs. It is, however, necessary to ensure that all interns, before being recommended for qualified teacher status, have developed a full range of basic skills necessary for satisfactory classroom teaching. For this purpose, a 'List of important abilities' – abilities seen as of priority importance for beginning teachers – has been developed on the basis of a consensus among Oxfordshire secondary school teachers (Aplin, 1987), and this list provides the main framework for diagnostic and summative assessment of interns' classroom competence; but from the beginning, interns are asked to explore for themselves the most satisfactory ways of meeting these imposed criteria. Later in the year, when they have demonstrated such basic competence, the task set for them is to evaluate and develop their teaching against criteria formulated by themselves.

Conclusion

From the foregoing analysis, it may be concluded that the questions raised by the Cambridge researchers in terms of their analytical framework, and the concerns which arose from their empirical studies, have in large measure been addressed in the planning and negotiation of the Oxford internship scheme. The large degree of consen-sus which has been demonstrated to exist between the two schemes extends also to the perceived implications for schools and training institutions and their staffs. For exam-ple, in emphasizing the unmatchable detail and sensitivity with which practising teachers can help student-teachers to understand the complex realities of classroom teaching, Furlong *et al.* note: 'Yet such understanding and help demands of teachers skills of explicitly indicating to students matters which many teachers only implicitly sense and which they rarely formulate consciously' (1988, 170), and they go on to recommend that 'appropriate forms of in-service training should be established so that teachers have the necessary expertise to carry out such training in a systematic professional manner (ibid, 206).

Correspondingly, in the Oxford scheme considerable importance is given to support and training of this kind for mentors and professional tutors, through the work of a field officer and the provision of an advanced diploma course specifically concerned with such skills and strategies.

There is similar agreement about the needs of university lecturers, with a common rejection of populist demands for 'recent and relevant experience' of classroom teaching: 'what lecturers require . . . is not current experience of teaching particular classes as if they were being equipped to do Level (a) work, but wide-ranging analytical experience of practice that is directed to elucidating matters of principle' (ibid, 195).

More generally, the apparent degree of consensus is confirmed by the finding that all but two of the twelve specific recommendations emerging from the Cambridge research are built into the Oxford scheme. One of these two exceptions, as has been noted, concerns experience of a variety of secondary schools. The other exception will be explored in the next part of this chapter.

THE CAMBRIDGE ANALYTICAL FRAMEWORK FROM THE PERSPECTIVE OF THE OXFORD INTERNSHIP SCHEME

Despite their independent development and their differing purposes, it is clear that a great deal of common ground is shared by the Oxford and Cambridge initiatives. As has been noted, almost all the measures recommended in the conclusions of the Cambridge research project had from the start been integral elements of the Oxford scheme. From the Oxford perspective, therefore, the practical judgements made by the Cambridge team seem generally very sound. It is none the less a disappointing research project in that it fails at a theoretical level to contribute to our understanding of the processes and problems of teacher education. The practical proposals, although mostly very sensible, are limited inevitably by the analytical framework developed to explain what was happening in the courses studied, and in terms of which conclusions were formulated. It is the value of the analytical framework that has to be questioned.

This part of the chapter therefore focuses on that analytical framework and examines it in relation to the alternative ideas offered by the Oxford internship scheme. A central concern of the analytical framework, as of the internship scheme, was with *integration*. Drawing especially on Hirst (1983), it construed the elements of professional education to be integrated in terms of four 'levels of professional training'; and it was primarily from Schön's (1983) conception of 'the reflective practitioner' that it derived ideas about the nature of the integration that would be appropriate. It is these central ideas, the elements to be integrated and the nature of the integration seen to be appropriate, which will be discussed in this section.

Levels of professional training

The four 'levels' which are used as the basic analytical categories for discussing teacher education programmes are differentiated in terms of contexts, outcomes and processes.

Level (a) is concerned with learning 'through direct practical experience in the class-room, school or community context', whereas Level (b) is concerned with similar kinds of learning 'in detached contexts'. Levels (a) and (b) are concerned with the acquisition of 'understanding, judgement and skills' for use in teaching, Level (c) with 'the acquisition of knowledge of the principles behind different professional practices and reflection on their use and justification', and Level (d) with 'introducing students to an essential content of theoretical knowledge' and/or 'developing students' own skills of reflection and analysis'. Two key differentiating concepts are those of *explicitness* and *generality*: at Level (a) 'training remains rooted in the specifics of particular concrete situations' but at Level (c) students 'begin to understand . . . that practical principles are inevitably general'; at Level (a) 'issues of professional principle and theory are entirely implicit', while the purpose of Level (d) work is 'to make explicit and critically examine . . . value judgements and theoretical assumptions'.

From the Oxford perspective, all these differentiating criteria are important in describing different kinds of useful learning in professional teacher education; but the rationale for this way of analysing training is none the less difficult to understand. There are of course many other ways in which types of professional training might be distinguished. Furthermore it is not obvious that the chosen criteria are correlated in the ways which their use in defining the four levels suggests: such correlation would need to be demonstrated (analytically or empirically), or else the need for many more categories should be recognized. Even if these problems were resolved, the distinctive advantages for 'purposes of considering the significance of school-based work in training' (Furlong *et al.*, 1988, 131) of categorizing training into the four given levels are not readily apparent.

There are four specific ways in which this 'levels of training' part of the analytical framework seems unsatisfactory from the perspective of the Oxford internship scheme.

First, the idea of *levels* of training is obscure and unhelpful. That there are quite different kinds of knowledge to be learned, different sources from which to learn, and different kinds of learning processes necessary is not in question. To what extent, and in what ways, these are hierarchically related is, however, far from clear. Some kinds of knowledge may no doubt be characterized as more abstract, others as more complex, and others still as more explicit; but what is clear is that *different kinds of discipline* are involved in the thinking underlying the practice of teaching, in considering the relative merits of different approaches to teaching, and in engaging in one or other of the 'foundation disciplines'. To suggest that forms of training may be ordered in terms of a single hierarchy, especially without any clear specification of the perceived underlying dimension, is to impose a specious simplicity which can only confuse one's thinking.

Unfortunately, the idea of 'levels of training' seems to be not an arbitrary confusion but rather an ideological one. The presentation of the levels makes very clear that the increasingly reflective, analytic, explicit and generalized nature of the training as one moves from Level (a) to Level (d) leads to a greater degree of enlightenment. Level (a), the type of training for which teachers are best placed to accept responsibility, and which is seen as an essential basis for other types of training, is none the less clearly the lowest level of training, upon which higher levels should build.

The Oxford internship scheme, in contrast, is founded on a very firm rejection of this kind of hierarchical view of different aspects of professional education and of the different kinds of knowledge on which they draw. The partnership between university and schools is secure only because teachers appreciate that the aspects of professional education for which they are best placed to help interns are recognized by university staff as of equal status to those aspects which are best provided in the university. The very general readiness which there has been among teachers to accept the complementary value of the different kinds and sources of knowledge and learning could not have been expected if the schools' contribution had been construed as Level (a) and the university's contribution as Levels (b), (c) and (d). Concern for diplomacy, however, although important, is not the primary concern. More important is the fact that there are no good grounds for giving primacy *either* to the learning that is possible from engagement with the practice of particular schools and classrooms *or* to that which is possible from exploring the decontextualized theoretical arguments, research evidence and explications of alternative versions of good practice available through university study: each provides essentials which the other cannot provide.

From the Oxford perspective, a second weakness of the categorization of types of training is the treatment of 'direct practical experience' as one undifferentiated category, while the more academic kinds of training are differentiated into three categories. This is especially surprising in a study concerned with 'the significance of school-based work in training'. Was, for example, the distinction between 'learning through practice and feedback' and 'learning how experienced teachers work' not sufficiently important to be worth making? The failure to make any such distinctions reflects a general neglect in the research project of major issues relating to school-based work. How, if at all, can experienced teachers make the sophisticated craftsmanship of their teaching accessible to student teachers? To what extent, and in what respects, is this craft communicated in conversations about students' lessons, or about their own lessons, or conversations of a more general nature? What different functions are and can be fulfilled by different kinds of classroom observation by students, at different stages of their training? What are the distinctive benefits of collaborative teaching for training purposes, and how may these benefits be optimized? How does the culture and organization of teaching facilitate and inhibit learning to teach? How can the similarities and differences among members of a school subject department (or of a primary school) acceptably and usefully be made available to help student teachers? These are some of the questions of priority concern within the Oxford scheme, or whenever the complexity of learning 'from direct practical experience' is recognized. Use of the undifferentiated Level (a) category reflects, and probably contributed to, the neglect of such questions in the Cambridge research.

A third weakness of the categorization of types of training is in the definition of Level (c) as involving 'the acquisition of knowledge of the principles behind different professional practices and reflection on their use and justification'. This formulation in terms of 'practical principles' is not one which can easily be related to what is known about how teachers approach their teaching (e.g. Clark and Peterson, 1986; Calderhead, 1987). It seems, too, to offer a very limited view of the range of kinds of knowledge to which lecturers should introduce their students. Hirst's (1983) account of the nature of practical principles in education is one which is entirely consonant with the rationale of the Oxford internship scheme. However, it remains open to question whether or not the articulation and evaluation of such practical principles is the only way through which more rational educational practice can be achieved. Furthermore, even if Hirst's view on this were accepted, what he has argued for in his 1983 paper is the *need to seek* and to test such principles, not that an adequate body of such principles is available for current use. Practical principles on which professional practices might be based should certainly be included in the knowledge to which students are introduced by their lecturers, but so too should such other kinds of knowledge as different ways of construing various aspects of teachers' tasks and situations, explorations of phenomena associated with schooling, and considerations of which account might be taken in schooling. Many issues are not best discussed in terms of 'practical principles'. From the perspective of the Oxford internship scheme, a more open view of university lecturers' contributions is necessary.

A final and, from an Oxford perspective, most fundamental criticism of the 'levels of training' framework is that it offers a very unbalanced view of the critical evaluation of principles and practices. There is complete agreement that a central concern of initial teacher education should be to help and encourage student teachers to develop skills and habits of submitting suggested principles or practices of schooling to critical evaluation. There is equal agreement that crucial criteria in any such evaluation should be those concerned with the clarity and justifiability of the values and assumptions implicit in suggested practices, and the coherence and validity of the arguments of principle upon which they are based; and, furthermore, that these criteria must be rooted in the disciplines of philosophy, psychology and sociology and that university lecturers should generally be best placed to induct student teachers into their use. It is what is missing from the Cambridge framework in this respect which must be criticized: there are many criteria other than those associated with the foundation disciplines which have to be taken into account in any adequate critical evaluation of schooling practices or principles, especially criteria concerned broadly with their *practicality*. Included in this general category are criteria of feasibility (in relation to constraints of, for example, time, resources, skills and power), of likely effectiveness within given contexts, and of social acceptability. In general, it is such criteria of practicality which are necessarily given precedence by teachers in schools, and it is they who are generally best placed to induct student teachers into their use. For professional educators, the intelligent use of such 'practical' criteria in evaluating proposed practices is as important as the use of 'academic' criteria; and for many student teachers, learning to use the 'practical' criteria may be the more difficult task. In the Oxford internship scheme, the critical evaluation of practices and principles against the whole range of 'academic' and 'practical' criteria is a central concern of the programme, a concern in which university and school staff are seen to have equally important, but different, roles.

In summary, while a more open formulation of the university lecturer's role would be preferred, the Cambridge characterization of major types of professional training is seen from the Oxford perspective to be flawed mainly in its hierarchical view of school and university contributions, and in its lack of recognition of the diversity and import-ance of the contributions which can most effectively be made from within the context of ongoing school practice. This difference has important implications. From both perspectives, it would be valuable for practising teachers to be able to spend more time on initial teacher education, and to develop further their skills for doing so. From the Oxford perspective, this means teachers being able to make fuller use, in a number of ways, of the knowledge and expertise which they already have as teachers in schools. From the Cambridge perspective, however, there is little recognition of such possi-bilities. Their conception of a fuller contribution from teachers is rather that teachers should develop the same kinds of analytic skills as university lecturers. This concern, and the associated relatively dismissive attitude to the practical expertise of teachers, are reflected in their recommendation (vi), one of only two Cambridge recommendations which are not incorporated in the Oxford scheme:

> To develop critical reflection, students need to be introduced to the analysis of the professional activities of the teachers with whom they work, or other forms of practice which they encounter and of their own attempts at practice. This involves the elucidation of practical principles and the critical assessment of practice, i.e. training at Level (c). How far teachers are equipped to undertake explicit analytical and critical work in the light of practical principles and to train students in these matters at Level (c) varies greatly. Without such expertise the practical Level (a) work which teachers undertake with students will be limited in character and concerned only with immediate practicalities. We suggest therefore that all teachers working with students should have the opportunity, through some form of in-service training, to develop the explicit use of the necessary analytical and critical skills of working with students at Level (c), at least in relation to their own practice and that of the student.
>
> (Furlong *et al.*, 1988, 206–7)

Integration of an appropriate nature

As noted earlier, the Cambridge group explain their ideas about the need for integration in teacher education, and about the nature of the integration needed, in terms of Schön's (1983) conception of 'the reflective practitioner'.

Central to Schön's conception of the reflective practitioner is the idea of 'reflection-in-action', the complex creative thinking which he believes professionals frequently use to formulate, reformulate and tackle the problems which confront them in their practice. Schön describes and analyses at length, and in thought-provoking ways, processes of reflection-in-action he has encountered in various professional fields. Although applied to 'professions' in general, however, his theories have been developed mainly in relation to architecture, psychotherapy, town planning and management, and have not been significantly based on, or tested in relation to, school teaching. Furthermore, unless the concept of reflection is very unhelpfully extended to include sub-conscious mental activity, the usefulness of 'reflection-in-action' as a general way of characterizing teachers' professional activity must be very seriously questioned; it is more plausible to argue that, because of the complexity of classroom teaching as a social activity, much of teachers' expertise has to consist in limiting the amount and nature of the reflection-in-action in which they engage during it. Calderhead's general conclusion would seem to apply with particular force to the work of Schön:

> For models of reflective teaching to have any constructive impact on teacher education, and to be influential in informing teacher education programs, they will most likely have to be grounded in a more detailed and empirically defensible interpretation of teaching and teachers' professional learning.
>
> (Calderhead, 1989, 46)

Even if Schön's concept of reflection-in-action were seen as an appropriate way of characterizing professional teaching, its relevance to learning to teach would not be obvious. (The Cambridge group do not refer to Schön's own *Educating the Reflective Practitioner* (1987), so it will not be discussed here.) Reflection-in-action, as described by Schön, depends heavily on professionals' already established repertoires for construing situations and appropriate ways of dealing with them. As the Cambridge group themselves quote him: 'When a practitioner makes sense of a situation he perceives to be unique, he sees it as something actually present in his repertoire. . . . The familiar situation functions as a precedent, or a metaphor or . . . an exemplar for the unfamiliar one' (Schön, 1983, 138). Defining the situation by reference to his repertoire, the professional responds in a way which leads to consequences which provide further information for interpretation through reference to past experience: 'This he does through a web of moves, discovered consequences, implications, appreciations, and further moves' (ibid, 131).

It is by extrapolating from this account of the professional activity of experienced practitioners to that of beginners that the Cambridge view of an appropriate kind of integration is derived:

> The recognition that teaching is an interactive process whereby one draws on one's past experiences and understandings to experimentally impose meaning on a situation applies equally to the novice as to the experienced practitioner. Even the most naïve student therefore comes to the PGCE with a stock of knowledge with which to 'define' classroom situations, as well as certain practical skills with which to deal with children. However inadequately, most students can 'survive' in the classroom even from the earliest days of training.
>
> (Furlong *et al.*, 1988, 125)

Given both an acceptance of Schön's account of professional reflection-in-action as a valid account of experienced teachers' practice, and also the extrapolation of this to provide a description of, and a prescription for, beginners' practice, the major object of initial professional education becomes the development of fluent, critical and effective reflection-in-action, and it is in relation to this purpose that appropriate and inappropriate types of integration can be judged:

> In such a reflective approach, students' direct practical training at Level (a) in the classroom and school is the heart of the matter. Other levels of training are used to develop increasingly more informed critical reflection and through that, progressively more effective professional practice . . . We came to appreciate how elements of training based on the inadequate traditional notion of practice as the 'application of theory' inevitably creates a psychological gap between theory and practice which no amount of practice can bridge. In contrast, elements of training based on the analysis of actual practice established no such gap and gave theoretical work at Levels (b), (c) and (d) its proper professional significance.
>
> (ibid., 203–4)

From an Oxford internship perspective, this conception of the kind of integration which is appropriate is dangerously narrow and seems to be based on seriously misguided assumptions. It is of course true that without any training students already have ways of defining classroom situations and that most of them can find ways of surviving in classrooms. It is also true that these initial ideas will be important in shaping their learning about teaching. However, the repertoires which beginning student teachers bring with them are of very different kinds from those of experienced teachers, and not having been developed on the basis of classroom teaching experience tend to be much less useful, both for teaching *and for reflecting on teaching*. In so far as they are asked to learn about teaching from their reflections on their own or others' practice, the limitations of student teachers' perceptions, information-processing, understandings and awareness of alternatives (cf. Berliner, 1987; Calderhead, 1988) are likely to restrict their learning about teaching as much as they restrict their teaching. Learning from reflection on teaching is certainly important; but to deny the value of more abstract learning as an input both to teaching and to reflection upon teaching is to restrict arbitrarily and very seriously the opportunities for learning which PGCE students are given in their limited year of training.

The Cambridge conception of integration is unsatisfactory also in its neglect of probably the most fundamental problem for those attempting to integrate theory and practice in teacher education, the tendency for student teachers to experience systematic divergence between the principles and suggestions of their university tutors and the practices and opinions which they encounter in schools. One way of trying to solve this problem is to select and train as supervisory teachers an unrepresentative set of teachers who engage in what is perceived from a university perspective to be good practice. The implicit solution of the Cambridge group, in contrast, is for the practice of schools and teachers to be the focus of critical analysis by student teachers and their university tutors. Neither of these approaches seems calculated to sustain a close working partnership between schools and university. Even more seriously, by sustaining the 'theory-is-superior-to-practice' attitude, and thus inviting the equally crude 'but-not-realistic' response, both approaches seem poorly judged for preparing student teachers to work as both realistic and reflective practitioners.

The Oxford internship conception of integration is based on the premise that it is inevitable and entirely appropriate that interns should encounter systematic divergence of views on many issues between schools and university: the sophisticated craft knowledge which teachers use in specific school contexts, and the practicality criteria which they are obliged to emphasize must clearly lead them to different conclusions from those to which university lecturers are led by the more generalized abstract knowledge and the academic criteria which their work involves. Consensus of view is not therefore assumed on any issue: it is only on what issues should be explored, and when, and how, that it is seen to be necessary to achieve consensus among the university and school staff involved in a programme. A second premise is that no views or practices, whatever their source, should be accepted as authoritative, but that all should be critically tested against the full range of academic and practical criteria. Integration is achieved through interns' use of the different opportunities available to them to examine ideas and practices in different ways, with particular emphasis on testing in school contexts the practicality of ideas emanating from academic sources as well as reflecting in academic contexts on the theoretical assumptions and educational values of practices encountered in schools. With the help of their tutors and their mentors, interns learn, for example, that the realization of their preferred educational goals may be dependent on conditions that they or their schools cannot fully provide, and that while trying to achieve these conditions one may be wise in the meantime to concentrate on more attainable goals.

Ideas of reflection on practice are certainly of importance for initial teacher education, but the Cambridge group's view of integration through reflection on practice is too narrow in two ways. First, it is seriously premature to tie ideas of reflection on practice to any single orthodox view, especially to that of Schön, questionable as its relevance is to teaching, and most of all to the teaching of beginners. Second, there is every reason to believe that an equally important emphasis in initial teacher education should be that of acquiring at an abstract level ideas for use in one's teaching, and of exploring, through observation, discussion with teachers and one's own teaching, the practicality of these ideas.

CONCLUSION

The practical insights gained through the Cambridge research project were considerable. These insights and the premises on which the Oxford internship scheme was based are mutually supportive and are reinforced by the successful experience of the Oxford scheme.

At a theoretical level, however, the analytical framework developed in the context of the Cambridge research project has a number of serious weaknesses. Prominent among these are an ideological emphasis on academic knowledge as the superior arbitrating kind of knowledge, with an associated lack of recognition of the importance and rich diversity of kinds of knowledge and of learning opportunities in the context of practice; and too great a reliance on a fashionable but untested and narrow view of how integration should be achieved. These weaknesses seem in part to follow from a neglect of available research-based knowledge about the processes and problems of learning to teach. They are important weaknesses primarily because they do not help us to ask more penetrating questions about these processes and problems.

In Oxford, there can be no sense that the problems of teacher education have been solved. It may reasonably be claimed, however, that an arena has been created, in terms both of a conceptual framework and of a practical partnership, where these problems can very fruitfully be investigated and tackled.

REFERENCES

Aplin, R. (1987) 'The assessment of interns for qualified teacher status'. SDES Dissertation, Department of Educational Studies, University of Oxford.

Benton, P. (ed.) (1990) *The Oxford Internship Scheme: Integration and Partnership in Initial Teacher Education*. London: Gulbenkian Foundation.

Berliner, D. C. (1987) 'Ways of thinking about students and classrooms by more and less experienced teachers', in Calderhead, J. (ed.) *Exploring Teachers' Thinking*. London: Cassell.

Bernstein, B. (1971) 'On the classification and framing of educational knowledge', in Young, M. F. D. (ed.) *Knowledge and Control*. London: Macmillan.

Calderhead, J. (ed.) (1987) *Exploring Teachers' Thinking*. London: Cassell.

Calderhead, J. (1988) 'Learning from introductory school experience'. *Journal of Education for Teaching*, **14**, 75–83.

Calderhead, J. (1989) 'Reflective teaching and teacher education'. *Teaching and Teacher Education*, **5** (1), 43–51.

Clark, C. M. and Peterson, P. L. (1986) 'Teachers' thought processes', in Wittrock, M. C. (ed.) *Handbook of Research on Teaching*, 3rd edn. New York: Macmillan.

Furlong, V. J., Hirst, P. H., Pocklington, K. and Miles, S. (1988) *Initial Teacher Training and the Role of the School*. Milton Keynes: Open University Press.

Hirst, P. H. (1983) 'Educational theory', in Hirst, P. H. (ed.) *Educational Theory and its Foundation Disciplines*. London: Routledge & Kegan Paul.

McIntyre, D. (1988) 'Designing a teacher education curriculum from research and theory on teacher knowledge', in Calderhead, J. (ed.) *Teachers' Professional Learning*. Lewes: Falmer.

McIntyre, D. (1989) 'Professional development through the Oxford Internship Model', paper given at Symposium on Professional Development in Education: Research, Policy and Practice, Centre for Professional Development in Education, The University of New England, Northern Rivers.

Schön, D. (1983) *The Reflective Practitioner*. London: Temple Smith.

Schön, D. (1987) *Educating the Reflective Practitioner*. London: Jossey Bass.

Section III

The Practice of Partnership

Chapter 10

Partnership and Reflective Practice in the Subject Training Group: Some Opportunities and Obstacles

Peter Lucas

INTRODUCTION

> It will take very little effort for them to transform the present levels of informal cooperation and collaboration into a lasting partnership beneficial to schools and colleges alike.
>
> (Proctor, 1984)

Even though he is writing about institutions that are '*committed* to teacher education' (his emphasis) Proctor nevertheless does seem here to be affected by the 'boundless optimism' to which Preen and Collier (1987) have made reference in examining official pronouncements on what can be achieved in initial teacher training. And the Department of Education and Science Circular 24/89, *Initial Teacher Training: Approval of Courses*, gives an impression that it is all straightforward provided that institutions have the will: 'Where possible, institutions should build long-term partnerships with individual schools which will foster collaboration and training opportunities. Arrangements should be reviewed regularly to ensure that the benefits to institutions and schools are maintained' (p. 13). Yet from initiatives that have been made and are continuing to be made it is clear that whatever successes can be claimed, unless the challenging nature of the task of establishing close partnership is accepted and clarified by those involved opportunities are going to be missed.

Unfortunately, this problem of mapping and analysing the demands of partnership is made significantly more difficult because of contending models of teacher desired: the skills-focused 'technician,' whose engine of professional development is seen as external to him or her and who is systematically 'updated'; and the more autonomous individual who gives primacy to self-monitoring 'reflective practice'. Within the context of initiatives such as the National Curriculum and local management of schools, together with low morale among teachers, the latter model represents a more developed form of professionality that seems increasingly vulnerable (Poppleton, 1988). It is appropriate, therefore, to examine the opportunities for and the obstacles to encouraging reflective practice within a developing type of partnership known as a subjecttTtt training group which is being explored in a university PGCE course one of whose explicit goals is to promote that model. But first the contexts need elucidating.

All students on the course in Sheffield University's Division of Education are being prepared for state secondary comprehensive schools. They have an initial two-week experience in a primary school, two block teaching practices in comprehensives, the first in the autumn term (during which they are 'paired' for much but not all of their teaching) and the second in the spring term; pursue separate and combined subject application courses as appropriate; a common-core professional and educational studies programme; and, in the summer term, an intensive short-course option (for example on non-verbal behaviour), and a five-week collaborative inquiry in which small 'research' teams of two to four students work on practical problems in association with staff in one or more schools. There are no formal written examinations: assessment is entirely by practical teaching and course work. The Division's concern to have a 'close working partnership' (DES, 1989, p. 7) with local schools is affirmed in a variety of ways: teachers help to organize and operate teaching practice (for example by sharing responsibility for supervising and grading students); they teach in the areas of subject application and professional and educational studies; become members of working parties and policy bodies; and help to interview and select candidates.

As an explicit goal, the encouragement of reflection as the regular and businesslike investigation of one's own practice may be perceived as a way of approaching 'research-based teacher education' (Rudduck, 1985). Because it is set within a university the course is part of an institution one of whose prime functions traditionally is sceptical, questing inquiry, and no matter what differences there may be between undergraduate and postgraduate courses, 'the chief academic aim of the university', as a university,

> is not to manipulate and mould students for specific vocational slots in the power-structures of professional or any other society but to teach them to think for themselves within the context of a certain expertise so that they can question, criticize and help to shape the power-structures which they join instead of being passive victims of them.
>
> (Perkin, 1969, 245, 246)

Thus, this context requires that initial teacher education tutors should bring to any partnership what Rudduck (1989) calls 'an analytic perspective that is fed by observation in a range of classrooms and sharpened by the evidence of research'. Equally importantly, teachers can contribute what Shulman calls the 'wisdom of practice' (1988). Whatever criticisms can be made of the tidiness of this distinction, it more or less accurately describes the opportunities available (or that ought to be available) to student teachers, whose task therefore is to learn to use what is happily termed the 'knowledge resources' (Huberman and Levinson, 1984) on offer. The question for tutors and teachers then becomes: what might a partnership between a school and a university-based training institution look like which can enable students to do this most effectively?

One response has been the establishment of training groups. Tutors in different subject areas in the Division of Education have set up and run such groups, a common feature being the involvement of the subject tutor(s) and staff from local schools used for teaching practice. The one which has been in existence longest is in history, set up in 1984/5. This embraces the students (fourteen registering for 1989–90) as well as teachers from schools in which they do their teaching practice. Other people are also invited: for example, representatives of advisory services. Five meetings are held each year. The first is an informal social evening when students and teachers can meet and talk at the beginning of the year. The last is normally in July and attended only by the tutor and teachers when the agenda is usually confined to making decisions about the nature and sequence of the individual method assignment programme for the following year. Students themselves are responsible for the content and activities for each of the other three meetings, and offer presentations on issues that are perceived by them as of significance and interest. The second and third meetings are held during an afternoon or evening within the first and second teaching practice periods respectively. The fourth meeting takes place at the end of the five-week 'collaborative inquiry' period and is devoted to the presentation by the student 'research' teams of the results of their work.

For their collaborative inquiry project, history students involve schools in the training group (although schools that are not members may additionally be used). Teachers from training-group schools are invited to attend method sessions, not necessarily to organize and run them (solely or jointly with the tutor), but to be present in three capacities: as a resource whose knowledge, skill and experience can be tapped as and when needed by students, as observers from the teaching community into which the students are to be placed (and therefore informal monitors of the course), and as participants learning alongside the students and tutor. Moreover, teachers from the training group schools are used whenever possible in the interviewing process.

This particular type of partnership is not being pushed as a 'solution'. For one thing, increasing uncertainty (up to the last minute) attached to teachers' attending meetings because of competing calls on their time and the difficulty of getting 'cover' for their classes is a problem. The experience of the group is being drawn on to explore some of the demands 'partnership' makes.

Because student teachers need to learn to use the 'knowledge resources' of each co-operating site, we can follow Huberman and Levinson (1984) and examine a partnership from the viewpoints of both knowledge transfer and linking theory and inter-organizational theory. For example:

Does knowledge (in the form of products or of processes) 'flow' from one partner to another? In which direction does it flow most strongly?

Who are the significant persons in this 'flow'? Who are the sources, the recipients, the blockages? Who takes the crucial role in the partnership's 'transactions'?

Does the 'flow' reshape courses?

Is it orderly, uninterrupted, and channelled, or is it irregular, intermittent, and meandering?

What sorts of 'knowledge resources' are mutually transferred?

Is knowledge narrowly channelled into the goal of improving performance, or does it also irrigate discussion of such issues as the worth of choices or the intra- and inter-institutional and external influences on performance?

Do the partners have a deal, or – because teachers are not legally obliged to help train student teachers – what is more aptly described as a 'psychological contract' (Handy and

Aitken, 1988)? What does each partner gain from it? Are the gains hard to detect and puzzling, or solid and clear?

How far are negotiations to set up the contract 'taken for granted' rather than painfully and slowly worked out in detail? What 'inter-organizational arrangements' are created for putting the partnership into practice?

Do these alter in any way the interconnections between the 'power' of one partner and the 'dependency' of the other?

What are the consequences for the partnership structure itself of any 'exchanges' that take place? (How does it prosper? Does it become more or less 'visible'? Does it become deeper-rooted? Does it become fashionable?).

How vigorously do the partners take it upon themselves to nurture their interactions?

Is the partnership able to rely on sufficient means (or 'clout') for its maintenance and development to be guaranteed?

What links have previously existed that now aid or could aid the partnership?

Is the enterprise 'orphaned' (i.e. is its intrinsic interest and significance 'symbolic' rather than 'real' for each partner?

Such questions (and they are not exhaustive) must, I believe, be among those faced by the designers and executants of any partnership structure. I propose to select (and employ) three that seem particularly important:

1   Who are the key persons in the partnership? Who takes the crucial role in the partnership's 'transactions'?
2   What does each partner gain from the 'psychological contract'?
3   How vigorously do the partners take it upon themselves to nurture their inter-actions?

WHO TAKES THE CRUCIAL ROLE? A RECONCEPTUALIZATION AND SOME IMPLICATIONS

Teachers and tutors may well believe that they are the critical persons in any partnership between school and training institution, but the commonsense view must be that the roles of both are significant and that it is the complementarity of those roles that needs most emphasis, not the differences between them. However, what I want to argue here is that the critical individuals are the students themselves. (I am not saying that teachers should put student teachers before their own pupils.) A student, whose training is the *raison d'être* of a partnership, spends more time in a school than a tutor and more time in a training institution than a teacher, and is therefore likely to be the most important channel of communication between the two. Whatever differences can be identified between 'expert' teachers and student teachers, the latter have opportunities not generally enjoyed by teachers to (i) capitalize on the latest knowledge and interpretations in their own subject specialism which they bring to initial training courses; (ii) seek out and pass on new knowledge from educational research, in such areas for example as pupil learning; and (iii) examine, use and analyse the effectiveness of resources (such as fresh textbooks and computer programmes).

Students can thus tap what have been identified as important sources for settling and extending teaching's 'knowledge base' (Shulman, 1988). Moreover – and this has a direct bearing on another such source, the 'wisdom of practice' – the students can model, albeit with varying degrees of success, appropriate reflective behaviours for an audience of pupils, teachers and tutors. True, this is not a role exclusive to student teachers. Co-operating teachers may themselves model reflective practice, but even where this is so they do not normally commit themselves to what should be the rigorous analytical demands of writing down their reflections and having this writing responded to by tutors and/or peers. And whilst student teachers may be critical of 'make work' and tasks whose relevance is perceived by them as doubtful, a method-assignment programme can be seen as worthwhile (Lucas, 1988b). Moreover, the importance to teachers wishing to reflect systematically of 'reading and writing the texts of their lives in classrooms' has been indicated (Proefriedt, 1988, referring to Miller, 1987). Method tutors and other supervisors may model reflective practice, too, but where this is the case, it is likely normally to be only in relation to their dealings with their students and not with children in schools. Finally, part of the role of a student teacher who is to be university certificated is to represent the university, to substantiate the 'chief academic aim' that students should 'think for themselves'.

It has been observed that 'most research on beginning teachers has been focused on their problems' (Veenman, 1987). With good reason, of course; but it is appropriate to look at the bright side, to examine the student-as-giver, especially as the theory that doing the job unavoidably 'washes out' the positive effects on attitude of initial teacher training is not without its questioners (Veenman, 1987, referring to Zeichner and Tabachnick, 1985): 'a loss of idealism is not an inevitable result of induction into teaching and . . . the efforts of formal teacher preparation programmes are not necessarily in vain' (Zeichner and Tabachnick, 1985, 19). The major implication of the thrust of my argument for any partnership arrangement is that it must include features that reinforce student teachers in their role as critical individuals.

WHAT DO THE PARTNERS GET OUT OF THE 'PSYCHOLOGICAL CONTRACT'?

What tutors get from the closer links made seems straightforward: the course is likely to appear more practical and more relevant in the eyes of students. And accreditation is more likely. It may also be easier to reduce students' vulnerability. This was made particularly clear in 1985. 'I have had so few encouraging comments that I can't actually remember any examples', one non-history student wrote in response to a questionnaire distributed within the Division of Education in the summer term. A history student, on the other hand, recorded a contrasting experience: 'The discouraging comments had little effect upon me, because they were far outweighed by the encouragement of [tutor] and the Training Group teachers' (Lucas, 1988a). This was during the period of the teachers' industrial action, but the need for such 'protection' seems no less strong today. However, given that teachers' goodwill is crucial, it is the question of what partnership might offer them that is chiefly being addressed here. Benefits to schools from association with the history method group have been identified by teachers (Davies, 1987; Lucas and Wilshaw, 1986; Roe, 1983), but what it is important to emphasize here is the need to investigate the extent to which, and in what ways, teachers profit from the 'analytic perspective . . . sharpened by the evidence of research'. This can only be touched upon. Within the training group an attempt is made to focus this perspective through assignments which seek to encourage collaboration between students and teachers.

An example of a recent team research project was one in which students tackled the issue of the accessibility of materials in all-ability classrooms. Two of the students early in the PGCE year had come to perceive this as an area of especial interest to them and one which had general significance. Aided by a workshop they attended at their first teaching-practice school, they subsequently did a presentation on the problem to the autumn meeting of the training group. They followed this up by selecting the problem for their collaborative inquiry, and for this were joined by a third student. Together, the students drew up detailed criteria for the production of materials, critiqued resources (both published and teacher-made) used in the school where two had done their first TP, produced what they saw as a model resource on the topic using the division's computer facilities, had that model resource in its turn critiqued by staff from several schools and their tutor, and also tested it out in class. Staff in the principal department concerned subsequently told the tutor how useful it had been to be involved in the inquiry: it wasn't just that the students' research had 'highlighted strengths and weaknesses of our resources. . . . When someone comes in like that you feel you really must do something . . . can't really justify carrying on with them year after year' (tutor's notes). In a previous year, another department then in the training group invited five students (in teams of two and three) to investigate selected departmental resources, critique, and improve/replace them. The head of department reported that although the staff 'had long . . . recognized' that the materials needed evaluating, it was not just that they 'had never found the time to carry it out', they had not 'been confident that [they] could perform the task with sufficient objectivity for the whole exercise to be worthwhile'. Critical probes have also been made by students into processes and attitudes. For example, a student 'research' team was invited by one school to examine teachers' use of small-group work. In activities such as these the role of the student teachers is dramatically inverted: they are no longer essentially vulnerable novices, mere 'apprentices', but 'significant others' – what Zeichner and Liston (1987) have termed 'user-developers of curriculum' – whose views merit attention and respect. At the same time, staff in host departments have to demonstrate courage, openness and a commitment to reflective practice in their dealings with their future fellow professionals. The students' report on the small-group work, with their recommendations, was 'of great value to the school, and is at present being widely circulated', wrote the senior co-operating teacher. Among the factors he attributed to the successful operation of the enterprise was 'a good relationship between school and students. The History Training Group, successful teaching practices and other pre-existing links ensured that this was the case'. His report went on to note that 'care must be exercised in involving teachers who are not familiar with the Training Group' (Lucas, 1988c). Staff in this inquiry took advantage of the opportunity provided by the training institution of 'an arena where people can take risks with ideas and where worthwhile failure is better than never trying anything different' (Ruddock, 1989). In this connection it is worth noting that the (voluntary) training group is not an inspectorial body with powers over the jobs of teachers.

In contrast to the team project, the value to teachers of the students' individual method assignments seems much less. This is unfortunate but not inevitable. The individual assignments – requiring the self-evaluation of teaching strategies used during teaching practice (Lucas, 1988b) – are designed partly to provide structured opportunities for discussion between students and class teachers. It may be that where teachers have been involved in making decisions about the method assignments their involvement in the classroom is likely to be greater. One snag is that not all schools are necessarily represented at that meeting. A more crucial point seems to be that some procedure is required to guarantee a particular teacher's availability for discussion in school with a student at appropriate points during teaching practice when action is being taken by the student and evidence being gathered. Are schools willing to 'protect' co-operating teachers' free periods for this purpose? Of course, it is not just a matter of securing time for discussion; how the discussion is to be structured is likely to prove crucial if the 'wisdom of practice' and the 'analytic perspective' are to be fused. What kind of framework might promote such fusion in this case? It has been suggested that 'rarely have schools ... been able to develop good strategies for understanding what and how teachers are learning from practice, and what they need to know in order to improve their practice' (Rudduck, 1989, 24). Two lines may be worth pursuing. One is to draw on the criteria used in the method course for assessing the quality of history students' reflective analysis:

> (i) the range and quality of the questions raised and/or used in the course of the writing (learners must question!); (ii) the nature, quality, and range of evidence drawn upon (statements must be grounded in evidence); (iii) the extent to which the analysis is balanced (i.e. the self-flagellation/complacency issue: the recognition of strengths as well as weaknesses); (iv) the quality of commitment to reflection (i.e. there must be some demonstrable redrafting of plans/materials rather than simply pointing out what would be done another time; also, there must be a determination to make one's ideas/observations/identified issues accessible by an emphasis on quality of presentation; (v) the extent to which educational literature has been used.

Criteria (i) and (ii) look particularly useful in this connection as a possible agenda for discussion between teachers and students. It would mean teachers accepting a wider role regarding such assignments than that of helping to set them up in school (for example by identifying particular children with whom a student could profitably work on an assignment) and being around for any questions. Would they want and would they be able to get the time to do this?

Potential links between the use of such assessment criteria for teaching-practice-based method assignments and 'clinical' methods of supervision should be clear and the latter might be the second line. Essentially, such methods involve supervisors gathering data about a lesson and then jointly analysing these data with the student teacher. The latter will have previously established an agenda by identifying questions to which answers are sought. A 'clinical' method weights 'power' less on the side of the supervisor, whose experience, knowledge, and skill can in traditional approaches be a block to student learning; the student has a more autonomous role as the supervisor learns to be less authoritarian; and both collaborate with the prospect of getting pleasure, exhilaration, and deeper understanding (Rudduck and Sigsworth, 1985). A 'clinical' type of approach is commonly used by the tutor with his history students, but no systematic attempt has been made to encourage the use of similar methods by co-operating teachers. Uniformity in such matters may be desirable, but the obstacles seem large: teachers generally are used to traditional 'judgemental' approaches (which may be reinforced by external pressures for more categorical grading); they do not usually have the time to spend with students that is required; they can experience difficulty in being reflective when (in the words of a student) they are 'caught up in the mechanics of it all the time'; and being in daily contact with students in school can make it harder for them than for training institution supervisors to remember that students are still beginners. However, the potential for professional development of regular reflection on non-judgemental, descriptive evidence where teachers are supervising students and students are observing teachers looks considerable.

HOW VIGOROUSLY DO THE PARTNERS NURTURE THEIR INTERACTIONS?

Picture this scene: groups of students and teachers had been asked by a collaborative inquiry team: 'What makes a good display?' The groups were then given the opportunity to critique photographs of actual wall displays (mostly in training-group schools). 'If you have this sort of thing at meetings the History Training Group will end up with only two!', the tutor is told informally at the time. This raises the very practical problem of handling analysis within a 'partnership'. Picture another occasion, this time captured on video. A team of three students have devised a computer simulation; a card simulation has also been devised because the team wanted to compare the effectiveness of computer-assisted learning (CAL) and non-CAL approaches. The simulations had been tried out with pupils of two different schools. In the Initial Training Centre there has been an exchange between a team member and a teacher who has raised the issue of pupils' 'physical task' in having to read single-spaced print on the monitor. Someone else joins in . . .

> (Transcript from a video recording of the meeting. ST = student teacher; OM = other members of the History Training Group.)
> OM2:   Which perhaps highlighted one of the points that actual simulations of that kind . . . are perhaps the least economic use of the computer . . . if you are using the computer to analyse statistics which is otherwise difficult . . . that's perhaps a better use of the computer . . . . Whereas if it was something that could be used on cards and the pupils read the information from the printed sheet . . . I would always find that easier than reading something from a screen.
> ST1:   . . . we haven't used a lot of graphics here. . . . I agree . . . it's . . . much more . . . user-friendly reading off cards and the pupils who did work in the large class with the card games . . . felt a lot more relaxed than the computer groups . . . a personal opinion. (Looks to other members of team.)
> ST2:   . . . it was a bit of a false situation because . . . [the pupils were] taken out as a group of six with one of us with a computer. . . . I don't think they felt that at ease anyway . . . difficult . . . to say how they would have reacted perhaps left on . . . their own a bit.
> OM2:   I just have my doubts as to whether a simulation exercise is . . . the best sort of thing for a computer . . . whether it . . . gives any advantage at all to a simulation exercise

OM3: whereas I can certainly see that a computer in terms of statistical analysis provides you with a facility that you simply would not have if you didn't have a computer.

OM3: (To the team) One of the things you were actually looking at was the nature of causation, weren't you?

STs: Yes.

OM3: (To OM2) Now I actually have to disagree with you and say there are far . . . more key pointers to a pupil in terms of the nature and weight of events given through that particular dimension . . . (To the team) you said you had eighteen paths and that's a sort of minimum that you could work towards. You can't facilitate the eighteen paths through a card development, at least I don't feel that you can. I think there are certain degrees of limitation within that not least of which is that like any piece of history whether it's delivered through a micro or whether it's delivered through card it's still your interpretation or the interpretation of other historians. I think the other element that might need drawing in is the flexibility and I think they [the students] just hinted at that, that pupils have choices to weigh those elements themselves which maybe they haven't got in another direction. It's, still, . . . part of the work today has been to just to look at the explorations [of those].

OM2: . . . I wouldn't actually accept that the nature of causation is best explored through a computer simulation as opposed to a classroom simulation and discussion. . . . I think you can do [the work] as effectively and perhaps more effectively through . . . a card simulation and . . . discussion. . . . I think a computer is a kind of optional extra on that. . . .

ST1: I think . . .

ST3: (Not a member of the research team) I think, sorry . . .

ST1: Go on.

ST3: . . . you're like saying the computers are an . . . optional extra . . . in a way for every teaching method you could actually say that about computing . . . most children will actually come across when they get older some form of technology. Quite a lot of them will be working in front of VDUs. It's essential . . . that that actually becomes . . . an integrated part of all teaching.

OM2: Ah well, yeah, I wouldn't disagree with that. I think that's another point.

ST3: But . . . by actually saying 'optional extra' . . . you marginalize it, . . .

OM2: That's not quite what I'm arguing, . . . I think in terms of that very specific example what I'm saying is maybe it's not such a good example in my opinion. Obviously [OM3] disagrees . . . with that. I wasn't arguing that . . . the use of a computer within a classroom is an, well it is an optional extra in some schools because they don't have the actual access to a computer in the way in which you would have here. I don't think in terms of information technology it's an optional extra, no, but what I think I'm saying is 'be very careful in terms of what you're using the computer for. Make sure it's purposeful.'

OM4: . . . in causation . . . it is better than using cards because you set me a load of cards and I'll cheat. I'll look through 'em all. I'll find them. . . . Mechanically you've got to go through this [the computer programme]. . . . You wouldn't do that with cards and in that sense it does exactly what the cards do only better because it forces you into a situation where you can't cheat.

ST4: And another thing about it is . . . this . . . [the computer] takes all the weight off the teacher's shoulders . . . teacher doesn't have to do a thing about administering cards or distributing cards or making sure they're in the right order . . .

OM2: . . . I accept that. . . .

ST4: . . . you can [then] . . . sort out the other problems [as they come?] through like who are the people mentioning . . . choices . . .

Specifically, in the above episode a way of working is challenged: economic and reading-ease arguments are introduced and counter-arguments include the facilitating of handling alternatives and flexibility for pupils to make judgements, the effective enforcement of appropriate behaviour, and an easier logistical burden for the teacher with the pedagogical gains resulting from it. One contributor reacts to the use of particular words and their perceived wider implications. More generally, students are submitting some of their work to public scrutiny. The work itself is the result of care and reflection, a series of purposeful steps during which they examined the results in a businesslike way. In the discussion, limiting factors are identified. In carrying a 'private discourse' (their own joint reflections during the inquiry and during the preparation of their written report) 'into discussion and debate with others', the students are – it seems reasonable to conclude – contributing to the construction of 'a critical community of enquirers' (Carr and Kemmis, 1986, 39–40).

Some other points are worth raising about such interactions. For a community, a partnership, properly to be 'critical', all the members must be committed to criticism. 'Why didn't they [the teachers] say anything?', students can ask (and on occasion have done so) in amazement when commenting subsequently on a presentation. Teachers themselves can (and do) express concern about those students who are not doing a presentation and who stay quiet. All participants have to be aware of their responsibility here. However, some measures are necessary to create a setting in which each person feels able to contribute. The 'power' problem is only partially met by the fact that students determine the content and activities. Recent students in written comments have suggested that there should be 'more student control over format e.g. introduce the meeting' (traditionally done by the tutor), and that teachers should 'present something as well' (which seems appropriate).

Perceived inequality of power is not the only issue. To what extent do partners know each other? This consideration underlines the importance of students' valid observations about the need for ice-breaking exercises. However, problems can arise when individuals know each other: there may be points to win, scores to settle, old battles to be refought. Students feel liberated when they hear and see teachers arguing, for they realize that there is no official line to which they must stick; at the same time, 'debate' can be perceived as of less value than 'discussion'. It is common for teachers to discuss with pupils rules of behaviour for discussion: open and systematic reflection on the very processes in which they are engaged must be important for the members of any partnership.

A final observation regarding such interactions: although students readily acknowledge the value to them (in spite of some anxiety!) of having to present and examine their views in public, they have not taken (and it cannot realistically be expected that they would take) the initiative to put themselves in such a situation. If it is a requirement – and in the summer term the presentations are part of the assessment – there is clearly a contradiction between this and the encouragement of reflective practice as an autonomous pursuit. Will the participation of teachers in joint presentations with students lessen this contradiction?

CONCLUSION

In this chapter an attempt has been made to tackle some significant issues related to the establishment of closer links between training institutions and schools and the idea of reflective practice, drawing on one developing type of 'partnership'. Obviously, many questions remain unanswered. Nevertheless, the opportunities in partnership are apparent, though to grasp them fully the difficulties ought not to be underestimated.

ACKNOWLEDGEMENTS

The author would like to acknowledge the co-operation of members of the History Training Group in the gathering of data for this chapter.

REFERENCES

Carr, W. and Kemmis, S. (1986) *Becoming Critical: Education, Knowledge and Action Research* Lewes: Falmer/Deakin University Press.

Davies, R. (1987) 'Teacher training and the history department', *Teaching History*, **47**, 23–5.

DES: Department of Education and Science (1989) *Initial Teacher Training: Approval of Courses* (Circular 24/89). London: DES.

Handy, C. and Aitken, T. (1988) *Understanding Schools as Organisations*. London: Penguin.

Huberman, A. M. and Levinson, N. (1984) 'An empirical model for exchanging educational knowledge between universities and schools'. *International Review of Education*, **30**, 385–404.

Lucas, P. and Wilshaw, D. (1986) 'Promoting partnership in initial and in-service training: a school-based simulation interviews programme'. *Cambridge Journal of Education*, **16** (1), 24–8.

Lucas, P. (1988a) 'Teaching practice placements, laying the foundations for a reflective training community'. *British Journal of In-Service Education*, **14** (2), 92–9.

Lucas, P. (1988b) 'Approaching research-based teacher education: questions for a reflective method assignment programme in initial training'. *Cambridge Journal of Education*, **18** (3), 405–20.

Lucas, P. (1988c) 'An approach to research-based teacher education through collaborative inquiry'. *Journal of Education for Teaching*, **14** (1), 55–73.

Miller, J. (1987) 'Teachers' emerging texts: the empowering potential of writing in-service', in Smyth, J. (ed.) *Educating Teachers: Changing the Nature of Pedagogical Knowledge*. Lewes: Falmer.

Perkin, H. (1969) *Key Profession: the History of the Association of University Teachers*. London: Routledge & Kegan Paul.

Poppleton, P. (1988) 'Teacher professional satisfaction: its implications for secondary education and teacher education'. *Cambridge Journal of Education*, **18** (1), 5–16.

Preen, D. and Collier, G. (1987) 'Beyond CATE: a future for the PGCE'. *Higher Education Quarterly*, **41** (2), 184–91.

Proctor, N. (1984) 'Towards a partnership with schools'. *Journal of Education for Teaching*, **10** (3), 219–32.

Proefriedt, W. (1988) 'Some thoughts about teaching and writing'. *Teachers College Record*, **90** (2), 281–91.

Roe, J. (1983) 'One school's challenge to a student: a residential field course'. *Teaching History*, **36** (June), 38.

Rudduck, J. (1985) 'Teacher research and research-based teacher education'. *Journal of Education for Teaching*, **11** (3), 281–9.

Rudduck, J. (1986) 'Ingredients of a good partnership'. *Times Educational Supplement*, **3655** (18 July), 20.

Rudduck, J. (1989) 'Teacher development and university–school system relations'. Unpublished paper for OISE Conference on Teacher Development: Policies, Practices and Research.

Rudduck, J. and Sigsworth, A. (1985) 'Partnership supervision (or Goldhammer revisited)', in Hopkins, D. and Reid, K. (eds) *Rethinking Teacher Education*. London: Croom Helm.

Shulman, L. S. (1988) 'Knowledge and teaching: foundations of the new reform'. *Harvard Educational Review*, **57** (1), 1–22.

Veenman, S. A. M. (1987) 'Problems as perceived by new teachers', in Hastings, N. and Schwieso, J. (eds) *New Directions in Educational Psychology: 2. Behaviour and Motivation in the Classroom*. Lewes: Falmer.

Zeichner, K. M. and Tabachnick, B. R. (1985) 'The development of teacher perspectives: social strategies and institutional control in the socialization of beginning teachers'. *Journal of Education for Teaching*, **11**, 1–25.

Zeichner, K. M. and Liston, D. P. (1987) 'Training student teachers to be reflective'. *Harvard Educational Review*, **57**, 23–48.

Chapter 11

A Training Course for School Supervisors: Two Perspectives

Martin Booth and Nicolas Kinloch

RUNNING A COURSE FOR SUPERVISORS

The current key words in teacher training are 'partnership' and 'school-based training'. From the early 1980s they have featured strongly in publications from Her Majesty's Inspectorate (HMI) and the Department of Education and Science (DES); they are stressed in the Council for the Accreditation of Teacher Education's (CATE) criteria for initial training. Many courses of initial training are being modified so as to give students far more contact with teachers and schools. In some cases, the student no longer undertakes a block teaching practice but spends regular periods of time in school throughout the year. Teachers are serving on advisory committees which oversee initial training courses; they come into the training institution to take seminars or give lectures. And lecturers are now required to spend time in schools regaining 'recent and relevant' experience of the classroom.

Schools therefore are playing an increasingly important part in initial teacher training; student teachers now have frequent and often sustained contact with serving teachers. Such enhancement of the role of the school has been actively encouraged by HMIs and the DES. They see the Postgraduate Certificate in Education course (PGCE) which is focused on the practicalities of teaching and where the students spend a large proportion of their time in school as the most effective way of improving the quality of the training; indeed the DES has introduced the idea of the Articled Student and the Licensed Teacher where trainees will spend most of their time in schools and be paid a modest bursary or salary.

The response to these initiatives, however, has largely been made by the training institutions; it is they who are suggesting the ways in which the licensed teacher or the articled student schemes might work and are redesigning their PGCE courses to increase student contact with schools and teachers. They are understandably anxious to retain a major control of the initial training of teachers. Yet the notion of partnership implies a shared responsibility and a shared professional ownership of teacher training; it also involves a clear understanding and delineation of the roles schools and training institutions must play in the training process.. Such evidence as is available suggests there are few institutions which are prepared at this stage to undergo a radical rethinking of their position and surrender some of their control; and research reported in this volume (Chapter 8) shows that many teachers are far from clear as to the role they should now be playing in initial teacher training and that they do not possess the knowledge and skills necessary to undertake the complex business of training and supervising student teachers in schools.

It was the issue of the teacher as trainee supervisor which was addressed by a group in the University of Cambridge Department of Education in 1987. The Cambridge secondary PGCE course adopts a traditional pattern in that there is a full term's block of teaching practice sandwiched between two terms which are largely department-based; students have a long period of time, therefore, when teachers in the schools have a major responsibility for their professional development. Increasingly, however, in the first and third terms students are spending regular time in schools observing, teaching and undertaking small-scale investigations of topics such as pastoral care or grouping policies. How could we enable our teacher supervisors to play a full and effective role in this training process and acquire a real sense of professional ownership for part of the course? With funding from the University Grants Committee (as it was then) an inservice training course for fifteen secondary history teachers was mounted during the academic year 1987/8; its success has led to the extension of the training of secondary geography and English teachers in 1988/9 and secondary mathematics and science teachers in 1989/90.

In 1987/8 the course consisted of twenty-two half days spread over the academic year with the weight of the course in the middle; the funding provided for supply cover, travelling expenses as well as the cost of a part-time course director. In 1988/9 full-day sessions were planned, as it was considered easier for schools to arrange cover. Originally ten days were scheduled but difficulties of release meant that this had to be reduced to seven. Most of the supply cover this year was met by the local authorities. The 1989/90 course has reverted again to half days with an introductory residential weekend (Friday to Sunday) in the first term. Supply cover for all teachers is being met by the local authorities concerned.

The underlying aim of the courses is simple: they are designed to enable the teacher supervisor to take full responsibility for the professional development of the student during the teaching-practice term. The concept of 'professional development' in this context, however, is not as straightforward as it sounds; the group responsible for the course found Schön's (1983) notion of 'reflection-in-action' helpful. The concept offered a way of marrying the theoretical underpinning of teaching with the practical realities of the classroom, of helping the supervisor to move beyond the immediate considerations of a particular class, a particular lesson to the pedagogical principles both general and subject-specific which should underpin teaching and be generalizable to other situations. The supervisor therefore acts as a mediator between theory and practice; he or she has to set up a dialectic for the student which will result in productive reflection and lead to the refinement of skills, the modification or enlargement of existing knowledge and the creation of a personal model of teaching which will have general application. The role of the supervisor therefore is complex and demanding. It goes far beyond current practice; it demands the teasing out and articulation of rationales and procedures which underwrite the teaching activity.

The first stage of the course is spent in exploring and discussing the underlying philosophies behind particular approaches. Department tutors talk about elements of the PGCE course and the links between the 'methods of subject teaching' course and the more general pedagogical components; the teachers discuss amongst themselves the aims and objectives of their subject departments ('the best lesson I have taught'; 'the best piece of equipment I have'; 'a justification of my subject to the school governors') and then make a presentation to the rest of the group.

The second stage involves the hammering out of the principles and practice of supervision – an activity shared by training institution tutors and teachers, thus stressing the notion of joint ownership of training. In the first instance this demands addressing the question: what should be the agenda for discussion with a student during supervision? The historians in 1987/8 felt that there were two interdependent areas. First and most important there was the issue of teaching the subject-specific skills such as working with historical sources (documents, pictures, artefacts and so on) and using them as evidence or developing an understanding of key methodological concepts such as cause and consequence or change and continuity. But secondly there are the general teaching skills of classroom organization and management – creating, maintaining and restoring order, the use of language, lesson introductions, group work, teaching for a range of abilities and so on. The historians felt that supervision should take a subject-specific item as the focus for supervision discussion – though inevitably one or more of the more general items would be addressed as well.

The historians therefore could articulate the essential nature of history teaching; the English teachers on the other hand seemed unwilling to talk about a subject-specific agenda with skills and concepts particular to English. Their concerns were with the general skills of communication and language and the ways in which these are intimately bound up with matters of classroom organization. In contrast the geographers, like the historians, had a clear list of subject-specific items which they felt had to be addressed. The mathematicians and scientists (only half-way through their course at the time of writing) have focused on content and have begun to address the specific skills and concepts with which a particular topic will be concerned.

In the third stage of the course, discussion moves from agendas for supervision to the issue of its conduct. The first and most important principle that teachers and tutors have laid down is that supervisions should be regular (at least once a week) and should be formal in that a specific period of time should be put aside for them and that there should be an agenda for the discussion. Supervisors' comments must be backed by evidence and the tenor of the supervision should be positive and supportive. But what should be the style of supervision? Two broad approaches have been identified: the clinical and the counselling. Both approaches are remedial in that they aim to improve the student's teaching, but the first is essentially didactic. The supervisor is the clinician who has the 'cure' or recipe which will solve the student's teaching problem. The relationship here is one in which the power is firmly in the hands of the supervisor who is the expert and has the answers. With the counselling approach the supervisor's role is more muted; there is more emphasis on allowing the student to explore and articulate the teaching style, with the supervisor encouraging a detailed analysis of the pedagogy underpinning the lesson. Teachers came to the conclusion that both approaches had validity and that a supervisor might at different times adopt one or other depending on the student and the circumstances.

The next stage is 'mutual observation'. The aim here is to give teachers experience of what it is like to be observed and then have one's teaching analysed in a supervision. All teachers and tutors pair up; one teaches, the other observes and then gives a supervision. The roles are then reversed. With the historians there was initially considerable opposition to this part of the course. The opposition was gently overcome; the reaction to the experience was unanimously favourable. For many teachers, teaching has been a largely private affair conducted behind closed doors. The paired experiment was a symbolic affirmation of the course's commitment to openness, to 'reflection-in-action', as well as allowing the teachers to experience at first hand the reality of being observed and supervised. A number of the historians then conducted a supervision with their student in public; agenda, style and utility were discussed. Videos of supervisions taking place were also observed. The English and geography teachers brought in their students on a course training day. Supervisors and students first met separately to discuss issues of supervision and then came together in mixed-subject groups to pool ideas.

During this stage of the course teachers and tutors also consider the issue of the overall programme for the student: the induction, the opportunities given for observation of other teachers within the subject department or in other departments, team teaching or small-group work and the student's involvement in the broader professional responsibilities of the teacher, for example for tutoring and pastoral care. They consider the profiling of the student's teaching and the criteria against which such performance should be judged.

The historians' course resulted in a package of materials, some of which are given below in their revised version – they were modified in the light of their use in 1988/9. The package opens with a teaching practice contract (the teachers' own phrase):

TEACHING PRACTICE CONTRACT

The purpose of making public a contract between school supervisors, students, the University Department of Education and Local Authority, is to make the PGCE course as coherent as possible for all students. Teaching Practice should build on and develop the pedagogical knowledge and skills which students have begun to acquire in the first term. The contract, therefore, concentrates on the development of the pedagogical knowledge and the procedures and styles most likely to foster its development. Students will be introduced to the contract early in the Michaelmas Term.

General

1   It is agreed that at the heart of pedagogical knowledge is the nature of the subject being taught. A summary is provided in the subject-specific agenda but individual schools may want to add to this (eg in the case of humanities teaching). Issues of management and control should be viewed within the context of teaching and learning history.

Observation and Teaching

2   Student and supervisor should observe each other's lessons. Students should also have the opportunity of team teaching with an experienced teacher.

3   The observer should always be aware of the teaching objectives and have a lesson plan before observing a lesson.

4   Students must keep a teaching practice file, using the pro forma provided. The file must be to hand at school at all times. The file must be kept up to date.

Supervision

5   There should be a regular weekly formal meeting between supervisor and student.

6   Discussion should normally focus on one aspect of the subject-specific agenda.

7   All comments, whether from supervisor or student, must be supported by clear evidence.

8   All formal meetings should begin and end positively.

9   Wherever possible supervision should be supportive and positive in order to foster a sense of progression and development.

10 Towards the end of each half of the term supervisor and student should meet for a longer period (normally a half-day session) in order to review progress and (in the case of the first of these meetings) to plan ahead. Forms are provided in order to set an agenda and to record the main points of these discussions.

It then moves on to give the agenda for supervision, a teaching practice file lesson plan pro forma, a form for the evaluation by the student of school-experience visits during the first term of the PGCE course, questionnaires to be filled in by both student and school supervisor for the exchange of information, guidance on dealing with subject-specific teaching problems (for example, difficulties in teaching source-based lessons), and finally an agenda for discussion between supervisor and student halfway through the term and an end-of-term profile form. An excerpt from the subject-specific agenda follows.

AGENDA FOR DISCUSSION BETWEEN STUDENT AND SUPERVISOR HALF WAY THROUGH TERM

This agenda is intended as a guide for discussion over a half-day or two or three sessions. Each item should be discussed, with the emphasis on reviewing progress and setting targets for the second half of term. An agreed statement should be entered at the time under each item. Disagreements should be indicated.

1   Working with sources

Consider the following points:

(a)   What sources have you used?

(b)   How have you used them?

(c)   What has been your *most* successful source-based lesson and why?

(d)   What has been your *least* successful source-based lesson and why?

(e)   Supervisor's comments.

(f)   Target for next half term.

Other topics included were: developing empathetic understanding, developing under-standing of concepts, general teaching skills and pastoral care and extra-curricular activities. These topics were then used as the basis for the end-of-term profile. Similar, though less ambitious, materials were produced by the English and geography teachers in 1989.

The courses were therefore concerned with philosophical underpinnings, the relation of theory and practice and the opening up of teaching to detailed scrutiny and analysis. They were above all a means of empowering teachers to take a full and effective part in the process of initial training. The reaction of all teachers on both courses was in the main extremely favourable. They felt they had reflected on their own practice with a seriousness and depth they had not before undertaken and that they had been given a far clearer idea about the role and purpose of the supervisor. They expressed this in terms of being 'more purposeful', more 'methodical' and 'thorough' and 'more formal and structured' in the conduct of supervisions. This was contrasted with the previous attitude of 'just keeping an eye on the student'. These comments and the production of teaching practice materials underline the key achievement of the courses: the creation of a genuine sense of partnership between the teachers and tutors. In the second half of this chapter, a history teacher who attended the 1987/8 course and has been supervising students for a number of years reflects on his particular experience of the course.

A TEACHER SUPERVISOR'S VIEW

In 1985, shortly after being appointed head of the history department of a large city comprehensive for children aged 11–18, I became a history teacher supervisor for the Cambridge University Department of Education. I knew that it would be my task to supervise PGCE students during teaching practice, but beyond this I had little idea of what the job involved. In this, I imagine, I was similar to other teachers used by the department. It was probably true even of those who had held the position for years. A certain anarchy seemed the prevailing philosophy. It was taken for granted that teacher supervisors, most of them, like myself, heads of department, would know how to train students. We had ourselves, after all, passed at one stage or another through the ordeal of teaching practice.

The reality was different. After two years I had evolved a rough and ready method of supervision. It lacked much coherence. It was almost exclusively centred on classroom management. I was somehow under the impression that provided a student's physical survival in the classroom could be guaranteed then the major objective of the practice had been achieved. Of course there was something to this. There is little point in producing an excellent lesson if poor classroom management does not permit it to succeed in its purpose. But I allowed the student's natural concern with this aspect of teaching practice to influence my own judgement unduly. I began to forget the simple rule that management is only a means to an end.

In 1987/8 the Cambridge course for teacher supervisors started to change much of this approach. The first two sessions of the course (each of a day) involved four teacher supervisors only – those who were responsible for looking after groups of history students who spent one day a week in schools during the first term of the course. Here the students both observed and taught lessons; on the following day they were able to discuss these with the teacher supervisor. In these initial two sessions the four of us had an opportunity to discuss the programme we were giving our students and the relationship of this to the rest of the Postgraduate Certificate in Education course. The students seemed both aware and appreciative of the closer co-operation between department and supervisors. They seemed less frustrated than students commonly do with theory. There was less indication than hitherto that students felt that what they heard in the lecture hall was irrelevant and that all they really needed were a few classroom tips. The observation and initial practice that they undertook were perceived to be purposeful and closely related to the methods of teaching history work they were engaged on in the Department of Education. The obviously closer relationship between the schools and the department was a source of confidence.

In the sessions which followed we were joined by a further eleven history supervisors. Each one of us would be responsible for a history student during his or her block teaching practice during the Spring term. For the original four it was the opportunity to pass on their experience and conclusions to the others. For many of the new supervisors it was a rare opportunity to meet with fellow heads of department: the joys of *glasnost* are by no means confined to the Soviet Union. For these supervisors the debate that had produced the course was new. Not all of them were instantly converted. There remained a few – by no means the oldest of them – who persisted in their belief that tips for teachers on classroom management alone held the key to a successful teaching practice. But even these were converted during the training. The initial part of this phase of the course was the establishment of precise objectives for the teaching practice of the second term. This meant that much time was spent in discussion. A consensus was eventually reached: there would be a heavy emphasis on encouraging students to develop particular skills in the pupils they were teaching. Of course there was still a place for assisting students with the basics of classroom management, but this was now to be put in a wider and more appropriate context. The whole emphasis of the supervision would reflect more accurately the 'revolution' that had overtaken history teaching since the mid-1960s, with its emphasis on the development of historical skills and concepts.

Accordingly a detailed list was compiled which covered those skills which it was thought that students needed to have some experience in teaching. These included source-based learning; the establishment of key concepts such as change, causation, similarity and difference; and more general principles of classroom organization such as group work, motivation and management. For teacher tutors such as myself this list was to become an extremely valuable asset.

A novel but important element in the course was the drawing up of a contract which would be agreed at the beginning of a teaching practice between the student and his or her supervisor (see pp. 146–7). It would, for example, be agreed that a regular meeting should take place between them; that every such meeting would end as constructively as possible; and that comment and criticism would be supported with evidence. For their part students would make and keep detailed lesson plans. This contrast was a useful device quite apart from its practical function. It symbolized the increased professionalism which was a function of the initiative.

We then went on to consider the question of the supervision of a student. What did the student feel like when being observed? How was the observation itself to be conducted? And what style of supervision would then be adopted in the debriefing session? There was some perturbation at the demand that we pair off and visit one another's schools in order to observe and be observed. This dismay was natural: for many of the supervisors it was almost the first time that they had ever been observed by their peers. It was, however, an instructive insight into the fear experienced by most students on teaching practice. It was moreover the first step in the process of compelling teacher supervisors to undergo the necessary re-evaluation of their experience and expertise.

There was another aspect of the earlier pattern of supervision which virtually everyone involved agreed needed to be changed. This was the element of assessment of teaching practice. Hitherto this had been done in the form of two brief reports. This brevity was in some respect an advantage for supervisors who often enough had little time to spend on the preparation of lengthy reports. But it meant that they were often vague to the point of incomprehensibility. We wanted something which reflected the new direction of the course. We were trying to establish a partnership between the department and the individual school, and between the school and the student. Thus the reports would be replaced with a profile, to be negotiated between student and supervisor. This was a major step. We knew that it would create a certain amount of havoc within the department. Administrators like short reports. They look less favourably on lengthy profiles, useful as these might be in terms of giving students the opportunity to comment on almost every aspect of their teaching practice. Perhaps we were too careless of this administrative burden. We were also, perhaps, too optimistic: it was neither possible nor ultimately desirable to remove the element of judgement from the profile. In the end we would still have to recommend to the examiners that they 'pass' or 'fail' the student. None the less the attempt to involve the student in this aspect of the practice underlined the whole philosophy of partnership.

But all of this would have been ineffective but for an element which permeated the course: the very much closer liaison formed with the university department. This was of course implicit in the direction given by the department to the whole course: but the links were closer than that. For the first time the department gave a clear indication of the content of its course; it was now possible for supervisors to gain some knowledge of the theoretical component of the students' training and thus to link it more closely to their classroom experience. This was now real partnership. Perhaps the greatest benefit of the course to the supervisors, as they prepared to receive their teaching-practice student, was the knowledge they now possessed of precisely what the student had or had not experienced. Too often in the past they had had to do without any indication of a student's actual knowledge or understanding. Now they were more easily able to devise an appropriate course of training during the practice.

For my own part, I looked forward with anticipation to my own teaching-practice supervision. Like my fellow supervisors, I felt that I had a better chance than before of doing a good job. But since, unlike most of them, I had been closely involved in the setting-up of the course, I would be unable to deny a considerable amount of responsibility should the supervision prove to be no more successful than in previous years. Anticipation was mixed with trepidation.

I need not have worried unduly. The student in question was, in any case, a very effective classroom teacher. I soon found that the framework of the practice could build effectively on the work that had been done in the first term and allow the student time for 'reflection-in-action'. It would have been pointless, for example, to suggest to the student that he undertake a piece of source-based work had I not already known just what he already knew and had experienced of this aspect of teaching. As the practice continued there was a clear feeling of both development and progression of which both student and I were aware. We could endeavour to fill in the inevitable gaps which had resulted from the first term's experience. Best of all, on occasion, we were able to use the theoretical knowledge obtained by the student in the lecture hall. Thus we could outgrow the common notion of teaching as a series of practical classroom tips. There can probably be no really good teaching without a theoretical basis: we began to see the truth of this.

As our contract provided, we met on a regular weekly basis. It is true that this ought to have happened anyway but as research has demonstrated, it happens much less often than is commonly supposed. During these sessions we were able to reflect on the experience of the previous week and to prepare for the next one. While I was critical I was, I hope, positive; and I tried never to end a meeting without some attempt at providing a constructive solution to the problems that had been raised.

At the end of the practice we worked our way through the profile. This was a larger undertaking than I think its authors (of whom I was one) had anticipated. It took a whole morning. Supply cover was paid for by the LEA, an advantage for a pilot course unlikely to be repeated in the new age of austerity and school financial self-management. Seen in retrospect much of the profile was too detailed. Even so, the student welcomed the opportunity to comment on all he had seen and tried. It is worth pointing out that in future many PGCE students will come from schools which have put in place records of achievement. Such students will be familiar with the idea of self-assessment and will believe, correctly, that negotiation with their tutors and supervisors is a right and not a privilege. Although the profile that we had designed needed substantial revision, it was surely a positive advance. The student, incidentally, was deemed to have completed his teaching practice satisfactorily.

The initiative, in my view, was highly successful in demonstrating that partnership between training institutions, schools and students is essential rather than merely desirable. It gave coherence to an otherwise fragmented course. It removed the basis for the oft-expressed student belief that 'theory is useless'. It enabled educationists and teachers to meet and exchange views, and to collaborate closely on a venture which is supposedly shared but had very rarely been joint. It enabled teachers to meet; to discuss their ways of working and to question them. Some even found that they had not always done everything so perfectly as they had perhaps supposed. The greatest beneficiary of all this interaction was the student.

The initiative did, of course, raise an important final question. When it ended, a large majority of those who had participated in it believed that partnership must be the way forward. They looked forward, in subsequent years, to refining the process and deepening the relationships that had been established. It was an irony that it was during the development of the initiative that the very ideas about teacher training which it sought to replace should have been given government sanction. The idea of the licensed teacher, trained on the job by old sweats, was seen by the Secretary of State as an adequate response to criticisms of the existing systems of training. Far from encouraging the exciting possibilities that the initiative had opened up, the Secretary of State sought to minimize the role of the training institutions and of the presumably irrelevant theories they espoused and taught. It is not surprising that many of those involved in the Cambridge initiative have found it impossible to agree with him.

REFERENCES

DES: Department of Education and Science (1984) *Initial Teacher Training: Approval of Courses* (Circular 3/84). London: DES.
DES: Department of Education and Science (1989) *Initial Teacher Training: Approval of Courses* (Circular 24/89). London: DES.
Schön, D. (1983) *The Reflective Practitioner*. New York: Basic Books.

Chapter 12

Practical School Experiences: Who Teaches the Student Teacher?

Colin Terrell

This chapter gives a brief account of a series of linked stages of an action research project which attempted to improve the quality of supervision offered to students on teaching practice[1] within a four-year BEd Initial Teacher Training (ITT) programme for intending primary school teachers. Initially the project focused on improving the ways in which college tutors might help students on teaching practice. As the work progressed, however, it became clear that students placed a higher value on advice from co-operating class teachers than from the college tutors. This was mainly because advice from a co-operating class teacher was usually given with the benefit of intimate knowledge of the ecology of the particular classroom in which the student was placed. Co-operating class teachers, however, were often wary of giving advice because they felt they may be interfering in an area which was the province of college tutors and they felt untrained in supervision skills. A pilot course of training in supervisory skills for co-operating class teachers was then developed and evaluated. College evaluators, local education authority (LEA) evaluators, students and co-operating teachers perceived this course to be successful. LEA representatives on the evaluative team, however, suggested that the LEA would gain further benefit if, once having been trained in analysing student-led teaching sessions, the co-operating teachers were given further training in how such skills could be used with teacher colleagues as part of in-school staff development programmes. Partnership in ITT was fostered between the college and the LEA when these two elements were incorporated into inservice courses – a partnership in which each side gains equal benefit.

To provide a context, some of the earlier preliminary work is described first. The account then focuses on a description of more recent work during which partnership in ITT between the college and two LEAs developed.

All the stages of the project took place between 1985 and 1989 and each single stage lasted approximately one term (eleven weeks). Ten stages have been completed so far (not all are covered in this chapter) and the project is still ongoing. This account is written chronologically and describes only how the broad thinking of the project team changed over time. More detailed reports of each stage of the project are available elsewhere (see references).

The chapter also discusses a number of possible 'myths' which often seem to underpin the way in which teaching practices are conducted in many ITT programmes. Cornbleth (1987) argues that a myth is 'a widely held belief with tenuous connections to pertinent evidence' (p. 187). The way in which a group – e.g. an ITT course team – plans a programme of studies may rely heavily on myths some of which may be held so strongly they cease to be questioned. At each phase of the project a number of myths of ITT were highlighted.

PRELIMINARY WORK

A description of an action research project should begin with some indication of 'Why was it done – what was the motivation?'

First, there was a significant external pressure to encourage ITT tutors to engage in research. It is Council for National Academic Awards (CNAA) policy that staff associated with ITT programmes should be involved in research. During a twelve-month period prior to the start of this project various ways of meeting this requirement were proposed at faculty meetings but none gained widespread support. As these discussions were taking place, a number of unrelated staffing matters resulted in an unusually large number of new appointments being made to one of the college's ITT programmes. Two primary teachers and three primary head teachers were appointed to teach on the ITT BEd programme, all straight from school. As is normal with almost all new appointments these candidates were selected in April/May on the basis of their teaching ability and remained in schools until July prior to taking up appointments in the college during September. Within three weeks all five were engaged in supervising students on a final teaching practice and this relatively large group (compared to the usual single new appointment) made it clear in the final examination board they had felt, and still did feel, under-prepared to supervise students. Some form of training should have been provided.

At the next faculty board meeting it was suggested that developing and evaluating ways of improving the performance of college tutors might be a useful group research project which might involve the whole ITT team and feed back directly into the main work of the faculty, i.e. training students to teach. This proposal seemed to gain the wholehearted support of the faculty for at least two reasons. The topic was central to, and of interest to, the work of every member of the faculty and the research was to be undertaken by members of faculty staff in practical situations (during teaching practices) using an action research approach, as opposed to appointing an internal or external 'research expert' to do the work.

The main overall aim for the first eighteen months of the project was to try and improve the quality of supervision offered by college tutors to students on teaching practice. There were very few instances in the literature to suggest that training college tutors is a common practice. A report by Her Majesty's Inspectorate (DES, 1987), part of a national survey of ITT programmes of study, found 'a variety of induction practices' offered by colleges to staff taking up appointments on ITT programmes. The report highly commended *one* college which, it suggested, provided training in 'methods of supervising primary teaching practice' (p. 40). Because of the project team's interest in the topic this was followed up, with some difficulty owing to confidentiality in HMI national reports. When contacted, the head of the ITT programme concerned stated that no such training course had ever existed. The explanation offered was that at one of the meetings between HMI and the college staff it had simply been suggested (by a member of the college staff) that some form of training 'might be a good idea'. This may be how one of Cornbleth's (1987) myths was first generated!

COLLEGE TUTORS AND SUPERVISION

The ITT team supporting the project decided on two initial exploratory action steps. The first was in the traditional mould: students were asked to complete a Likert-type questionnaire (one featuring five-point attitude scales) focusing on supervision of teaching practice. Second, to provide a qualitative check on the findings of the question-naire, a team of three non-participant observers were to be present at every in-college and in-school meeting between individual students and the college tutors assigned to them throughout a five-week teaching practice. Six student and college-tutor pairs took part (for a full report see Terrell, Tregaskis and Boydell, 1986). Surprisingly, to the project team, observing college tutors in the workplace seemed a relatively novel approach. Although there are many investigations in the literature concerning the activities of college tutors almost all rely on some form of 'testimony', i.e. college tutors are required to fill in questionnaires and/or are interviewed about aims, objectives, styles and so on. It seemed very rare for college tutors to be followed into the workplace to find out whether what they claimed they did bore a relation to what they did. Only one other paper was identified which followed college tutors into the workplace and this focused only on one college tutor (see Zimphner, deVoss and Nott, 1980).

In brief, students' responses to the questionnaire indicated a very high degree of student satisfaction with college tutors. However, the fieldnotes of non-participant observers, who followed college tutors into the workplace, suggested that college tutors put almost all their efforts into providing students with positive support – loosely translated this meant they were universally nice to students and wary of upsetting them. The project team interpreted these two findings from differing sources of data in the following way.

From interviews with college tutors it was clear that they viewed teaching practice as a stressful time for students and questionnaire responses from students indicated this to be an accurate perception. Because college tutors perceive students as being under stress, they endeavour to offer as much moral and personal support to students as they can. One way of doing this is to avoid being critical of student teaching, even when there may be good reason for criticism. For example, it was not unusual for a college tutor to tell the non-participant observer after an observation session that a particular student had not done well and to acknowledge that this had not been mentioned to the student during the post-lesson discussion. College tutors almost invariably rationalized this failure to provide candid criticism by claiming that 'special circumstances' surrounding the session made it unwise, in their opinion, to offer criticism. For example, even if students themselves sometimes said that things had not gone well, college tutors might often provide supportive reasons for the failure outside and beyond the student's control, e.g. children always play up on rainy days, or it's always difficult to get them to settle after PE, or it's a very difficult class/school/area and so on. College tutors were invariably supportive, almost irrespective of what happened during student teaching sessions. Moreover, college tutors' rationalizations for avoiding negative criticisms nearly always made sense to non-participant observers.[2] It was the sheer frequency with which college tutors avoided criticism that makes this general observation important.

Course documents, and evidence from pre-practice interviews with college tutors, emphasized that one of the main aims of teaching practice was to relate theory taught at college with student classroom teaching. Non-participant observers, however, witnessed few instances when college tutors linked theory with student-led sessions in schools (despite making over thirty-six visits to classrooms alongside college tutors). The lack of theory–practice links was perhaps one of the most significant findings of this phase of the project.

College tutors did frequently offer advice to students, usually in the form of 'tips-for-teachers'. For example, telling a student of an artefacts-lending service operated by the county library or advice on how to distribute fifteen small pots of glue with the minimum of mess. Moreover, in interviews students stated that they appreciated this sort of practical, concrete advice. However, the evaluators did not feel 'tips-for-teachers' was linking theory with practice, at least not as described in pre-practice interviews with college tutors or in the course programme documents. Descriptions from both these sources suggested theory–practice links to be something rather more profound. For example theory–practice links were described as providing specific examples from observed student teaching and illustrating how they did, or did not, accord with aspects of educational theory as taught during college-based sessions.

There is in fact very little *evidence* (other than claims by organizers of ITT courses) on which to base the assertion that teaching practice is where theory–practice links are made explicit, i.e. this is an assertion which has all the elements of a Cornbleth (1987) myth. This finding has since been checked in two other institutions by a different investigator who reported substantially the same results (see Menter, 1988).

Following college tutors into the workplace and then interviewing them, class teachers and students, provided some evidence for another possible myth. All the ITT programmes concerned provided information for college tutors, co-operating class teachers and students on the aims and purposes of teaching practice – and how class teachers might assist students. This was usually in the form of booklets setting out policy statements and briefing notes. There was, however, from interviews with class teachers, little evidence that class teachers had read them. It was not uncommon for the papers to have been sent to the school but not to have reached the co-operating class teacher. There was also evidence that many college tutors had not read them, nor had some students.

When these points were made to college tutors, co-operating class teachers, students and the organizers of the ITT programmes the most common reaction was a wry smile and comments which indicated lack of surprise. The participants in teaching practices perceived briefing notes to be simply a ritual of teaching practice – and ineffective.

There is abundant evidence in the literature to indicate that simply providing policy statements and/or briefing notes (even when read by recipients) is not an effective way of ensuring workplace trainers do (or even have the skills to do) what the writers of the briefing papers wish. (For a review of effective inservice training methods see Joyce and Showers, 1980.)

Many ITT course organizers acknowledge the ineffectiveness of briefing papers (see above). However, ITT course organizers are not free agents, and higher levels seem to accept the myth that policy statements are effective. The DES Circular No. 24/89, *Initial Teacher Training: Approval of Courses* (commonly called the CATE Criteria),[3] demands that: 'Institutions [with ITT programmes] should have a written policy statement which sets out the roles of tutors, head teachers, other teachers, employers, and students in relation to students' school experience' (p. 8, para 2.5).

The commentary supplied with the Criteria tends to reinforce the view that CATE, at least, actually believes the myth – i.e. 'The statements [policy statements on teaching practice] should be in sufficient detail to be of practical assistance to all concerned in the arrangements' (p. 15, Annexe B). The rest of the CATE Criteria papers do not provide evidence to support the proposition that more detail (in written papers) will be of more *practical* assistance – a myth.

TRAINING COLLEGE TUTORS IN SUPERVISION

The next stage of the project was to report the findings of lack of candour and theory–practice links to the college tutors on this particular ITT programme. They were sceptical of the findings.

In an attempt to raise awareness (or show that the members of the project team were incorrect) college tutors were paired and asked to shadow each other on at least one visit to a student in school. Each pair of college tutors was also asked to discuss the visits. More than twenty college tutors were involved. Discussions between pairs of college tutors were always confidential so there was no final report on this part of the project. However, informal comments from college tutors indicated that they found shadowing a very helpful experience in terms of their own staff development. Even those with years of supervisory experience had never been observed nor had they observed any other college tutor. In addition, the project team noted that, after completion of this exercise, college tutors, while not wholly convinced, were less sceptical of the above findings concerning lack of candid criticism and lack of theory–practice links.

The next phase of the project was to ask college tutors to introduce candid criticism into post-lesson discussions and to attempt to relate theory to practice (as suggested in the course programme documents). College tutors were again followed into schools. In general, college tutors still remained very reluctant to offer candid criticism. As before, even in circumstances where college tutors reported privately to the non-participant observer that the student had not done well, they would once again generate a variety of reasons as to why offering candid criticism would not have been appropriate. On the few occasions when college tutors did offer criticism, it was often so buried in a welter of surrounding praise as to be almost unnoticeable – at least to the student. Although college tutors readily attempted to relate theory to practice there was no consistent coverage; each college tutor seemed to peddle his or her own unique brand of theory–practice with little reference to the practices of other college tutors, or to the educational theories outlined in the course documents. It ought to be added that student comment to the non-participant observer on the quality of supervision was consistently positive. (For a full report see Mansfield, 1986.)

During this stage of the project the research team began to have doubts about the wisdom of asking college tutors to be more candid and forthright. It would be easy to envisage a situation where supervisory procedures in terms of honesty and forthright-ness of criticism were tightened up to such a degree that a course might end up with a high proportion of unhappy, demoralized, nervous students. This was not an exercise – these were real students on real teaching practices and there was evidence in plenty that students (the customers) were content with present arrangements. Pressing college tutors to change (even though the project team might think for the better) might produce an unhappy group of students and unhappy anxious students were unlikely to learn a great deal, nor would it enhance college relations with schools.

These feelings of disquiet by the project team resulted in a change of direction. The next stage attempted to investigate what might constitute good supervisory practice which would not provoke undue levels of anxiety in students. Groups of those con-cerned with supervision – head teachers, teachers, college tutors and students – simultaneously observed a series of lessons over a period of ten weeks. Lessons were taught by different volunteer teachers or students each week. A specially arranged room available at the college enabled large numbers of observers to see the same lesson. (Cronshaw (1986) provides a more detailed account of this phase of the project.) During the lesson each observer was asked to write comments as supervisory advice to the teacher. In addition, at the end of each teaching session a volunteer from the group of observers acted as a college tutor and conducted a post-lesson discussion with the teacher. This was also observed by the rest of the group.

The intention was, first, to attempt to identify commonalities in written comments of observers and, second, to focus group discussion on *the quality of the post-lesson conference* in terms of how helpful it might be in improving the teacher's performance. In this way it was hoped to identify styles of supervision which were both helpful in terms of improving teaching performance and which students would judge as non-threatening.

Content analysis of the written comments of observers showed little commonality or consistency. Some were even wholly contradictory. For example, commenting on a story read to the children one observer wrote, 'Moving around whilst reading helped retain interest and attention. They followed you everywhere with their eyes.' Another wrote, 'It is not a good idea to move around while reading a story. The movement distracts children.' Both observed the same lesson.

It also proved difficult to get observers to write comments on how they would help the teacher improve his or her *teaching technique*. Most preferred to extol the virtues of how *they* would have taught/organized the session.

One set of simple procedures used by two college tutors was picked out by students as being particularly helpful. If, in a short *pre-lesson* discussion, the college tutor asked *whoever was to do the teaching* to identify an element of the lesson to be a focus for post-lesson discussion, this seemed to reduce anxiety and/or resentment on the part of the teacher even when negative comments were made afterwards. The teacher being observed had, in a sense, been geared up to expect criticism in one particular area and this had the effect of reducing anxiety. This also seemed to allow the observer to feel more comfortable offering negative comment because it was within an area where comment had been specifically requested by whoever was doing the teaching.

As this phase of the project progressed, a common theme began to emerge from student comment on the post-lesson conferences. Students noted that in these circum-stances there was little difference in the value (to students) between college tutors' comments and the comments class teachers brought into college to join these observational sessions. Neither were as useful as comments received from co-operating teachers assigned to students during teaching practice because the co-operating teacher on teaching practice *had intimate knowledge of the class*. Student concerns about teaching tended to centre on elements specific to the ecology of a particular school/ classroom. For example, what do I do if a specific child is insolent, lazy, aggressive? How do I fit in with the way my co-operating teacher organizes reading? I know nothing about the history of the local church but it has been suggested that I arrange a visit as part of my project on medieval England. Therefore, the most useful comments, according to students, were from co-operating class teachers *in school* who had intimate knowledge of the particular school/class within which the student was placed. College tutors and the practising class teachers brought into college for this research exercise almost inevitably provided only general advice because they did not know the specific ecology of a class. To a student the most helpful advice comes from an observer who can comment on teaching technique within the context of the unique ecology of the class in which the student is placed.

As a result of these findings the research team agreed a major change of direction: the project should endeavour to involve co-operating class teachers more closely in the supervision of students. Moreover, it would be unfair to ask class teachers to take on this function without training. (It has already been pointed out that briefing papers, as training, are ineffective.) A small pilot scheme was implemented during a fourth year final teaching practice during which a group of co-operating class teachers were asked to become more closely involved in supervision and offered some training. The training took the form of a college tutor being seconded to the school for the duration of the teaching practice to work alongside class teachers and with students in the classroom. The college tutor also conducted small group sessions with class teachers and college tutors on lesson observation and analysis. Results indicated that teachers were enthusiastic to become more 'professionally involved'. Furthermore, the students involved felt the form of advice offered by class teachers was more helpful following training. (For more details of this pilot study see Terrell and Winstanley, 1988.)

TRAINING CLASS TEACHERS IN SUPERVISION

This section focuses on the evaluation of two courses[4] aimed at training co-operating class teachers in supervisory skills. For brevity both courses are considered together and the account divided into four sub-sections: an introduction, an overview of the organization and main findings of each course, a summary of the main points from evaluations of both courses, and finally a brief description of a new course being planned.

Introduction

One of the few areas on which there is general consensus in initial teacher education is that in-school experience is the most important element of ITT programmes. However, it has already been shown that those responsible for dealing with students on teaching practice (co-operating class teachers and college lecturers) are rarely provided with any training. On both the courses evaluated here co-operating teachers were asked to undertake a formal supervision session, once weekly, with the student placed in his/her classroom. Formal supervision was defined as comprising three simple stages.

1   A pre-lesson meeting was to be held where the student to be observed explained to the observer the aims of the teaching session.
2   The teaching session was then to be observed.
3   A post-lesson discussion was to be held during which the observer was expected to analyse how far aims for the session had been met and make suggestions how the student could improve *his or her style* of teaching.

It is often assumed that repeated sequences of the above three steps are routine on all teaching practices, but work at the college and in other institutions refutes this (see Terrell, Tregaskis and Boydell, 1986; Menter 1988). Briefly, this work has shown that once co-operating class teachers are satisfied a student can 'cope' with discipline they tend to confine their involvement to 'I pop in and out to make sure everything is okay' rather than becoming heavily involved in exactly what is being taught and how. These courses were aimed at increasing co-operating teacher involvement by providing training in the above three steps.

Overview of the organization and main findings of each course

Both courses were organized and led by the same college lecturer.[5] For the first course eight co-operating primary school teachers together with the third-year (BEd) initial training students assigned to their classrooms for a four-week teaching practice volunteered to participate. The four college tutors who had been assigned to the students (two students each) also joined the course. Students, class teachers and college tutors attended college once a week on a series of ten half days before, during and after the teaching practice. The eight teachers were from four schools (two teachers from each school). This pairing of teachers was to facilitate in-school discussion of supervisory experiences as part of the learning experience.

Interviews with students indicated that they perceived the high level of teacher involvement in supervision as being more challenging and more useful than their experiences on previous teaching practices. Class teachers, however, had reservations. Although they enjoyed the course and felt it had helped students, they did not feel it had influenced their professional practice in any significant way. This meant that the LEA, although supportive of the course in general terms, was reluctant to fund further courses at full cost because it did not appear to have much influence on the professional practice of the teachers involved. In other words this was not a partnership: only the college gained – schools/LEA did not.

To meet LEA requirements it was proposed that the course be redesigned such that the first five weeks concentrated on training teachers in supervisory skills (with students) whereas the second half concentrated exclusively on helping each pair of teachers within a school to use their new skills on each other as part of a programme of inservice development of classroom skills. The first half of the course, five half-day sessions involving eight students and eight co-operating class teachers, was planned for a fourth-year teaching practice (five weeks). The second half of the course, also five half-day sessions (but involving the eight co-operating class teachers only) took place after the teaching practice had finished.

Summary of main points from evaluations of each course

Fuller reports on each of the courses are provided by Coles (1988) and Hoye (1988). Students and college tutors on both courses valued the fact that class teachers became formally involved in supervision. They felt that class teachers were ideally placed to offer supervisory advice for three main reasons. First, seeing the class teacher operate successfully in the workplace gave the teacher high credibility. Second, student response to any negative criticism of classroom performance (a chance to put it right) was likely to be *witnessed* by the class teacher later in the practice. Third, the class teacher shared with the student an intimate knowledge of the 'ecology' of that particular classroom and its pupils. The college tutor is rarely in such a strong position on any of these three factors.

The class teachers on both courses came to value the greater responsibility they were encouraged to take in the training of students although they were initially sceptical about formalizing their involvement in supervision. For example, at the beginning of both courses a typical class teacher comment was 'we do it anyway ... formalizing things will sour friendly relationships with students'. However, by the end of the courses a typical comment was 'I felt as if I was professionally involved ... my opinion was valued.' One class teacher commented 'I felt we were being treated as professionals. It's the first time I've felt part of a team responsible for training students.'

The major training material for the courses was a series of specially prepared video recordings of complete formal supervisory sessions. These included full-length recordings of pre-lesson discussions, the associated lesson as taught in the classroom, and the post-lesson analysis between teacher and student. During these college sessions teachers, students and college tutors were asked, in a group situation, to comment on and discuss how they might have improved the quality of supervisory advice offered in a post-lesson discussion seen on video. This was more difficult than expected. For example, teachers, students or college tutors, when commenting on the video, all showed a tendency to discuss how they would have taught the lesson rather than concentrating on the supervisory strategies. Strong leadership was often needed by the course leader to ensure that discussion remained centred largely on the 'skills of supervising students' and not exclusively on the 'process of teaching pupils'. Although both may overlap, they are different.

A major element in the course was that the person being observed (be it student or teacher) was allowed freedom to select a particular element of his or her teaching for detailed observation and analysis by the observer. As was suggested above, it is not so helpful if the focus is decided for him or her. Worse, and as often happens, the observer decides unilaterally on a string of foci during the observation session and in the post-lesson discussion fires them at whoever has been doing the teaching. Less anxiety is generated in whoever is doing the teaching if a focus for observation is negotiated beforehand.

In early sessions there was resistance by teachers to students' selecting topics for the observation. Comments were: 'Students will select things they are good at or trivia . . . a focus is only a part of a lesson.' In practice students suggested foci which teachers thought very sensible, e.g. 'on-task between-pupil' conversation in a science lesson. Because students almost invariably chose topics which teachers thought worthwhile the idea of students selecting foci gained almost unanimous approval as the courses developed. After experience of allowing students to choose foci teachers commented: 'Analysing how a student dealt with specific elements of teaching with my class caused me to think about what I do . . . some of the things I wanted to criticize were things I realized I did . . . . I developed new ideas watching the student.' In this sense formal supervision of students seemed an effective way of helping teachers reflect critically upon their own teaching.

Teachers on the first course (where they did not go on to analyse colleagues' teaching) thought it unnecessarily long. 'You could do all this in a day . . . just tell us what to do during a pre-practice meeting and let us get on with it . . . its easy . . . we do it all the time anyway.' The evaluators, however, thought there was considerable improvement in the technical application of formal supervision by these teachers as the course progressed (despite the fact that teachers felt they had not improved). For example, at the beginning of each course the teachers rarely questioned whether what they thought they did with students matched what they actually did. For example, if a negative comment was delivered in a friendly manner and with a smile it was generally assumed by the teachers that the comment would be received and interpreted as supportive – yet there were a number of occasions when the student being criticized clearly did not share the same interpretation. This occasional failure of the teacher tutor to understand the viewpoint of a student is illustrated by the following brief account of an interchange between a co-operating class teacher and a student during one of the group sessions.

A co-operating teacher explained how important it was to offer challenges to the student after a difficult teaching session and that her way of doing this had been to outline a list of alternative teaching strategies and offer the student 'freedom' to select/ try one of them. The student placed in this teacher's classroom, however, responded that selecting from an offered list was not a challenge. The challenge was generating a solution for oneself. Moreover, the student added, what was really needed was the freedom to generate a solution for oneself, the opportunity to try it out – and failure tolerated.

The group then began discussing circumstances where effective supervision might best be, 'knowing when to hold back and let the student make and learn from mistakes' or 'giving the student freedom to work out their own solution'. These can be difficult skills for the college tutor and the co-operating teacher, particularly if he or she feels they have a ready-made solution.

Although teachers on the first course felt it too long teachers on the second course thought it was too short, particularly when they became involved in the second half of the course where they were expected to observe and analyse each other's classroom teaching using the skills learned through helping students. However, despite the pressure of time these teachers felt the course had, overall, been successful both in terms of what students had gained and in terms of what they had gained in relation to their personal development as teachers.

The evaluators, however, did not feel the latter half of this course had entirely met its objectives. For example, the level of analysis of teaching between pairs of teachers was often thought to have been superficial, involving a lot of what might be described fairly as ritual congratulation. There was a tendency for the teacher being observed to 'play safe' and select a focus which involved the observer having to pay attention almost exclusively to aspects of pupil behaviour rather than teacher behaviour. It was also noted that when involved in group discussions (i.e. all eight teachers together in college) there was a tendency for only the member of the pair who had undertaken the teaching to contribute to the discussion. Teachers who had acted as observers, who might have been expected to be the major contributors, made little contribution. There was little evidence to suggest that the in-school, post-lesson discussions between pairs of teachers (in private) were characterized by any more rigorous, or more candid, analyses of teaching. The evaluators interpreted this as teachers opting for 'safe strategies' which would avoid conflict. It might take considerably more time than was available on this course for teachers who are also colleagues to achieve candid levels of critical appraisal and analysis.

Both these pilot courses achieved some degree of success and this model does seem to represent a step towards a true college–LEA partnership. Both sides gained; students perceived themselves to have gained from the increased involvement of the co-operating class teachers; the skills learned by the teachers were perceived by them to be of benefit to their own professional practice.

A new course

A new programme of studies leading to BEd is currently being planned which will incorporate and extend many of the ideas gained from the above project. Briefly, students on this new BEd route for intending primary teachers will spend 50% of course time in schools. Co-operating teachers will be trained as 'school tutors' (largely as described above) but the training will take place entirely in school, as opposed to in college. In addition 'curriculum laboratories' will be set up in specially designated 'teaching schools' to support the ITT programme. These curriculum laboratories will be large teaching spaces in the teaching schools where groups of up to eighteen students will be able to work with pupils alongside the school curriculum leaders[6] and college tutors. It is hoped this will increase the degree of partnership between college and schools/LEA so that both sides will derive benefit.

For example, from the college side, this high degree of involvement in schools will enable college tutors to work with children on a regular basis. This form of work in schools will also count as renewal of professional experience for college tutors. Students will benefit from increased practical involvement with teachers in schools.

From the school/LEA side the presence of students in greater numbers and for longer periods in schools (usually a full term) will provide staff with many more semi-qualified extra hands. Curriculum leaders will be able to 'try out' (on students) differing styles of staff development pertinent to particular school initiatives prior to introducing them to school staff.

This BEd ITT programme also hopes to attract mature students who live locally but who may have small children of pre-school or school age which limits the times at which sessions can be offered, i.e. all sessions will be timed between 10:00 a.m. and 3:00 p.m. This should benefit local LEAs by increasing the supply of local teachers.

This account has described one ITT course team's attempt to improve the quality of supervision offered to students. Some of the findings will be generalizable to other courses. Moreover, the ITT course team gained considerable insight into college teaching methods through the process of undertaking this form of action research. It is hoped that this description of the method of attempting to achieve solutions will be as generalizable as many of the findings.

NOTES

(1) The term 'teaching practice' is going out of fashion in many ITT programmes mainly because the word 'practice' implies that the major element of skills learning takes place prior to the period the student spends in school. Terms like 'block school experience' have replaced it within the college which supported this project. However, 'teaching practice' is retained here simply because it still has a common meaning.

(2) It is important to point out that the observers were all college tutors. Non-college tutors unfamiliar (unsullied?) with the culture of teaching practice might have been less understanding.

(3) The Council for Accreditation of Teacher Education which undertakes scrutiny of all courses of ITT. Without accreditation courses cannot be offered.

(4) The Council for National Academic Awards Development Fund provided grant aid to support this phase of the project (grant no. 1015).

(5) Each course was evaluated by a non-participant observer (a different evaluator for each course) who attended each in-college session, visited the schools to observe teachers supervising students and interviewed all major participants before, during and after each course. An action research framework (Elliott, 1976–7) was used to adapt and alter both courses in the light of comments from evaluators and participants.

(6) 'Curriculum leader' is a term commonly used to describe teachers in primary schools who specialize in a particular subject area.

REFERENCES

Coles, D. (1988) 'Teacher reflection and analysis in the classroom: collegial collaborative development', in Terrell, C. and Coles, D. (eds) *Recent Innovations In Initial Teacher Training for Intending Primary School Teachers* (College Monograph 3). Cheltenham: College of St Paul & St Mary Press.

Cornbleth, C. (1987) 'The persistence of myth in teacher education and teaching', in Pokewitz, T. (ed.) *Critical Studies in Teacher Education*. Lewes: Falmer.

Cronshaw, W. (1986) 'An account of the third phase of one college's research project into school practice supervision', in Terrell, C., Mathis, J., Winstanley, R. and Wright, D. (eds) *Teaching Practice Supervision in Primary Schools: Conference Proceedings* (College Monograph 2), pp. 117–24. Cheltenham: College of St Paul & St Mary Press.

DES: Department of Education and Science (1987) *Quality in Schools: The Initial Training of Teachers*. London: HMSO.

DES: Department of Education and Science (1989) *Initial Teacher Training: Approval of Courses* (Circular 24/89). London: DES.

Elliott, J. (1976–7) 'Developing hypotheses about classrooms from teachers' practical constructs: an account of the Ford Teaching Project', *Interchange*, 7 (2), 1–22.

Hoye, L. (1988) 'Observations on collegeal appraisal during an inservice course on teacher reflection and analysis in the classroom'. Unpublished MEd Dissertation, College of St Paul & St Mary, Cheltenham.

Joyce, B. and Showers, B. (1980) 'Improving inservice training: the messages of research', *Educational Leadership*, 37 (5), 379–85.

Mansfield, P. (1986) 'Patchwork pedagogy: a case study of supervisors' emphasis on pedagogy in post-lesson conferences', *Journal of Education for Teaching*, **12** (3), 259–71.

Menter, I. (1988) 'Profiling supervisory practice', in Terrell, C. and Coles, D. (eds) *Recent Innovations In Initial Teacher Training for Intending Primary School Teachers* (College Monograph 3). Cheltenham: College of St Paul & St Mary Press.

Terrell, C., Tregaskis, O. and Boydell, D. (1986) 'Teaching practice supervision in primary schools: an ethnomethodological perspective', in Terrell, C., Mathis, J., Winstanley, R. and Wright, D. (eds) *Teaching Practice Supervison in Primary Schools: Conference Proceedings* (College Monograph 2), Cheltenham: College of St Paul & St Mary Press.

Terrell, C. and Winstanley, R. (1988) 'Cooperating teachers and supervisory skills', in Terrell, C. and Coles, D. (eds) *Recent Innovations In Initial Teacher Training for Intending Primary School Teachers* (College Monograph 3). Cheltenham: College of St Paul & St Mary Press.

Zimphner, N., deVoss, G. and Nott, D. (1980) 'A closer look at university student teacher supervision'. *Journal of Teacher Education*, **31**, (4), 11–15.

Chapter 13

A Double Vision: The Experiences of a Head and Principal

Ray Stirling

The 'double vision' of the title alludes to the unusual nature of my personal experience. As the principal of a college of education and as the head of two comprehensive schools, I have been able to view the relationship between the school and the training institution from two different angles. There is a further duality which arises from differences in time. My first headship was in the 1960s, my second in the 1980s. Undoubtedly there have been changes in the relationship between schools and initial teacher training institutions over these decades, but there is also an element of *plus ça change, plus c'est la même chose*, for the theme of 'partnership' in teacher training is certainly not new. The James Report (DES, 1972) recommended close liaison and the sharing of responsibility between the colleges and schools:

> The [colleges] would form a new and closer relationship with schools. . . .
> The schools and the teachers in them would be asked to undertake new roles in teacher training. . . . Teachers in schools would be more closely involved . . . in planning and supervising practical work . . . they should be associated with the selection of students.
>
> (paras 3.45, 3.47)

It was also a feature of Circular No. 3/84 (DES, 1984):

> Institutions in co-operation with local education authorities and their advisers should establish links with a number and variety of schools and courses and should be developed and run in close working partnership with those schools.
>
> (Annex, para. 3)

There are, however, significant differences between the Report and the Circular. The former recommends partnership and places it within the context of a holistic view of teacher training. In the Circular, partnership is mandatory, and ends are postulated but means are omitted.

THE 1960s: THE VIEW OF A HEAD TEACHER

It is not surprising that partnership has been a recurrent theme for debate, for it is implicit in the training process. In order to train teachers, colleges and departments of education need schools, just as schools need the training institutions to meet their need for new staff. 'Partnership' is therefore born of necessity. But shotgun marriages do not always make for happy liaisons. Despite the formal bonds, there may be few shared interests, few values held in common.

It was my dissatisfaction as a head with the form which 'partnership' took in the 1960s which determined my move into a college. At that time, relationships between school and college were always civilized and friendly, but they were also cursory and narrowly functional. It was not so much a partnership that the training institutions appeared to want as a ticket of access to the classroom. It was a bonus if we, the teachers, were invited to contribute to the assessment of the student, and I cannot recall a single occasion when we were asked for our views on the criteria of that assessment. Nor were we given any information about the theoretical element of the student's course. We had no sense of the college views on the theoretical underpinnings of classroom practice. Theory and practice were estranged. Other relationships were cosmetic: the token head on an academic board, the occasional lecture to the students given by a senior teacher. But perhaps most dispiriting was the immense cultural gap between the two types of institution. As teachers at the chalkface we were humorously cynical about the inhabitants of the ivory towers. Only rarely did our worlds meet in common endeavour for only rarely, so it seemed, were we fired by common professional interests.

It was the events of the 1960s which forced a reassessment of this relationship. The expansion of teacher training and the advent of comprehensive education, and the subsequent interaction of these two developments, threatened to disturb a relationship in which the balance of power and control between the two sides had been far from equivalent. The desirability of a new form of professional partnership had been evident to the schools for many years. Now it became imperative.

THE CHANGING ALLIANCE

The expansion of the colleges initiated an intensive recruitment drive for new staff: academically qualified staff to meet the requirements of the new BEd degree, but also teachers from school whose practical expertise would, it was hoped, come to the aid of the institutions which were to be thrown into dizzy disorientation by the new form of school organization. Of necessity, the colleges were now having to adjust their training to meet the needs of the schools. This was, potentially, a reversal of the old relationship. Mixed-ability teaching, the anti-school values of some pupils, the changes in social groupings within the school and the attendant behavioural problems which were characteristic of some comprehensives, and later the raising of the school-leaving age all created a challenging new world. To some of us it seemed a brave new world, but to many in the training institutions it was one for which their experience was no longer pertinent. (I well remember a lecturer who arrived late at the school. He was profuse in his apologies, having mistaken our large building for Gilbey's, a gin emporium with a similar glass facade!) The colleges needed to be freshly inducted into the aims and activities of the new comprehensive schools if their students were to be able to identify with the range of pupils they would be required to teach.

But if the colleges were obliged to liaise more closely with the schools, so also were the schools suddenly in need of the help and guidance of the colleges. The curriculum was discovered, it seemed for the first time. How it should be taught was no longer the preserve of academics. Teachers needed more than their outmoded certificates in education and a set of dog-eared notes. They even talked about the curriculum in the staff room and expressed uneasy concern which at times became a shout for help. The introduction of CSE and particularly Mode 3 introduced a new form of assessment with new goals, new rules and a need for new skills which teachers did not necessarily possess. Strange things were afoot to which the old pragmatism was an inadequate response. New methods demanded new initiatives in professional development; the gap between theory and practice was getting narrower.

In short, there emerged in the 1960s and flowed into the 1970s a need for professional interdependence which seemed destined to transform school–college co-operation into a more broadly based professional partnership. There remained of course a whole range of fundamental issues which needed to be addressed if this promise were to be fulfilled. How could lecturers and teachers work together to satisfy both sets of needs? How could institutional barriers be broken down or at least made more flexible? How could the stereotypes of theorist and practitioner be destroyed, their common interests and perspectives be developed?

In the end this rich promise came to nothing – and its failure paved the way for the National Curriculum. At a time when the tide was flowing in favour of a partnership firmly located in curriculum development, the majority of teacher training institutions remained aloof, locked into their traditional limited relationship with the schools. It would be easy to blame introverted attitudes for the perpetuation of this situation. But the major constraint was the nature of the respective role prescriptions. The division between tutor and teacher meant much more than different conditions of service; it also meant specialization in different practices, and the ownership and transmission of different types of knowledge.

A further constraint on the emergence of any new form of partnership was the grouping of the colleges within the area training organizations (ATOs). The primary function of the ATOs was to monitor courses and awards. Additional tasks were to provide short inservice courses for serving teachers, and facilities for further study and research. But the institutes developed particular strengths, some in research, some in student teaching, some in inservice work. Owing to a lack of inservice provision at the local colleges, my staff had to travel to the Institutes of London and Cambridge to satisfy their professional needs; and so an opportunity to further links between school and training institution was lost. Instead a different form of partnership emerged, though it was still within the field of curriculum development. It had less to do with student training and more to do with teachers beginning to accept responsibility for their own professional development. During my time with the Schools Council, I saw real partnership in action. The colleges became professional centres, information centres, research centres, bringing teachers and lecturers together in development projects; and in the teachers' centres also, irrespective of their institution, teachers and educationists came together in common enterprise.

THE 1970s: THE VIEW OF THE COLLEGE PRINCIPAL

It would probably be true to say, however, that the 1960s ended and the 1970s began with the schools and colleges locked into a time warp. The pattern of partnership remained largely untouched by the changes in professional needs referred to earlier. Occasionally the more erudite and articulate of my staff gave the odd lecture to a PGCE group. Teachers carried on as supervisors and teaching practice tutors continued to flit into school.

Then came the James Report. At long last the mould of traditional roles was to be broken. Initial training and professional development, schools and training institutions were to be shaped into a new unity. The three cycles of personal education, pre-service training, and induction and inservice training opened up a new vista. Here was the grand design, and part of that design was a new partnership, a partnership *par excellence*. The pre-service training, though based in an institution, was to be specifically related to a teacher's needs on taking up a first appointment. The second year of the second cycle would be spent largely in school with one day a week on release to attend a professional centre. Every school would have its professional tutor who had the task of advising the new 'licensed' teacher. The narrow initial training role of the colleges would be given a new dimension.

All this too when spare capacity in the training establishments was forecast and the demand for higher education on the increase. The signs and portents promised the favour of the gods. But in the event, the gods turned out to be fickle.

In the four years that I was a principal of a college, I was able to participate in its metamorphosis from a monotechnic to a multifaceted institution, with all the implications of this for the liaison between college and schools. When I went there, the college was already a good example of the best sort of partnership a single purpose college could generate. It had done all the right things within the confines of teacher training. Nevertheless, seen from the other side, the basic recipe was just the same though it had been spiced up a bit. Heads were well-represented on our school practice committee and they helped to draw up the criteria for assessment. We invited students' supervisors from the schools into the college. But best of all, some lecturers had not only built up sound links with schools, but they had credibility as practitioners because they chose to teach some part of a school timetable. In exchange for this input, teachers led college tutorials. The two cultures, theory and practice, were fusing.

But it was during the latter part of my time at the college, when we painfully grew out of our monotechnic role into a more broadly based institution, that I became convinced that a genuine partnership cannot be achieved within the confines of an establishment devoted solely to initial training. This is because of the nature of teaching itself. It is a total enterprise which involves both practical skills and theoretical justification. There are no sides; it is a seamless garment. Teaching is holistic. In their practice, teachers unify their initial training, their teaching experience, and their professional development. It is an accident of history which created separate institutions to minister to this continual growth. Teacher education is a continuum embracing initial training, inservice and research and development, and all of these are interdependent. We are forever compartmentalizing these elements. Initial training institutions by their very remit could do little for the needs of established teachers, and they were therefore reduced to the role of supplicant begging co-operation and masquerading as partners. True partnership requires interdependence, a meeting of one another's needs. We needed therefore to alter the context of initial training.

The James Report's third cycle was designed to do just that. Its effect on the college and its relationship with schools was most significant. The opening up of the college to inservice courses for teachers, and the introduction of the part-time DipHE, meant an influx into the college of teachers eager to profit from the contact. They were doing no one any favours. The opening up of the college library as an information or resource centre, the creation of a primary reading centre available to anyone in the community, moved trainers and teachers some way towards the communality of interest which had been lacking. The participation in curriculum-development projects of lecturers along-side teachers and LEA advisers, all on equal terms, was real professional partnership. Teaching practice continued in its traditional form but in a richer context.

The James Report flickered brightly but briefly. Its ambitious proposals were dampened by public expenditure cuts and, later, a fall in the birth rate. Attention shifted from the substance of training to the rationalization of the system as contraction set in. Yet from the ashes of the Report there did emerge new forms of institution which linked the three cycles into a whole and so facilitated real partnership: the institutes of higher education which combined teacher education with other higher education courses provide good examples of a professional continuum and mutual dependence. Similarly the schools of education associating initial training and inservice education, research and development created a climate conducive to the growth of partnership. It is a pity that this is not universally the case. (I cannot help contrasting this aim with the experience of a member of my staff who was forced to take an MEd out of the area, because the local university does not undertake inservice work. Continuity of training was lost and with it the opportunities for sustained partnership.)

TOWARDS PARTNERSHIP: THE NEED FOR RESOURCES AND A CHANGE OF ATTITUDE

In the post-James era, we were only tinkering with partnership and the constraints which had frustrated me as a head teacher continued to do so as a principal. The major problem was that neither college nor school had a financial remit to underwrite the development of partnership. The basic principle of teacher participation in training had been axiomatic for years, but it rests on the naïve assumption that a sort of *quid pro quo* exists which enables teachers to give the required time because they have been relieved of teaching time by the presence of a student. It is the 'feet up in the staffroom' image. In reality, everyone knows full well that this is not an accurate representation, and that to do the job of supervising students conscientiously and professionally is demanding of extra time. Such is the good will of teachers that in the past they were able to find that time.

The situation today is manifestly different. The changes with which schools are grappling are without precedent in my thirty-six years in the profession. Urgent professional needs which should be beneficial to partnership are being created. Instead, they are threatening such partners as exist. The good will has not been eroded nor has the professionalism. We have simply run out of time. The same government which issued Circular No. 3/84 also initiated professional contracts and conditions of service. The 1986 Education Act ushered in the new governing bodies which have to be serviced, and with the 1988 Education Reform Act came Local Management of Schools (LMS).

Yet initial teacher training institutions are being exhorted to generate still more teacher participation. We have come a long way from the perfunctory contact of the 1960s and I am certain that the principle of teacher participation and partnership is right, but only if the important role of schools in initial teacher training is acknowledged in the distribution of resources. The most precious resource we have is time. On its availability depends the quality of the relationship between school and college or department. It can no longer be assumed to be available; nor can it be rewarded by honoraria. It has to be bought and yet so far it has not been suggested that the participation of schools in initial training should feature in the formula for the distribution of resources. It seems quite likely that the advent of LMS will further exacerbate the underfunding of partnership schemes. The expenditure of every penny will be scrutinized, and non-essential expenditure rigorously denied.

Underfunding is perhaps the most immediately pressing constraint, though in some ways it might be the easiest to overcome. It only requires an act of political will, and teacher shortage might well be the necessary spur to action. The cynical cleavage of cultures that I alluded to earlier is less easy to remedy. I had thought that it resided mainly in school staffrooms but I found it just as ingrained in the college common room. When we talk of partnership it is reasonable to assume that we are talking of equality. Yet in reality we are a divided and hierarchical profession. We have different salary scales, different conditions of service and the pupils or students are of different status. The established attitude is that one is 'promoted from' or even 'escapes from' school to training institution. Of course one deprecates this, and murmurs 'difference of function, not better, not worse'. Yet the fact remains that I did not see many queuing up to get back into schools. Today, in the 1990s, the wariness and negative attitudes persist in my staffroom as they did in the staffroom of the 1960s and the common room of the 1970s.

Structures alone do not explain them. There is a fundamental divide between 'pure' and 'applied', between 'academic' and 'professional', between 'theorist' and 'practitioner'. It is a malaise which is at the heart of our training system. But it can be tackled and certainly alleviated if not eradicated. Is it baying for the moon to hope for a unified profession with a common salary structure? Differentials have narrowed and conditions of service grown close. Exchange of roles has long been recognized as a means of creating common values. One's attitudes are changed by participating in another culture, by swapping staffroom for common room and vice versa. Having done it, I can vouch for the effectiveness of the exercise. In my college, the exchange of teachers and lecturers was limited to occasional sorties and these were often disruptive to both establishments. It is just as true today. Good teachers are like birds of rare plumage, only observable in flight between INSET courses, examination moderation, National Curriculum meetings and consortia working parties. None the less, it is an improvement on the one-way traffic which used to pass for partnership.

Professional fluidity between schools and colleges based on the abolition of fixed tenure is not designed to create confidence in partnership. But there are developments which would make it possible to overcome structural barriers and avoid the problems of tenure. The practice is now widespread of seconding teachers to initiate or sustain curriculum developments for periods of up to twelve months or occasionally longer. It is usual for the teacher to be seconded to the LEA. The problem of staff replacement in school could be avoided by the secondment for research purposes being made to a training institution and by a mutual secondment back to the school. I have in mind, too, such secondments from my staff recently. Had these been mutual exchanges between school and department, the professional development of both parties would have been enriched and valuable bridges built. Such arrangements would of course require a mutual willingness to participate, and so we are back to attitudes.

Other developments are promoting partnership. Colleges are beginning to work with schools on research and development – on the testing of new forms of assessment, for example, or by participating in 'in school' inservice Baker Days. The National Curriculum Council's working groups are bringing together theorists and practitioners, teachers and lecturers. However, the immediate need to service the National Curriculum has had the effect of reducing substantial individual professional development. Teachers are too valuable to release for higher degree courses. Instead the provision of inservice training is uncoordinated as LEAs, departments and colleges try to compensate for this by mounting short courses. The subsequent haphazard pattern of provision is causing a crisis in our schools where classes are left to the ministration of supply teachers to a disturbing extent, and is fragmenting relationships between schools, LEAs and training institutions. We cannot go on servicing curriculum development in this uncoordinated way. The latest panacea is for teachers to work longer to accommodate their inservice needs. The opposite is needed: entitlement planned release and purposive professional development. How to deliver INSET in a sensible, planned way is one of the major problems facing us in schools. The current situation is certainly a far cry from the planned partnership of the James Report.

Yet all the ingredients are there for that partnership to re-emerge. The present ferment in education is a time pregnant with possibilities for a new covenant of partnership based on mutual need.

REFERENCES

DES: Department of Education and Science (1972) *Teacher Education and Training* (The James Report). London: HMSO.

DES: Department of Education and Science (1984) *Initial Teacher Training: Approval of Courses*. (Circular 3/84). London: DES.

Name Index

NOTE: Page numbers printed in italics refer to entries in the References sections at the end of each chapter.

Aitken, T.   134, *141*
Alexander, Robin J.   11, 12, *22*, 72, *73*
Aplin, R.   118, *126*
Ashton, P.   46, *55*

Baker, Kenneth   31, 47, *55*
Barton, L.   46, *56*
Bell, Andrew   25
Benton, P.   *126*
Berliner, D. C.   125, *126*
Bernbaum, G.   *23*
Bernstein, B.   111, *126*
Beyer, L.   49, *55*
Board of Education   69, *73*
Bonnett, K.   *23*
Booth, M.   87, *98*
Boydell, D.   *165*
Bromley, S.   *23*

Calderhead, J.   123, 125, *126*
Carr, W.   140, *141*
CATE (Council for the Accreditation of Teacher Education)   18, *22*, 46, *55*, 164
Caudrey, A.   62, *73*
Clark, C. M.   121, *126*
CNAA (Council for National Academic Awards)   9–13 *passim*, *22*, 33–42, *42*, *43*, 47, *55*
Coles, D.   161, *164*
Collier, G.   *141*
Collins, M.   28, *32*
Cornbleth, C.   154, 156, *164*
Cronshaw, W.   158, *164*

Davies, R.   136, *141*
Day, C.   30, *32*
DES   3, 8–9, 11, 13, 18–19, 20–1, *22*, *23*, 29, 38–9, *43*, 46, 47, 49, 51, 52, *55*, 59, 62, 67, 69, *73*, 87, *98*, *109*, 131–2, *141*, 143, 154, 157, *164*, 166, 170, *172*
Durham, M.   52, *55*

Eggleston, J.   15, *23*
Elliott, J.   12, *23*, *164*
Everton, T.   46, *55*

Foucault, M.   47–8, *55*
Furlong, V. J.   47, *55*, *86*, 88, 97, *98*, 110, 111, 115–16, 118, 120, 123, 124, *126*

Ginsburg, M.   49, *55*
Gorbutt, D.   9, *23*

Handy, C.   134, *141*
Hargreaves, D. H.   52, 53, *55*, 62, *73*, 87, *98*
Henderson, E.   *55*
Hillgate Group   52, *55*, 87, *98*
Hirst, P. H.   8, *23*, *55*, *86*, *98*, 111, 112, 119, 121–2, *126*
HMI   17, 18, *23*, 87, *98*
Hoye, L.   161, *164*
Huberman, A. M.   132, 133, *141*

Impey, G.   46, *55*

Jessop, B.   21, *23*
Joyce, B.   156, *164*

Kemmis, S.   140, *141*

Labour Party   *98*
Lancaster, Joseph   25
Lawlor, S.   87, *98*
Letwin, O.   53
Levinson, N.   132, 133, *141*
Levitas, R.   45, *55*
Ling, T.   *23*
Liston, D. P.   136, *142*
Lucas, P.   136, *141*

McCulloch, M.   11, 12, *23*, 34, *43*
McIntyre, D.   15, *23*, 110, 114, *126*, *127*
Mansfield, P.   157, *165*
Menter, I.   45, 46, 49, *55*, *56*, 156, 160, *165*
Merritt, J.   *55*
Miles, S.   *55*, *86*, *98*, *126*
Miller, J.   135, *141*
Mortimer, D.   *55*

Nokes, A. G.   35, *43*
Nott, D.   155, *165*

O'Hear, A.   27, *32*, 52, 53, *55*, 87, *98*

Patrick, H.   10, *23*
Perkin, H.   132, *141*
Perry, P.   53, *55*
Peterson, P. L.   121, *126*

Pocklington, K.   *55, 86, 98, 126*
Pollard, A.   46, *55, 56*
Poppleton, P.   131, *141*
Preen, D.   *141*
Pring, R.   6–7, *23*
Proctor, N.   14, *23*, 99, *109*, 131, *141*
Proefriedt, W.   135, *141*

Reid, K.   *23*
Reiss, M.   *98*
Richert, A. E.   100, *109*
Roe, J.   136, *141*
Ruddock, J.   132, 137, 138, *141*
Ruthven, K.   *98*

Schön, D.   111, 119, 123, 124, *127*, 144, *152*
Scottish Education Department/General Teaching
   Council of Scotland   39, *43*
Secretary of State for Education (1989)   87, *98*
Showers, B.   156, *164*
Shulman, L. S.   100, *109*, 132, 135, *142*
Sigsworth, A.   138, *141*
Smith, F.   25, *32*
Smith, R. N.   *43*
Socialist Teachers' Alliance   *55*

Stow, David   26
Sutton, C.   6, *23*

Tabachnick, B. R.   135, *142*
Terrell, C.   155, 159, 160, *165*
Thatcher, Margaret   20, *22, 23*
Tickle, L.   12, *23*
Tregaskis, O.   *165*

Veenman, S. A. M.   135, *142*
deVoss, G.   *165*

Warnock, Baroness M.   52, 53, *56*, 87, *98*
Webster, J. R.   8, *23*
Whitaker, P.   30, *32*
Whittaker, J.   11, *22*
Whitty, G.   45, 46, *56*
Wilshaw, D.   136, *141*
Wilson, P. S.   *23*
Wilson, S. M.   100, *109*
Winstanley, R.   159, *165*
Wragg, E. C.   26, 30, *32*
Wren, D.   30, *32*

Zeichner, K. M.   135, 136, *142*
Zimphner, N.   155, *165*

Subject Index

ACSET (Advisory Committee on the Supply and Education of Teachers) 17
Apprenticeship training 24–32, 68, 76, 87; *see also* Licensed teacher scheme
Attitudinal issues 63–5, 109, 155, 170–2; *see also* Politics and partnership

'Bournemouth Scheme' (Exeter University) 31
Briefing notes 156

CAL (Computer-Assisted Learning) 138–40
Cambridge Analytical Framework, the 88, 110–27, 144, 148
  appropriate integration 123–6
  levels of professional training 119–23
CATE (Council for the Accreditation of Teacher Education) 18, 24–5, 28, 46, 59, 62, 87, 143, 157
Circular 3/84 (DES) 3–4, 38–9, 46, 99, 166, 170
Circular 24/89 (DES) 3, 13, 18–19, 67, 131–2, 157
CNAA (Council for National Academic Awards) 9–13 *passim*, 33–42, 47, 154
  Development Fund 164
  the development of partnership 34–5
    the early 1980s 38–40
    the late 1980s 40–2
    where next? 42
  dimensions of partnership 35–7
  importance of work in schools 37–8
  involving teachers 33–4
Conceptual issues 67–72
Conservatism, the New 20, 21, 45; *see also* Politics and partnership
Context of partnership 1–56
  changing partnership 44–56
  CNAA perspective 33–43
  development in the UK 3–23
  two routes into teaching 24–32
Co-operating teachers 159
Cox Report, the (DES) 49
Cross Commission (1888) 25–6, 31
Curriculum laboratories 163

Development of partnership 3–23, 44–56
  early days 4–12, 45
  the 1980s 12–16, 48–54
  the political context 16–21, 45, 46–8

Economic and Social Research Council 99
Educating the Reflective Practitioner (Schön) 123
Education Act (1986) 170
Education Observed No. 7 (DES) 29
Education Reform Act 1988 28, 40, 54, 170
Exeter University 31

Funding inservice training 39–40, 41, 164, 170–2

'Gallery lessons' 26
Glasgow Normal Seminary (1837) 26

Headteacher's experience, a 166–72
  the changing alliance 167–8
  the 1960s 166–7
  resources and attitudes 170–2
HMI (Her Majesty's Inspectorate) 17, 18, 29, 31, 46–7, 52, 87, 98, 143

Initial BEd Courses for the Early and Middle Years (CNAA) 35
Initial Teacher Training Approval of Courses (DES)
  (Circular 3/84) 3–4, 38–9, 166, 170
  (Circular 24/89) 3, 13, 18–19, 22, 131–2, 157

James Report, the (1972) 10, 16, 24–5, 28, 34, 166, 169
Joint Regional Courses (DES) 25

Learning to Teach (SED/GTCS) 39
Licensed teacher scheme 20–1, 24–32, 39, 152, 169
LMS (Local Management of Schools) *see* Education Reform Act 1988

McNair Report, the (1944) 8, 69
Mature students 163

National Curriculum, the 28, 32, 131, 168
National Curriculum Council 172
New Right, the 20, 21, 45; *see also* Politics and partnership
New Teacher in School, the (DES) 52
Newcastle Commission (1861) 25

Oxford University Internship Scheme, the 15, 16, 110–27
  the analytical framework 111–13
  the scheme 113–18

Partnership
  the context of 1–56
    changing partnership 44–56
    a CNAA perspective 33–43
    development in the UK 3–23
    two routes into teaching 24–32
  the practice of 129–72
    experiences of a head and principal 166–72
    practical school experiences 153–65
    reflective practice 131–42
    training school supervisors 143–52
  the principles of 57–127
    confronting the issues 59–73
    Oxford and Cambridge models 110–27
    the students' views 87–98
    the theory–practice relationship 74–86
    training student history teachers 99–109
Personal issues 65–7
Perspectives on Postgraduate Initial Training
  (CNAA) 35
PGCE (Postgraduate Certificate in Education)
  38, 100, 113, 143
Politics and partnership 16–21, 45, 46–8
Presentations, student 140, 148, 161; *see also*
  'Gallery lessons'
Principal's experience, a 166–72
  the changing alliance 167–8
  the 1970s 168–70
  resources and attitudes 170–2
Profiles, student 151

QTS (Qualified Teacher Status) (Green Paper
  1988) 24, 51

Records of achievement 151
Reductionism 28
Reflective practice 31, 36, 92–3, 131–42
  nurturing interactions 138–40
  the 'psychological contract' 135–8
  a reconceptualization 134–5
  students' views on 92–3

Resources and attitudes 39–40, 41, 164, 170–2
Respect 65–6

Schools Council, the 168
Self-assessment 151
SPITE (Structure and Process in Teacher
  Education) (Patrick, Bernbaum and Reid) 10
Structural issues 60–3
Student history teachers, training 99–109
  aims and structures of the courses 101–2
  effectiveness of the courses 102–6
  evaluation of the courses 101
  recommendations 106–9
  the research project 99–101
Students' views on training 87–98
  background 88
  practice 88–92
  reflection and discussion 92–3
  theory 93–6
Supervisors, school 104
  practical experiences 153–65
    college tutors 155–7
    preliminary work 154–5
    training class teachers 159–64
    training college tutors 157–9
  training 143–52
    running a course for 143–8
    a teacher supervisor's view 148–52
Sussex, University of 11, 16

Teacher supervisors *see* Supervisors, school
Teaching in Schools: The Content of Initial Training
  (HMI) 17
Teaching schools 163
Theory–practice relationship 5, 69–71, 74–86

University Council for the Education of
  Teachers 11

Video presentations *see* Presentations, student